THE UNITED STATES PONY CLUB
MANUAL OF HORSEMANSHIP

Also by Susan E. Harris

Horsemanship in Pictures
Grooming to Win, Second Edition
Horse Gaits, Balance and Movement

THE
UNITED STATES PONY CLUB MANUAL
OF
HORSEMANSHIP

BASICS FOR BEGINNERS / D LEVEL

written and illustrated by

Susan E. Harris

Ruth Ring Harvie, USPC Editor

HOWELL BOOK HOUSE
New York

Howell Book House
Simon & Schuster Macmillan Company
15 Columbus Circle
New York, NY 10023

MACMILLAN is a registered trademark of Macmillan, Inc.

Library of Congress Cataloging-in-Publication Data
Harris, Susan E.
    The United States Pony Club manual of horsemanship : basics for beginners / level / written and illustrated by Susan E. Harris : Ruth Ring Harvie, USPC editor.
        p.   cm.
    Includes index.
    ISBN 0-87605-952-3
    1. Horsemanship.   2. Ponies.   3. United States Pony Clubs.   I. Harvie, Ruth Ring.   II. United States Pony Clubs.   III. Title.   IV. Title: Manual of horsemanship.
    SF309.H369   1994
    636.1'6—dc20
                                                                93-34438
                                                                CIP

5   7   9   10   8   6   4

Printed in the United States of America
Book design by Susan Hood

Contents

Contents

Foreword

For many years I have watched Pony Clubs provide grassroots instruction and activities essential to the development and nurture of future participants in the international equestrian disciplines. Although some children aspire to represent their country in competition, others choose a path of teaching, training or simply a lifetime of dedication to a sport in which they take continuing pleasure.

This manual speaks to a variety of goals and interests. The subject matter is designed to accommodate children's attraction to, fascination with and affection for horses as it introduces them to ever-increasing depths of knowledge. The emphasis on responsible use and care of horses at all times and in all phases of horsemanship should instill in young people a sense of pride and accomplishment based on high, yet attainable standards.

Susan E. Harris writes with charm and style, which speak to different ages directly and honestly. Her background as a teacher, trainer, author and clinician makes this book attractive and useful to all those who teach children and horses. Her continued interest in and respect for the basics of good horsemanship worldwide should keep professionals, amateurs and volunteers of both categories fresh, inspired and informed. More importantly, her style promises to make this manual and the forthcoming manuals the "best friends" of children who love horses.

DONALD W. THACKERAY

A Note from The United States Pony Clubs, Inc.

We suspect that the first requests from USPC members for a manual of their own were received in 1954, when the first U.S. clubs were founded. By 1979, when the Instruction Council rewrote the USPC Standards, it was determined that there was a need for one source of information members could consult as they progress through the rating levels. The British and New Zealand manuals have served our members well, but thanks to the foresight of the USPC Board of Governors, its officers, staff and instruction committees in the late 1980s and early 1990s, we finally have a text that matches our standards, uses terms specific to North America and is written at a reading level comfortable for the majority of our members.

Author and illustrator Susan E. Harris, an experienced and successful riding instructor, has received guidance from an advisory panel that represents years of teaching, coaching, and examining riding and horse management skills within the USPC. We wish to express our thanks to consulting editors Laurie Chapman-Bosco, H. Benjamin Duke III, and Dru Malavase, as well as to editorial assistants Jessica Jahiel and Anne Colahan.

Carol Urbanc, formerly of the USPC National Office, has been a source of technical support and personal comfort to the advisory panel.

Madelyn Larsen, of Howell Book House, has been the patient, professional reason we have a manual available at long last.

Melanie Heacock, while Vice President, Instruction, and now President of the USPC, has provided support and wisdom beyond the call of duty.

USPC editor Ruth Ring Harvie, as chairman of the Manual of Horsemanship Committee and Curriculum Standards Committees, and through terms on the National Testing, Educational Resources and Instruction Committees, has served tirelessly to correlate, coordinate, update and incorporate input from these vital educational groups, and has acted as the primary liaison between the USPC Susan Harris and the publisher.

Although we do not claim to cover all special-interest areas, we have carefully listened to and seriously considered all suggestions. We are grateful to all the members of the committees who have directly influenced this manual, especially Judith Fannin and the D and C Standards Committee.

Col. Donald W. Thackeray, who wrote the Foreword, has long been a friend, adviser, and committee member of the USPC, despite his duties as United States representative of the Fédération Equestre Internationale and his activities as an "I" level dressage judge. For his tutelage and interest, we are extremely appreciative.

Plainly, this manual represents several years of research, reference checking, philosophical discussion, consultations with experts, proposals and counter-proposals, and dozens of exchanges of letters. We hope that young riders everywhere enjoy Susan Harris's exceptional work as much as we do.

Introduction for Parents

Pony Club started in Great Britain in 1928 with 700 members. By 1992 there were more than 125,000 members in 27 countries, making it the largest junior equestrian group in the world. Each club is run by a volunteer District Commissioner and other elected officers. At this writing, the United States Pony Clubs have over 11,000 members in more than 500 clubs.

This *USPC Manual of Horsemanship* is written especially for Pony Club members and for the volunteers who lead and teach them, but it will also be helpful to anyone who wants to learn or teach good horsemanship. In this manual, and in the two to follow, the emphasis is on how children learn, rather than on subject matter for its own sake. Progress along a continuum of learning is stressed, not the mere acquisition of facts.

This manual provides an introduction to the curriculum of the USPC and will help children meet the current USPC Standards of Proficiency. However, the levels of proficiency required by the standards cannot be achieved by book work alone. Much practical hands-on learning is essential, as is good mounted instruction at all levels. As in any course of study, effective teaching and learning require outside reading and supplemental material. Material from the USPC's most recently published standards and reading lists, as well as individual teachers' resources, will be necessary to augment this manual.

Pony Club supports the ideal of a thoroughly happy, comfortable horseperson, riding across a natural country, with complete confidence and perfect balance on a horse or pony equally happy and confident and free from pain or bewilderment.

USPC's Mission

The United States Pony Clubs, Inc., an educational organization for youth, provides a program which teaches riding, mounted sports, and the care of horses and ponies, thereby developing responsibility, sportsmanship, moral judgment, leadership and self-confidence.

USPC's Guiding Beliefs

- USPC is an educational organization which progressively develops the well-rounded horseperson.
- The well-rounded horseperson is capable of riding safely and tactfully on the flat, over fences, and in the open.
- Knowledgeable care of horses and ponies (horse management) is basic to the well-rounded horseperson.
- USPC is committed to the well-being of the horse.
- Fair and friendly competitions develop teamwork and sportsmanship.
- Fun and friendship are part of Pony Club.
- USPC requires parental and volunteer involvement and support.
- USPC is committed to safety.
- The local club is the core of USPC.

This book is not intended as a substitute for professional advice and guidance in the field of horseback riding. A young person should take part in the activities discussed in this book only under the supervision of a knowledgeable adult.

All USPC tests in this book are current as of 1994.

PART 1

ABOUT PONY CLUB, LEARNING TO RIDE AND SELECTING A PONY

The ideal of Pony Club is a happy, comfortable rider with confidence and balance, on a pony equally happy and confident and free from pain or bewilderment. *Photo: Neena Ewing.*

CHAPTER 1

♦♦♦

For Children and Parents: Getting Started Right

Pony Club is for anyone up to twenty-one years old who is interested in horses and riding. It was started in England in 1928 to teach horsemanship, horse and pony care, safety and good sportsmanship to young people who could not otherwise afford expensive lessons. The United States joined the program in 1954. Today there are over 500 local Pony Clubs, with more than 11,000 members.

Pony Club mounts may be horses or ponies. In Pony Club, the word "pony" is used for all mounts used by young people, regardless of size or breed.

Pony Club teaches English riding, emphasizing the Balance Seat. There are nine levels, called "ratings," with clear standards for each level. Pony Clubbers start out as "unrated." They learn at their own pace and take the test for each rating when they are ready. Each rating includes riding tests (in the ring, in the open and jumping), stable management and oral testing. Testing for the first five ratings (D-1 through C-2) is done by local examiners. The C-3 rating is tested by regional examiners, while the three highest levels (B, H-A and A) are national ratings tested by national examiners. They require a high degree of skill, knowledge and horsemanship experience.

This book covers the Pony Club D Level, which includes the D-1, D-2, and D-3 ratings. This level introduces the fun and challenge of riding, while building a foundation of safety habits

3

Dismounted instruction at a working rally. Here an older Pony Clubber demonstrates bandaging. (However, no one should kneel near a pony.) *Photo: Neena Ewing.*

and knowledge of the daily care of a pony and his tack. In the D-1 through D-3 levels, Pony Clubbers learn to ride independently, with control, with a secure position at the walk, trot and canter and over low fences, in the ring and in the open. (The next manuals will cover the C Level and the B and A levels.)

The core of the Pony Club program is the "working rally" (or mounted meeting). Club members come to this meeting with their ponies for riding lessons, horse management instruction, mounted games and other activities. Working rallies are held regularly and emphasize learning, safety and fun. Pony care and safety are always stressed, and members are expected to take care of themselves and their own ponies as much as possible (with adult supervision). There are also unmounted meetings for various projects, learning and fun!

Local Pony Clubs may send teams of members to local, regional

Teamwork. Pony Clubbers set up their equipment at a competitive rally. Parents may not help or coach their children at competitive rallies. Instead, children must work as a team, helped by Horse Management judges. *Photo: Neena Ewing.*

and national "competitive rallies" in combined training, show jumping, dressage, mounted games and the tetrathlon (a competition that includes riding, running, swimming and marksmanship). In Pony Club competitions, teamwork, horse management, good horsemanship and good sportsmanship are just as important as performance. Parents are not allowed to help or coach their children during a competitive rally; instead, Pony Clubbers work together as a team and help each other (with adult supervision).

Many Pony Clubs sponsor clinics with well-known instructors, or take part in such activities as foxhunting, polo, distance riding, vaulting and driving. Camping with ponies is also popular, and often includes special clinics or activities. Know-Down, which is like a quiz contest, is an unmounted activity Pony Clubbers enjoy, especially during the winter.

A week-long Pony Club Festival is held every three years at the Horse Park in Lexington, Kentucky. It includes the Pony Club Championships, along with several days of clinics, workshops and special activities for Pony Clubbers and their parents. Many families like to attend the Festival as a family vacation.

Pony Clubs are active in more than twenty-seven countries

around the world, and there is an exchange program for members of Pony Clubs in the United States and other countries.

If you want more information about Pony Club, or if you would like to join a Pony Club or start one in your area, write to

> The United States Pony Clubs, Inc.
> The Kentucky Horse Park
> 4071 Iron Works Pike
> Lexington, KY 40511

Or you can telephone (606) 254-PONY (7669).

Mounted games are popular Pony Club activities that are fun for children and ponies, too. *Photo: Neena Ewing.*

WHAT YOU NEED TO LEARN TO RIDE

This book and this level of horsemanship are about good basics, or getting started right. You will need lessons before you can think about having a pony of your own. It is much easier to learn and have fun with good instruction, and it is kinder to your pony. The right pony, instructor, equipment and place to ride can make a big difference in how easy it is, how safe you are and how much you and your pony enjoy it.

A Good Instructor

Look for a good instructor first—preferably an experienced USPC instructor who will be familiar with the Pony Club's programs, requirements and methods of teaching. Good instructors will be safety-minded, know their subject and make it easy to understand, and care about ponies and young people. A good riding program will be safe and well organized, with ponies that are well cared for, and a clean, safe and orderly stable and riding area. Above all, the program should teach good horsemanship—which means understanding, handling and caring for ponies—not just riding.

The Right Pony and Equipment

You should start out on a reliable beginner's pony. Such a pony is quiet and well trained and will respond correctly when you ask him in the proper way. Being "overmounted" means riding a horse or pony that is too much for you. This is frightening, dangerous and no fun at all! As you become a better rider, you will be ready to ride a more advanced pony.

When you get a pony of your own, you will need the right tack and equipment for the kind of riding you are doing. The Pony Clubs recommend an all-purpose balanced seat saddle, which must fit both the rider and the pony. (For more information about choosing tack and equipment, see Chapter 12.) Tack does not have to be new or expensive, but it must be in good repair and condition and fit your pony.

Dress for Safety

To learn to ride, you need clothes that are safe and comfortable for riding and working around ponies. The most important item is a properly fitted safety helmet, which must be made to Standard

7

A child's pony should be gentle, friendly and easy for a child to handle. *Photo: Neena Ewing.*

F1163 of the American Society for Testing Materials (ASTM) and tested by the Safety Equipment Institute (SEI). (Look for the ASTM/SEI label inside the helmet.) This *must* be worn with the chin strap fastened *whenever you are on a pony.* In case of a fall, it could prevent a serious head injury or even save your life!

You will also need safe shoes or boots, long pants and comfortable, washable clothes. (See page 283 for details.) These don't have to be expensive show clothes. Many Pony Clubs have used tack and clothing exchanges, where you may be able to find "outgrown" items at bargain prices.

Where Will You Ride?

Where you ride depends on where you live and what kind of space you have at home or nearby. You will need a fairly level area about 60 by 120 feet or larger for basic ring work, and you will also want to ride in an open area like a large field or pasture and on trails. Streets and roads are a poor place to ride a pony, and they can be quite dangerous. If you don't have a good place to ride at home, you may find that it is better to keep your pony at a stable that has safer places to ride.

8

Safety

Whenever people and horses are together, safety must always come first. No one wants to get hurt or to injure someone else or to see an animal get hurt. The best way to be safe around horses and ponies is to become an educated horse person, and to follow good safety practices *all the time.* In Pony Club, safety is taught from the very beginning and checked in everything you do at every level. Far from stopping the fun, this lets everyone enjoy riding and being around horses and ponies without unnecessary risk.

A horse or pony is a big, powerful animal with feelings and a mind of his own. Even the most gentle pony thinks and acts like an animal, not like a machine or a person, and any animal can surprise you. Most accidents happen when someone doesn't know enough about horses and safety, doesn't think, or gets careless about safety practices. A knowledgeable adult should always be in charge of any activity that involves children and horses.

Like any other sport, riding is about as safe as you make it. Every rider should start with a good foundation of basic skills and knowledge and have plenty of experience and confidence at one level before trying to move up to the next level. However, some people get into trouble because they want to try more advanced activities before their basics are solid, or because they are in a hurry to compete or to get the highest possible rating as quickly as they can. This can lead to being overmounted or trying to do difficult and demanding kinds of riding before you or your pony are ready. This is dangerous, unfair to your pony and no fun at all! If you take time to learn everything in each level thoroughly before thinking about a higher rating, and don't get carried away by competition, you and your pony will be safer and will enjoy your riding much more.

The Balance Seat

There are different seats or styles of riding for different purposes. The USPC teaches the Balance Seat, which is an all-purpose seat. It is riding by balance, not by strength or force. This kind of riding is based on a modified dressage seat and includes riding on the flat (ring riding), jumping and riding in the open (trail riding and cross-country jumping). With a good basis in the Balance Seat, a rider can adapt to any style of riding.

9

A PONY OF YOUR OWN?

Most horse lovers dream of having their own horse or pony, but it is not necessary to own a pony to join a Pony Club or to take part in Pony Club mounted activities. You may be able to use a lesson pony or a leased or borrowed pony if you do not have your own. However, you are expected to take as much care as possible of any pony you use.

Are You Ready for a Pony?

If you want to have your own pony, you will have a lot of planning to do. Can your family afford to keep a pony? The cost of feed, health care, foot trimming or shoeing, maintaining the stable and equipment and other expenses will add up to more than the cost of buying a pony. Do you have a good place to keep a pony at home, or will you board him someplace else? Do you know an experienced horse person who will help you learn all you need to know about keeping your pony safe, healthy and well cared for? Above all, do you have the time and interest to work with your pony and take care of him *every day,* even on days when you can't ride him?

No matter how much you want a pony, take your time and make sure you are ready for all that owning involves. It is better to take riding lessons and learn good basic pony care first. This can be fun, and it may help you convince your parents that you really are ready for a pony of your own.

Leasing a Pony

Leasing a pony is one way to have a pony without buying one. Sometimes owners will lease a pony to a good home, even if they do not want to sell him. A lease is for an agreed-on period, usually a year or longer.

Leasing a pony means that you must take good care of the pony and pay for all his expenses, including feed, shoeing, veterinary care and board if he is kept at a boarding stable. Some owners ask to be paid for the use of the pony, others don't. Some owners will only lease a pony if he stays at their stable, so they can supervise his care. Before your parents lease a pony, you should try out the pony to be sure that you can ride, handle and care for him, and your parents should get all lease arrangements in writing.

ESPECIALLY FOR PARENTS

Parents who are experienced horse persons will already know what owning a pony entails, particularly if they are familiar with Pony Club. The following information will help parents who are new to horses and riding.

What Are the Benefits of Riding?

Riding, and especially owning a horse or pony, is not a cheap sport, but it can have great benefits for children and families. Riding is a healthy outdoor sport; it can be enjoyed alone, in a group, as part of a team or as a family activity, and this enjoyment can be lifelong. Children are naturally attracted to animals and to the challenge of riding. Riding and caring for a pony can teach them kindness, patience, responsibility and perseverance, while taking instruction and working with other young riders can help instill self-discipline, good sportsmanship and self-esteem. Of course, these virtues don't come automatically from taking riding lessons or buying a pony; they require guidance, leadership and, ideally, family participation. Sharing the joys, work, growth and challenges of riding is a good way to bring children and families together, and it gives children a healthy and positive outlet for their interest, time and energy.

For some children, riding may be an avenue for high achievement or even a career. While the challenge of competition is important to some, riding can be enjoyed simply as a wholesome recreation that puts us in touch with nature and with a wonderful and responsive animal.

At What Age Should a Child Begin Riding?

To be ready to learn to ride, according to Dr. Doris Bixby Hammett of the American Medical Equestrian Association, your child should have:

* An interest in ponies and the desire to ride and learn.
* Enough muscle strength to maintain a safe and balanced position, and neck muscles strong enough to support properly fitted protective headgear.
* The balance to stay on the pony in motion.
* The ability to understand instructions and follow directions.
* A long enough attention span for instruction.

While some very young children enjoy petting, brushing and being around ponies (with careful adult supervision), and being led around on a pony for short periods, most are not ready to begin regular riding lessons in a group until they are seven or older. Your child will enjoy riding and Pony Club more if you wait until he or she is ready and eager for the experience.

How You Can Help Your Child

Your child's start in riding and his first pony will involve some new responsibilities. You don't have to be an expert horse-person to see that your child has the necessary adult help, guidance and supervision, or to be in touch with how he is getting on with his riding, pony care and handling, and his confidence and enjoyment of the whole experience. Providing the pony and the equipment is only a start; continuing parental interest, guidance and support are what make it work.

Here are some things you might do for your child:

Read this book along with your child, and help him learn and follow good horsemanship and safety practices.

Include your child in discussions about riding, Pony Club and getting a pony. It can help him learn about being prepared and organized and how to budget time and money. Be frank with your child about how much you can afford to spend for essentials and for optional items and special events. It is reasonable to expect your child to work to earn "nice to have" extras and optional activities. (Some clubs raise funds to defray the cost of special events like clinics.) You may want to set up a calendar and help your child plan time for stable chores, riding, Pony Club and special events, as well as his nonriding activities, schoolwork and other responsibilities.

Start out with the right pony. If you are new to horses and riding, *please* don't start out by buying a pony. Read the section on choosing a suitable pony, and above all, get expert advice—preferably from the instructor who will teach your child.

Get the right equipment. You do not need to buy an expensive show outfit, but your child must have safe and suitable clothing and equipment. Often good used equipment is a better buy than very cheap new tack. Ask your Pony Club instructor for help in choosing the right equipment, making sure it fits both child and pony, and checking it for safe condition. Many Pony Clubs have a used clothing and equipment exchange.

Enforce safety! Insist that your child wear a properly fitted ASTM/ SEI safety helmet (with the chin strap fastened) *whenever he is on a pony.* This rule can prevent a serious head injury or even save your child's life! Don't let your child work around a pony or in the stable in sandals, sneakers or bare feet. (Set a good example by following the rules yourself; don't visit the pony or enter the stable wearing sandals, etc.)

Spend time with your child as he works with his pony, and give him hands-on help and supervision. Learn the basics of leading and handling the pony safely, and be aware of how well your child follows the safety rules he has been taught. Lead the pony while your child is learning to stop, steer and control it, then be on hand to watch once he is able to ride on his own. If your child's instructor suggests that he practice certain things, you can encourage this practice at home.

Check on the pony's health, well-being and care daily. Check his water supply, that he is fed the right amount, that his stall is clean and that care and chores are being done properly and on time.

Help by providing a regular source of feed, veterinary care, shoeing and equipment repairs as needed. Children can't drive to the feed store, pay a vet bill or replace a broken stirrup leather by themselves. They must be able to count on parental support for basic essentials for the pony, for emergency help (like calling a veterinarian) and for repairs and maintenance that require adult help.

Insist on consideration for the pony. In their enthusiasm, children sometimes forget to give the pony a rest. They may overdo things that are fun for them but hard on the pony. When children get frustrated, they may make a mistake and lose their temper. If you suspect that the pony is being misused, whether through thoughtlessness or ignorance, you *must* intervene.

Downplay competition. Some children (and some parents!) can get carried away and put too much emphasis on competition— passing ratings as quickly as possible, qualifying for competitive rally teams, winning and achieving at any cost. This can undermine the fun, sportsmanship and spirit of cooperation that Pony Club is all about, and it can ruin the whole experience of riding and Pony Club. Try to help your child discover other important values like fun, friendship, learning at his own pace and reaching his own goals—not just winning or passing ratings for their own sake.

Be a good communicator. If a "people problem" arises (with instructor, other children, or adults), don't jump to conclusions— try to get the facts first. (Children may not understand a situation or may bring home a different version from what is really occurring.) Taking time to understand a problem and then addressing it clearly and in a positive way often works wonders.

Get Involved in Pony Club

Pony Clubs can only exist with the involvement and commitment of parents of members and other volunteers of all ages. The more you put into Pony Club, the more your child is likely to get out of it. As a parent, consider, for example:

- Providing food or beverages at meetings or rallies.
- Painting or setting up jumps; building cross-country fences.
- Providing transportation for a field trip.
- Providing horse/pony transportation to a rally.
- Helping with fund-raising projects.
- Chaperoning field trips or at out-of-town rallies.
- Helping prepare and maintain the grounds for your local Pony Club meeting place.
- Running unmounted meetings or even mounted meetings; arranging for a speaker or instructor.
- Acting as chairperson for a rally or other club activity.
- Working at a rally as a coach, chaperone, organizing secretary, fence judge or other helper.

You may become interested in taking a more active role in organizing and helping with your local club, or in helping to organize Pony Club activities.

Choosing a Suitable Pony for the D Level Rider

When you are looking for a pony for a novice rider, you should have an experienced horse person as an adviser (preferably your child's riding instructor). Determine how much you can afford to spend and then consult with your adviser about what kind of animal you can expect to find in your price range.

A novice rider needs a good beginner's pony, even though he will probably move on to another mount someday. He may outgrow the pony physically as he gets taller, and he may need to move up to a more advanced mount as he becomes a better rider. Don't buy a pony that is too advanced (or one that is too "green" or inexperienced) for your child at this stage in the hope that he will "grow into it." This very dangerous situation often results in a child being overmounted, frightened and put off riding forever and in the pony being ruined. If you choose a good pony that is suitable for D Level work, there will always be new riders who need this kind of pony when your child is ready to move on to a more advanced mount.

TEMPERAMENT AND MANNERS The most important qualities in a beginner's pony are temperament, manners and suitability for a child. The first pony can make or break a child's confidence, enjoyment of riding and ability to learn.

Look for a pony that is friendly, quiet and unflappable. He should be easy to handle and willing to do what he is asked. He must not have any bad habits like nipping, kicking or aggressive behavior, and he should not be easily frightened or upset. A beginner's pony must be able to tolerate some mistakes while his young rider is learning. If he is too quick and sensitive, or if he is nervous, spooky or too eager to go, he will be easily confused and upset and will be hard, if not dangerous, for a beginning rider to control. Avoid ponies that are very stubborn, willful or irritable; even if they are safe, they will be no fun to ride.

Don't accept a pony with a bad habit or a questionable temperament in the hope that he can be re-trained. Training will not change a pony's basic nature. If he is quick and sensitive, after training he may be well trained, but he will always be quick and sensitive. Re-training a problem pony is a long process that requires an experienced rider, and it is not always successful.

AGE, EXPERIENCE AND TRAINING The less experienced the rider, the more experienced the pony should be. A pony for a D Level rider should be a mature "solid citizen" who knows his job well, *not a young or "green" pony*! Young ponies, no matter how gentle, are still maturing and must have their training confirmed under an experienced rider. They can be confused and upset by an inexperienced rider, and will become difficult to ride and handle. Both pony and rider may have a bad time and be unsafe.

A pony for Pony Club work should be at least five years old (seven to ten is better), and older ponies are often the best mounts for beginners. Many ponies are sound and useful well into their teens and even beyond.

A good Pony Club pony should go quietly at the walk, trot and canter, in a ring and outside, alone and in a group of ponies. He should go quietly and easily over ground poles and low jumps (up to about 2'6"). It is easier to learn good riding from a pony who responds correctly to the aids. Because he will be handled by children, his ground manners are most important: he must be easy for a child to catch, lead, groom and handle. Since your child will want to take his pony to mounted meetings and other events, it is important for the pony to be easy to load in a trailer and unload, and to stand quietly when tied.

SIZE A horse or pony should be of a good size for your child to ride and handle, and to carry his rider easily and safely. For security, your child's feet should reach at least halfway down the pony's sides, and the pony should not be so wide that it is uncomfortable for a child to get his legs around it. A child's feet should not hang below the pony's barrel, and pony and rider should be in proportion to each other.

A small child mounted on a too-large horse will have difficulty keeping his balance and being secure in the saddle, and mounting and dismounting without help. The long gaits and big movement make it harder to stay in balance with his mount, and the speed of the gaits and big movement of a jump may be frightening. It will also be very hard for a small child to safely groom, saddle, and care for a horse that is too big for him.

A child that is too large for a pony often feels insecure and top-heavy, as if he might topple forward over the pony's head. If the rider is too heavy for the pony, he will have balance problems and the pony may develop foot and leg trouble or a sore back.

HEALTH AND SOUNDNESS The pony must be healthy, sound, and strong enough to do the kind of work you want of him. A lame pony or one with chronic problems can be a heartbreaking and expensive disappointment. Your veterinarian should examine any pony you are seriously considering (called a pre-purchase examination). This should include a blood test (called a Coggins test) for Equine Infectious Anemia. This test (and certain other inoculations) are required by most stables and Pony Clubs before you may bring your pony to mounted meetings.

Although perfect soundness is always desirable, a pony for D Level Pony Club work should not have to pass the kind of soundness tests expected for a race horse or a three-day eventer. He should be sound for riding lessons, ring and trail work, and low jumping. Some good, useful ponies have blemishes (like a scar or

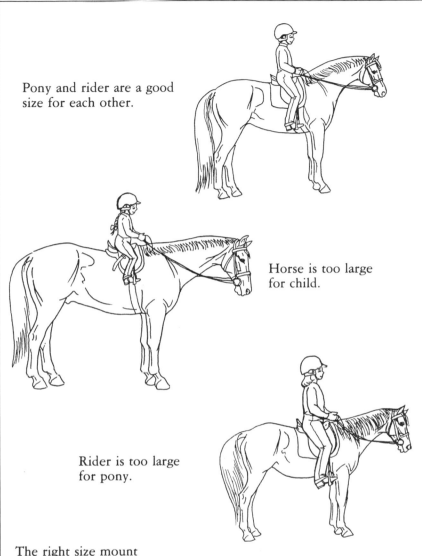

Pony and rider are a good size for each other.

Horse is too large for child.

Rider is too large for pony.

The right size mount

evidence of an old, healed injury), or a mild chronic condition that poses little or no problem with good management. Your veterinarian is your best adviser. Be sure he evaluates the pony in light of the work you plan to do with him, and how you will keep him.

GAITS, MOVEMENT AND JUMPING A pony with good gaits will make your child's riding easier and more enjoyable. He does not have to move well enough to win in the show ring, but he should move freely, with steady and even gaits that are comfortable for your child. Ponies should walk, trot, and canter. Those that perform a pace, running walk, or other special gaits are less suitable for this kind of riding.

Ideally, the pony should be a steady, experienced jumper that will jump quietly and easily over a variety of obstacles up to about 2 feet 6 inches high, in the ring and outside. A quiet, willing pony that is well trained on the flat but inexperienced in jumping would be preferable to an experienced jumper that is excitable or too strong for a beginning jumping rider.

SEX Mares and geldings are equally suitable. Some mares may be irritable around other ponies for the few days they are in season each month, but a quiet, well-trained mare should not be hard to manage. Stallions, no matter how well trained, are not safe for D Level children to ride or handle, especially in a group. They cannot be brought to Pony Club mounted events.

CONFORMATION AND BREED In a Pony Club mount, "Handsome is as handsome does." Good conformation is always desirable, but sound, functional conformation is more important than show-ring quality. Some conformation points to consider are the structure and straightness of the legs, the strength of the back and hindquarters, the pony's balance and proportions, and the length, shape, and balance of his neck and head. Conformation defects that can lead to performance or soundness problems (such as poor feet or crooked legs) are more important than "pretty" points, like the size of the ears, the shape of the head, or color. Ask your Pony Club instructor or an experienced horse-person to evaluate a pony you are considering, but emphasize the pony's real purpose—don't put conformation ahead of health, safety, and temperament.

A good Pony Club mount might be of any breed or combination of breeds. This is a matter of personal preference. It is more important to find a pony that suits your child than to insist on a particular breed of pony.

Trying Out a Pony

When you are looking for a pony, it's important to have an experienced horse-person along (preferably your child's riding instructor).

The first thing to observe about a pony is how he behaves in his home environment. How does he act in his stall, in a pasture, during grooming and tacking up? Can your child catch him, lead him, pick up his feet and tack him up (with assistance)? Does your child feel confident with him or intimidated by him?

Watch the pony as he is led in a straight line toward you and away from you. Does he travel straight and freely, or does he move crookedly?

Have someone else ride the pony first while you, your child and an experienced horse-person watch. How does the pony behave during mounting and as he is ridden? Does he move freely and evenly? Does he seem to respond easily to the rider's aids, showing good manners and a pleasant attitude, or does he resist or act up? How does the rider's experience compare with that of your child? If the pony is of a suitable size, you may want to ride him yourself or have your child's instructor ride him before you put your child on him.

The real test of a pony's suitability is how he performs for your child. It may be a good idea to keep the pony on a lead line or a longe line until you are sure that your child is confident and in control. He should try walking, stopping and turning before mov-

The real test of a pony is how well he performs for a child. This is a perfectly matched pair! *Photo: Susan Sexton.*

ing on to a faster gait. See if the pony is quiet and easy to ride on loose reins as well as on contact, and if he will stand quietly with the reins relaxed. If your child has experience in jumping, try the pony first over ground poles and work up gradually to the size jumps he and the pony are comfortable with. Try the pony in a ring and outside, alone and with other ponies.

Some owners will permit you to take a pony on trial for a week or longer, but this is a rare privilege, as a pony could be ruined in a short time in the wrong hands. Sometimes you can lease the pony for a month or so, which amounts to a trial period. If not, you may want to return for a second trial ride. In any case, you should insist on a veterinary examination (and an evaluation by your child's riding instructor) before accepting the pony. Take plenty of time to decide, because the pony will be your child's companion for a long time, and you want to find the right one.

PART 2

LEARNING TO RIDE

CHAPTER 2

D-1 Level:
Beginning to Ride

Safety is a concern at any level, but it is especially important at the D-1 Level. What you do now will help you establish good habits for later on.

SAFETY RULES FOR BEGINNING RIDERS

1. Dress safely for riding.
   - ASTM/SEI-approved safety helmet (properly fitted, with chin strap fastened).
   - Riding shoes or boots with a hard, smooth sole and a definite heel.
   - Long pants that don't wrinkle, rub or bind.
   - Shirt or sweater that tucks in.
   - No loose scarfs, pins or barrettes in hair, earrings, bracelets, rings, or waist packs. No candy or gum in mouth while riding.
2. Ride only with supervision, in an enclosed ring, until your instructor says you are ready to ride safely by yourself.
3. Ride a pony that is suitable for you and that you can handle and control safely.
4. Have a responsible person check your tack before you mount (both sides of the saddle and bridle).
5. Keep a safe distance (at least one pony length) between your pony and any other pony.

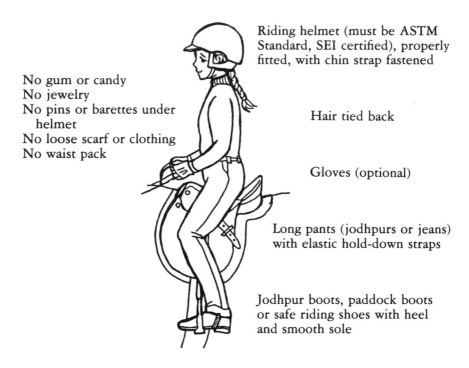

Riding helmet (must be ASTM Standard, SEI certified), properly fitted, with chin strap fastened

No gum or candy
No jewelry
No pins or barettes under helmet
No loose scarf or clothing
No waist pack

Hair tied back

Gloves (optional)

Long pants (jodhpurs or jeans) with elastic hold-down straps

Jodhpur boots, paddock boots or safe riding shoes with heel and smooth sole

Dress safely for riding

6. Run your stirrups up whenever you are not mounted. Keep the reins from dragging on the ground.
7. Pay attention to your pony and how he is feeling and acting. Always take good care of your pony after you ride him.

MOUNTING AND DISMOUNTING
How to Do a Tack Safety Check

Always do a safety check before mounting.

Put the reins over the pony's head.

Starting on the *right* side, check that the saddle pad is straight and that the girth is buckled correctly. Pull down the right stirrup. Check the right side of the bridle. All buckles should be fastened properly, with nothing twisted.

As you go to the *left* side, check the left side of the bridle. Check to be sure that the girth is tight enough and that the saddle pad is straight. Pull down the left stirrup.

Check:

Noseband, throatlash, bit and curb chain fit properly.
Strap ends are in keepers.

Check:

All parts of bridle are straight and buckled properly.
Bit and bridle fit correctly.
Strap ends are in keepers.

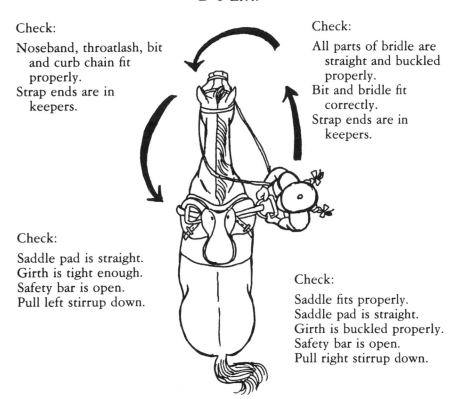

Check:

Saddle pad is straight.
Girth is tight enough.
Safety bar is open.
Pull left stirrup down.

Check:

Saddle fits properly.
Saddle pad is straight.
Girth is buckled properly.
Safety bar is open.
Pull right stirrup down.

How to do a safety check

How to Check Stirrup Length

Put your knuckles (in a fist) against the stirrup bar and stretch the stirrup leather along your arm. The stirrup iron should just reach your armpit. Make sure both stirrups are the same length before you mount.

How to Mount

Stand next to your pony's left shoulder, facing the tail. Hold both reins in your left hand on top of his neck, with the reins snug enough so that he won't walk off. Put the extra loop of rein (called the "bight") on the far side. With your right hand, take the back of the stirrup iron and turn it toward you. Put your left foot all the way into the stirrup with your toe down, so you won't poke the pony in the belly with your toe.

Put your right hand on the pommel (the front of the saddle) or in the middle of the seat. Never put your hand on the cantle (the back of the saddle), as this can pull the saddle over. Turn so

The stirrup should just reach into your armpit. Make sure both stirrups are the same length before you mount. *Photo: Ruth Harvie.*

you are facing the pony's side and spring up from your right foot, to "stand" for a moment with both legs together and your weight on your hands.

Swing your right leg over the pony's rump. Be careful not to kick him. Catch your weight on your knees and sink *gently* into the saddle. Never come down hard on his back!

Put your right foot into the stirrup and take your reins in both hands. Don't let your pony move off until you are ready.

If you are short or your pony is tall, you can get help from soneone or stand on a step, a mounting block or a hay bale. You can also let the left stirrup down so it is easier to reach it. (Don't try to climb on from a fence or from anything that might tip over.)

How to Dismount

Put both reins (and stick) in the left hand, with the end of the reins (the bight) on the right side of the pony's neck. Take both feet out of the stirrups. Put your right hand on the pommel or on the pony's neck.

Lean forward and swing your right leg over the pony's rump, making sure it doesn't touch his rump. Turn and slide down with your side against the pony, so that you land facing forward.

After dismounting, take the reins over your pony's head and run both stirrups up. If you are not going to remount right away, loosen the girth a hole or two.

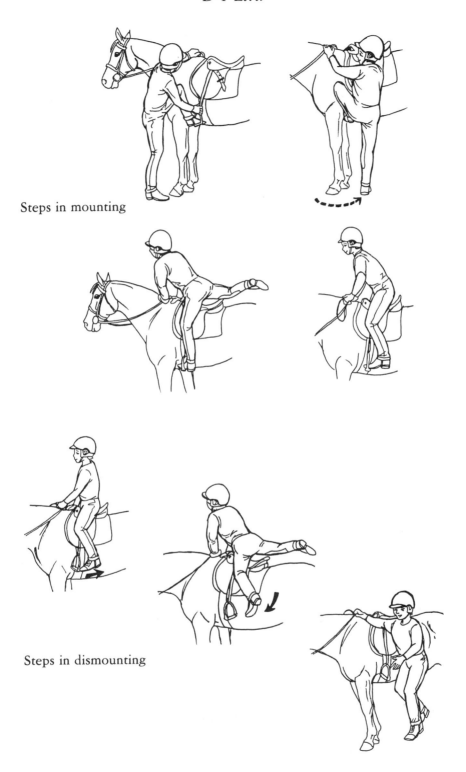

Steps in mounting

Steps in dismounting

Never dismount by swinging your leg forward over your pony's neck. You have to let go of your reins to do this, and if the pony moves off you could land on the back of your head.

BASIC POSITION FOR THE BALANCE SEAT

The way you sit makes all the difference to your riding. A good riding position makes it easy for you to stay on your pony and to ride in balance, and it is comfortable for you and for your pony. Sitting wrong makes it harder to ride and can make you sore, and can give your pony a backache. It takes time and practice to learn to sit the right way, but it is worth it.

Seat

Sit on your seat bones, deep in the center of the saddle. If you rock your seat a little, you will feel two bones like the rockers of a rocking chair. Sit on your seat bones, not on the front of your seat or on your buttocks.

Sit deep and tall in the saddle. If you take a deep breath, you will feel your back get taller and more relaxed and your seat get deeper. Let your legs hang down long and relaxed, and your head balance over your shoulders. Sit evenly in the middle of the saddle, not off to one side.

Stirrups and Feet

When your legs hang down, the bottom of the stirrup irons should touch just below your ankle bones. If your stirrups are too long, you will bounce and dangle your legs. If the stirrups are too short, they will push your legs forward and your seat backward.

Your stirrup should be under the ball of your foot, and your heels should be down (this will take some practice). Your toes should point out a little (about as much as your knees). They should not be turned in or stick way out.

Legs

Your legs should hang down so that they lie gently against the saddle and the pony's sides. They should not grip or pinch the saddle (this makes you stiff), but they should not stick out, either. The inside of your calf should be lightly touching your pony's

Good balanced position:

    Eyes up
    Arms hang beside ribs
    Knees and ankles relaxed
    Head balanced
    Back straight
    Balanced on seat bones
    Feet and legs under body
    Heels down

Problem positions:

WRONG
"Slumping"
Head and eyes down
Round back
Sitting on buttocks
Rider out of balance
Arms out ahead of body
Knees pinching
Heels up, toes down

WRONG
"Chair seat"
Back straight, but feet
  and legs ahead
Rider out of balance
  backward
Knees tight
Heels level

WRONG
"Perching"
Too far forward
Stiff, hollow back
Sitting on front of
  seat (crotch)
Knees tight
Legs too far back
Heels level or up

The Balanced Seat

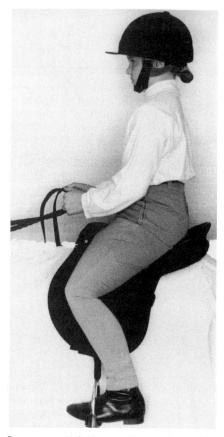

A balanced position. This rider's feet and legs are under her body, and you can draw a vertical line through her ear, shoulder, seat and foot. *Photo: Ruth Harvie.*

Incorrect "chair seat" position. Although she is sitting up straight, this rider's legs and feet are ahead of her seat, putting her out of balance. *Photo: Ruth Harvie.*

side. Your toes should be just under your knees, not out ahead of them. Your feet should hang underneath your seat.

Head and Eyes

Your head is quite heavy; it controls your balance. If your head tips down or to the side, your pony will feel it and may think he is supposed to stop or turn. Your eyes steer your head. If you look up and out over your pony's head, it helps your head (and the rest of you) stay in balance.

Shoulders, Arms and Hands

Let your shoulders hang down wide and relaxed. Your arms hang down under your shoulders, close to your ribs. Keep a gentle bend in your elbows. Do not stick your forearms stiffly out ahead of you or poke your elbows out to the sides. Keep your hands low, with your forearms and knuckles pointing toward the pony's mouth.

Some tips for good position and balance:

- When you take a deep breath, it relaxes your seat and back and helps you sit up tall, without making you stiff or sloppy.
- Look at a "target"—something at eye level in line with where you are going. Turn your eyes and find a new target whenever you turn your pony. Never look down. This helps balance your head and "aims" your pony where you are looking.
- Don't grip with your knees or thighs. Let them lie relaxed against the saddle. This helps them move with your pony and take up the bounces.
- To find your balance in the saddle (at a halt), try a "teeter-totter" exercise. Tip your body (from the seat bones up) back a little and forward a little until you feel yourself straight up and down in the middle of the saddle, sitting on your seat bones.
- Let your feet rest on the stirrups without pushing against them. Try to keep your heels back and down, not forward.
- To help remember the best length for your reins, you can put a piece of tape on your reins at the spot where you should hold them.

HANDS AND REINS
How to Hold the Reins

To pick up your reins, lay the reins on your pony's neck. Put your thumbs together, palms down. Pick up the reins and turn the ends of the reins forward, with your thumbs on top. Your little finger may be inside the rein, or the rein may go between your little finger and your ring finger. Your hands should be closed in a soft fist (not with open fingers, which can let the reins slip, or with tight, hard fists).

Shortening and Lengthening the Reins

To make your reins shorter, hold the tail end of your left rein with your right hand while you slide your hand down the rein.

Then hold the tail end of the right rein while you slide your right hand down the rein. Put your thumbs on the ends of the reins so they won't slip.

To make your reins longer, open your fingers a little and let the reins slide through.

How to pick up the reins:

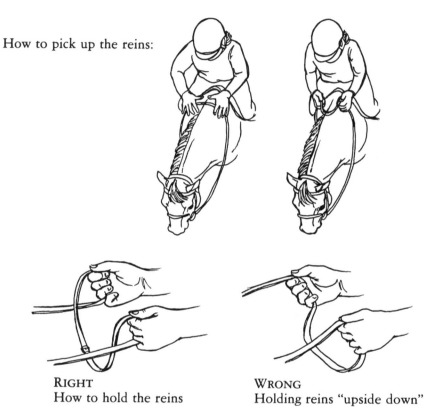

RIGHT
How to hold the reins

WRONG
Holding reins "upside down"

Holding the reins

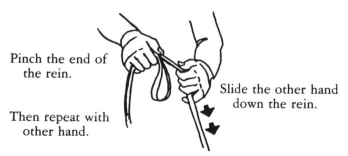

Pinch the end of the rein.

Then repeat with other hand.

Slide the other hand down the rein.

How to shorten the reins

Proper Length of Rein

Keeping the reins at just the right length takes some practice, but it makes a great difference in how easy it is to ride and control your pony. Your reins should be long enough so that you can keep your hands over your pony's withers, with your elbows bent. When your pony is going along as he should, there should be a gentle sag in the reins, but you should be able to tighten them by squeezing your hands into fists.

If your reins are too short, your pony will be unhappy and may

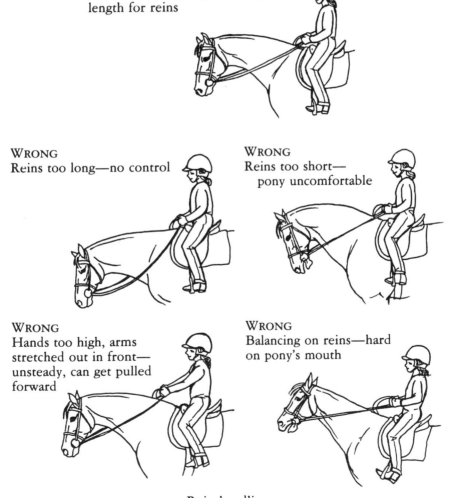

RIGHT
Hands in the right position, good length for reins

WRONG
Reins too long—no control

WRONG
Reins too short—
pony uncomfortable

WRONG
Hands too high, arms stretched out in front—unsteady, can get pulled forward

WRONG
Balancing on reins—hard on pony's mouth

Rein handling

pull or toss his head. You can also get pulled forward. If they are too long, your pony will not pay attention and it will be hard to stop or turn him.

LEARNING TO WALK AND CONTROL YOUR PONY

When you first begin to move, just relax and let your body get the feel of the pony's movements. Someone should lead your pony until you have found your balance and are comfortable at the walk, and have learned how to control your pony. The walk is a four-beat gait (it sounds like "one, two, three, four," or "clip, clop, clip, clop"). It is quite smooth and easy to ride.

Basic Control—the Aids

Ponies can't understand human talk the way we can, but we must have some way to communicate with them. The "aids" are the signals you use to help your pony understand what you want him to do. They are your legs, your hands, your seat, and sometimes your voice. Since a pony is trained to obey certain signals, you have to learn how to give the proper aids, or signals, so he can understand you and do what you want. If you don't give him the right aids at the right time, he will be confused.

The simple aids are:

Legs A short squeeze of both legs (using the calf muscle) or a nudge with the heels means to go forward. A squeeze with one leg means to turn that way.

Hands Your hands hold the reins, which are attached to a metal bit in the pony's mouth, so use them smoothly and gently. Both hands squeezing backwards (like squeezing water out of a sponge) means to stop or slow down. One hand moving out to the side means to turn that way. To let the pony move forward, both hands must relax.

Seat Your pony can feel your seat through the saddle. When you relax your seat and sit up deep and tall, it tells him to slow down or stop. When you look to one side and turn your head and your body, he knows he should turn the way you are looking.

Voice Your voice is only used to help out the other aids and not used instead of them. A low, gentle "Whoa" or "Easy" can help calm down a nervous pony, and a short "cluck" sound may help get a lazy pony to move on. Remember to praise your pony with a "Good boy" and a pat on the neck when he does what you want.

Aids should be short, like a heartbeat. You use an aid and then relax it right away. If your pony doesn't pay attention, give him another short aid, a bit stronger, but not longer. Sometimes it may take four or five aids before he understands and starts to obey you. As soon as he begins to obey, ease up on your aids.

LEARNING TO WALK, STOP AND TURN
To Walk On

First, look ahead where you want to go. Make sure your reins are short enough so that you can just feel your pony's mouth. Squeeze your legs against your pony's sides once to make him listen, then give him two short nudges with your legs to tell him to walk on. Let your hands go forward a little to "follow" his head as he starts to walk.

To Stop (or Halt)

To stop your pony, take a deep breath and sit tall, with your shoulders back. Close your legs in against your pony's sides and keep your heels down, then stop following with your arms and

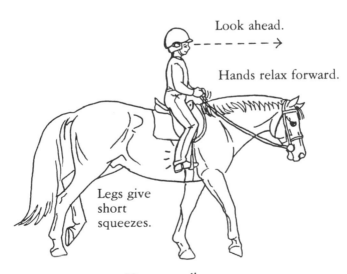

Look ahead.

Hands relax forward.

Legs give short squeezes.

How to walk on

hands, and squeeze your fingers several times, like squeezing water out of a sponge. Squeeze as strongly as you have to in order to make it work. Let your hands and legs ease up as he stops.

To Turn

First, look the way you want to turn. Sit up tall and turn your seat a little bit, and take your hand out to the side (away from the pony's neck). This asks him to turn his head and shows him where to go. Your other hand must ease up enough to let him turn. Use both legs to keep him going, and let your outside leg (the one you are turning away from) slide back a little. This helps to control his hindquarters.

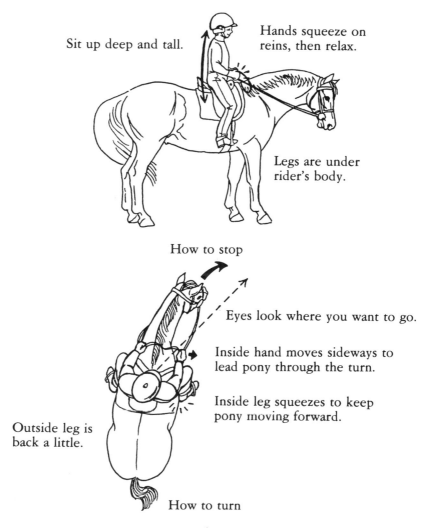

Sit up deep and tall.

Hands squeeze on reins, then relax.

Legs are under rider's body.

How to stop

Eyes look where you want to go.

Inside hand moves sideways to lead pony through the turn.

Inside leg squeezes to keep pony moving forward.

Outside leg is back a little.

How to turn

To Keep Your Pony Close to the Rail

Many ponies like to cut their corners and come into the center of the ring. To keep your pony on the track (next to the rail), first look ahead where you want him to go. Next, squeeze or nudge with your *inside leg* (the leg toward the center of the ring) as you steer him out toward the rail with both hands.

To Change Direction

When you turn and go the other way, it is called a "change of direction," or a "reverse." Before you change direction, your pony should be walking straight, next to the rail.

To change direction, look across the ring in the direction you want to turn. Make a turn across the ring. In the middle of the

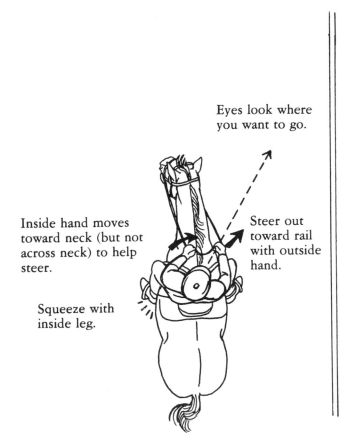

Eyes look where you want to go.

Inside hand moves toward neck (but not across neck) to help steer.

Steer out toward rail with outside hand.

Squeeze with inside leg.

How to keep pony close to the rail

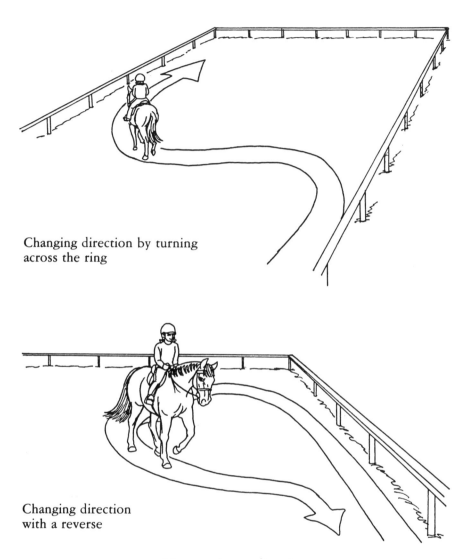

Changing direction by turning
across the ring

Changing direction
with a reverse

How to change direction

ring, look the other way. Turn your eyes, your seat (just a little), and your hand toward the new direction, and use your legs to keep your pony going. As you get to the rail, you will be going the other way.

To practice turning and changes of direction, it helps to set up cones, buckets or other markers to steer around, to help you remember where to turn.

LEARNING TO TROT
Your First Trot

When you are comfortable and can ride with good balance and control at the walk, you may learn to trot. A trot is a two-beat gait (it sounds like "One, two" or "Clip, clop"). It is a little faster and more bouncy than the walk. Someone should lead your pony at first, or your instructor should control your pony with a longe line, until you get your balance and can control your pony in a trot. Hold onto the pommel of the saddle or a neckstrap, so that your hands won't bounce up and down and hurt your pony's mouth, or make you lose your balance. At first, try a short, slow trot (just a few yards) several times, instead of trotting too long or too fast.

The aids for the trot are the same as for walking. Shorten your reins a little, squeeze with your legs once to make your pony listen, then give two short squeezes or nudges—as many as it takes to get your pony to trot. Be careful not to pull back on the reins, or the pony won't trot. If you don't hold onto the saddle

Riding a trot for the first time

or neckstrap and your hands bounce around, you will jerk on the pony's mouth and he may stop short.

When you ride the trot, it helps to breathe deeply, relax and sit up tall. Keep your shoulders back and let your legs hang down. Let your knees, hips and ankles be soft and springy to take up the bounces.

When you get used to trotting, you can put the reins in one hand and hold the pommel of the saddle with the other. Be sure to keep the hand that holds the reins down low against the pony's neck, so that it doesn't bounce and jerk. You can pull on the pommel to get your seat deep into the saddle. When you can keep your seat deep and your rein hand still and quiet, you can try letting go of the saddle and holding the reins in both hands. But if you start to bounce or lose your balance, catch the pommel quickly so you don't hurt your pony's mouth. Practice with short, slow trots until you are quite comfortable sitting at the trot. It's a good idea to practice trotting on a longe line, with an instructor controlling your pony while you learn to sit and go with the movement of the trot.

Half-Seat (Jumping Position)

Half-seat is a balancing position in which you are half sitting and half standing, not standing all the way up. Half-seat is also called jumping position. It is used for posting trot, for jumping and for riding up hills. It also helps you learn to balance and to keep your heels down.

To get into half-seat, tilt your body forward from your seat bones (not from your waist). Your seat should sink backwards a little as your shoulders go forward, just over your knees. Let your heels sink down and your knees stay springy, and keep your weight on your thighs, with head up and your eyes looking ahead. Don't stand up or lean out over your pony's neck. You should balance with your seat close to the saddle.

While you are learning to balance in a half-seat, you should rest your hands on the pony's neck or use a neckstrap. This keeps your hands from bouncing and pulling on his mouth by mistake while you are getting your balance. As you get better at riding in half-seat, you can practice at a walk and then at a slow trot, letting your knees, ankles and hips take up the bounces.

Half-seat

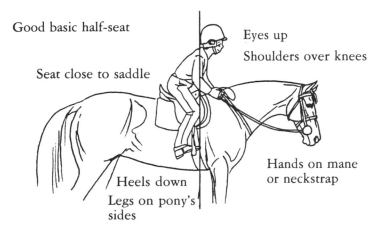

Good basic half-seat

Seat close to saddle

Eyes up
Shoulders over knees

Hands on mane
or neckstrap

Heels down
Legs on pony's
sides

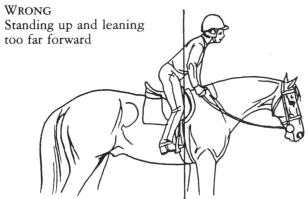

WRONG
Standing up and leaning
too far forward

Posting (Rising) to the Trot

Posting (also called "rising") is an easier way of riding a faster or bouncy trot. In a posting trot, you let your pony lift you up with one bounce and sit down with the next. This is easier on his back and is less tiring for you when trotting long distances.

To learn to post or rise to the trot, you will need good balance and control at the trot first. At a steady trot, count with your pony's rhythm: "One, two; one, two; one, two . . ." You will feel him lift or push you up with every other bounce (on "one"). You sit back down on the next step (on "two"). When you are balanced just right and catch his rhythm, it feels like you are "with" him perfectly and posting is easy. Remember, the bounce of your pony's trot does all the lifting—don't try to lift yourself up and

Let your pony lift you up
on one beat.

Then sit down for the
next beat.

Posting trot

down. You should only post as high as he lifts you, which is usually
very close to the saddle, not standing up high.

When you are learning to post, keep your hands on the pony's
neck or hold a neckstrap, so your hands don't bounce and jerk
his mouth or make you lose your balance. Keep your eyes up and
look ahead, and let your heels sink down. It is much easier to
post if your pony trots steadily along the rail than if he slows
down, speeds up, or cuts into the center. It may be easier to
practice your posting in a longe lesson, with your instructor controlling your pony. To help you feel his rhythm, you can hum or
sing along with his trot. To help your balance, you can practice
half-seat at a walk or at a slow trot.

IMPROVING CONTROL
Transitions (Changes of Gait)

A transition is a change. When you walk on from a halt or trot
on from the walk, it is called an "up" transition. When you slow
down from a trot to a walk or halt from a walk, it is called a
"down" transition.

Transitions should be smooth and gradual, so they are easy on
you and your pony. He will take several steps to slow down from
a trot to a walk or to stop. You and your pony should be in balance
during transitions, so that you feel secure and your pony can go
forward, stop or turn easily.

To make a good transition, you must *prepare* your pony by sitting up deep and tall, closing your legs on his sides and having your reins short enough to feel his mouth. This tells him to get ready. You ask for "up" transitions with short squeezes or nudges of your legs (being sure to look ahead and to relax your hands to let him go forward). For "down" transitions, sit deep and tall, take a deep breath, keep your shoulders back and give short squeezes with your hands on the reins. Remember to ease up on the pressure as soon as he starts to obey your aids.

Rating (Changing Speed) at the Walk and Trot

Sometimes you may want your pony to go faster or slower in the walk or trot, without changing to another gait. This is called "rating," or controlling his speed in a gait.

To go faster, give short squeezes or nudges with your legs in rhythm with your pony's walk or trot. Your hands must let him stretch his neck out more in order to move faster.

To go slower, sit deep and tall, take a deep breath and keep your shoulders back while you give short squeezes on the reins in rhythm with your pony's walk or trot. Keep your legs closed on his sides so that he doesn't stop instead of slowing down.

Getting the Best from Your Pony

Each pony is special and a little different from every other pony. Your pony should be trained to obey proper aids, but you will have to learn just how to give the aids in the best way for him. Some ponies are quite sensitive and respond quickly to a soft, light touch of your hands or legs. They may get upset if you use your aids too hard or too quickly, or if you are not smooth and quiet with your aids. Other ponies are a bit lazy. They need a "wake-up call" (like a firm squeeze of your legs) to get them to pay attention when you give them an aid, and you may have to use your aids more firmly.

Always use the lightest aids that will get the job done. Start out with a light aid, then make the next one stronger if you have to. If you start out with strong, hard aids, it can upset your pony and make him difficult to ride.

Some ponies want to have their own way. They will try to find out if they can ignore your aids and if you will give up. If a pony acts stubborn, you must not lose your temper, but you should not give up, either. He might be confused because you made a mistake in using your aids. Try again, giving him a very clear, correct aid. If he still does not do what you ask him, give the aids again several times, a bit stronger each time. Be as strong as you have to to get him to obey, but remember that getting angry or losing your temper doesn't work and is unkind to your pony. Remember to reward him with a pat and a "Good boy" as soon as he starts to obey you.

If you are having trouble with your pony and you find yourself starting to get upset with him, *stop, dismount and take time to calm down.* Don't try to ride a pony when you are upset or angry, and *never* lose your temper with him. Instead, ask your instructor for help with the problem.

GETTING READY TO LEARN TO JUMP
Jumping Position

Jumping position is the same as half-seat, which you learned before the posting trot. It is used for jumping, for riding up hills and as an exercise to help you learn to balance and to get your heels

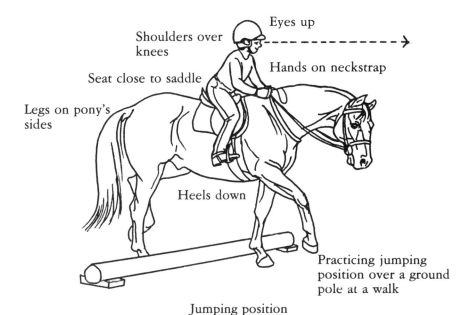

Eyes up

Shoulders over knees

Hands on neckstrap

Seat close to saddle

Legs on pony's sides

Heels down

Practicing jumping position over a ground pole at a walk

Jumping position

44

down. This position is important because it keeps you in balance with your pony when he goes over poles or jumps. It makes it easier for him to stretch his neck out to see where he is going, to round his back and to pick up his feet.

When you practice jumping position, you should balance close to your saddle, not standing up. Your heels must be down and your knees springy. Your head and eyes must look up and ahead, and your hands should be on the pony's neck or holding a neckstrap. You will need to practice jumping position at a standstill, at a walk and at a slow trot before you are ready to go over poles.

Practice with "Invisible Jumps"

You can practice control and steering over "invisible jumps" before you start riding over ground poles or real jumps. An "invisible jump" is made by setting up two jump standards as if for a jump, but without a jump pole between them. This is a good way to build your confidence and to practice jumping skills safely.

You will need to learn to "aim" your pony with your head and eyes. Pick out a "target" that is in line with the center of the invisible jump, and at your eye level (something like a spot on the wall or a tree branch). As you turn toward the invisible jump and ride straight down the line, keep your eyes on your target. Be careful not to peek down, even for a second!

At the end of the line, stop your pony while you keep your eyes on your target. If he is a little crooked or off the line, use your leg on his side to make him move over until he is lined up with your target. Then pat him and walk on. Practice aiming at your target with your eyes until you can ride him over the center of the invisible jump at a walk or a trot without looking down.

Now you are ready to practice in jumping position or half-seat. Keep your eyes on the target while you walk and then trot over the invisible jump. Keep your hands on your pony's neck or hold the neckstrap over the invisible jump.

Riding over Ground Poles

A ground pole is a pole on the ground, about 4 to 6 inches thick and 10 to 12 feet long. It should be fixed in place so it can't roll under your pony's feet if he should hit it. Ground poles are the lowest and easiest jumps. They help you and your pony get ready for bigger jumps.

When you ride over a ground pole, do it just as you have practiced. Steer with your eyes on the target as you walk on in a half-seat (jumping position), so you will feel balanced. As your pony steps over the pole, he should stretch his neck out and look where he is stepping. Your hands must stay firmly on his neck or neckstrap so they don't pull on his mouth. He may want to slow down, so your legs may have to squeeze to keep him walking forward. As he picks up his legs over the pole, his back may feel rounder and he may lift you up a bit. Let your heels sink down while your knees and hips take up the extra bounce. Remember to ride straight, to sit up and stop him at the end of the line and to give him a pat for doing what you asked him to.

You should be in half-seat every time you ride over a pole. This makes it easier for your pony to pick up his feet properly. You should have lots of practice walking over ground poles in

◆◆◆

USPC D-1-LEVEL RIDING TEST REQUIREMENTS

To pass the D-1 riding test, child should ride in an enclosed area without a lead line, demonstrating correct basic position at the halt and ride with control at the walk and trot.

1. Mount and dismount, with assistance if necessary.
2. Hold reins correctly at the halt.
3. Shorten and lengthen reins correctly at the halt.
4. Demonstrate correct basic position at the halt.
5. Ride at the walk and trot with control, keeping the pony on the rail.
6. Demonstrate a simple change of direction at the walk and trot.
7. Perform gradual transitions from walk to trot and walk to halt.
8. Walk over poles on the ground in jumping position.
9. Child will discuss with Examiner the reasons for different positions when riding on the flat and over fences (ground poles at this stage).

◆◆◆

half-seat before you try trotting over a pole or walking over a bigger pole.

COMMON PROBLEMS FOR D-1 RIDERS
The Pony Pulls

Some ponies pull on the reins with a jerk. This can hurt your hands, especially if the reins get pulled through your fingers, or if you are leaning forward, you could get pulled down onto the pony's neck.

The reason most ponies pull is because somebody has pulled on their mouth and hurt them, or because you are holding the reins too short. This can happen if your hands bounce or if you grab the reins for balance. If you have trouble with your balance, put your hands on your pony's neck or hold a neckstrap, so you won't pull on the reins by mistake.

Sit up deep and tall, with your shoulders back, so you won't be pulled forward. Keep your fingers closed on the reins and your thumbs on the end of the reins, so they can't be pulled through your fingers. Give your pony enough rein so that he can relax his neck and his mouth, especially when he is standing still. When you use your hands to turn, slow down or stop your pony, give short, gentle squeezes, not long, hard pulls.

It also may help to wear gloves when you ride.

The Pony Eats Grass

If your pony tries to eat grass while you are riding, he may put his head down suddenly and give you a jerk. If you let him eat grass when he should be working, he will want to eat instead of work, and he may get stubborn about it.

To keep him from eating grass, sit up deep and tall and keep your shoulders back. If he puts his head down to eat, keep your seat down in the saddle and your elbows bent, and hold the reins firmly. This makes him pull on his own mouth instead of pulling you forward.

If your pony gets his head down and will not stop eating, pull sideways and up instead of straight back. You may have to tap him with a crop to get his attention. Use your legs to make him move on.

In lessons only, a pony that is very stubborn about eating grass may have to wear a special check rein (called "grass reins"). CAUTION: Never use grass reins on a pony that is jumping or going over ground poles. In competitive rallies, grass reins are considered too dangerous to be used at all.

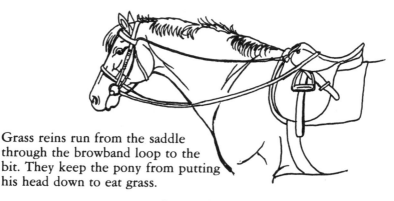

Grass reins run from the saddle through the browband loop to the bit. They keep the pony from putting his head down to eat grass.

Grass reins

CHAPTER 3

D-2 Level:
Improving Your Riding

Riding on the flat to D-2 Level standards will offer you new challenges and each will help you improve your skills even more. First, however, you must develop a good seat.

WHAT IS A GOOD SEAT?

Your "seat" means the way you sit, your balance and the way you use your body when you ride. A good seat helps you stay on your pony, makes you more comfortable and makes it easier for your pony to carry you.

A good seat is relaxed and supple, not tight and tense. It comes from balance, not from gripping with your muscles. An "independent" seat means that you can ride without using your hands for balance or to hold on. It also means that moving one part of your body (like your arms) does not make the other parts of your body (like your legs or seat) move out of position. Without an independent seat you will get bounced around, and you may grab the reins to keep your balance. Bouncy, unbalanced riders, tight, tense riders and riders who grab the reins for balance are hard on their ponies, even though they don't mean to be.

To develop an independent seat, you must get used to riding in good balance and position, and let your body go with your pony as he moves. This takes practice, but it helps you ride better.

BALANCE AND SUPPLING EXERCISES

At first, you may get sore muscles after riding, because your muscles are not used to the work. These exercises warm up your muscles and make them stronger and more supple, so you won't get so sore. They will also help your balance, confidence and control of your hands and legs. They are fun, too!

Always do a new exercise first at a halt, with someone holding your pony and watching out for you while you learn the exercise. Start gently and slowly, to let your pony get used to it. Later you can do exercises at a walk while someone leads your pony, or during a longe lesson (with your instructor controlling the pony on a longe line).

When your feet will be out of the stirrups during some exercises, you should cross your stirrups in front of the saddle. This keeps them out of your way and keeps them from banging against your pony's sides. (If you pull the stirrup leather buckle about 6 inches out from the stirrup bar, you can fold the stirrup leathers flat as you cross them over.) When you do exercises with your hands off the reins, tie a knot in the end of the reins to make them shorter, so that they will lie on the pony's neck where you can reach them.

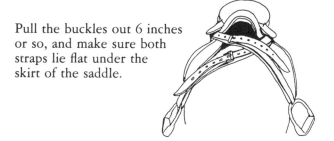

Pull the buckles out 6 inches or so, and make sure both straps lie flat under the skirt of the saddle.

Crossing stirrups

DROPPING AND PICKING UP STIRRUPS

1. Drop your stirrups (slip your feet out).
2. To pick up your stirrups, turn your toes in and slip your feet into the irons, without looking down at your stirrups

or using your hands to help. Practice until you can pick up your stirrups quickly at a halt and then at a walk.

FOOT CIRCLES AND ANKLE STRETCHES

These supple your ankles and help keep your heels down.

1. With both feet out of stirrups, draw circles in the air with your toes. Circle both feet one way, then the other.
2. Point your toes down toward the ground, then point them up as high as you can. Repeat several times.

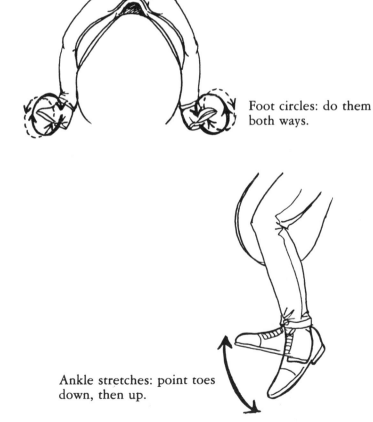

Foot circles: do them both ways.

Ankle stretches: point toes down, then up.

Foot and ankle exercises

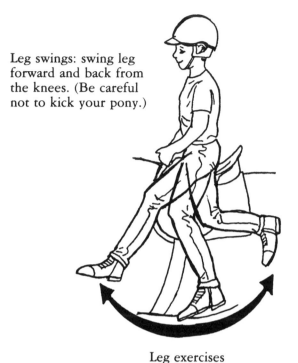

Leg swings: swing leg forward and back from the knees. (Be careful not to kick your pony.)

Leg exercises

LEG SWINGS

These relax your knees and loosen the muscles in your lower legs.

With feet out of stirrups, swing one leg forward and the other leg back, from below your knees. Then swing the other leg forward and back. Let your toes hang down, to relax your legs. Be careful not to kick your pony.

POLL AND CROUP TOUCHES

These are good for suppleness and for confidence. Try to keep your legs in position even though your upper body and arms move.

1. With feet in stirrups, reach forward with one hand as far as you can along your pony's mane, and try to touch his poll. (Don't touch his ears—he may not like it.) Your other arm stays behind you. Then, sit up.

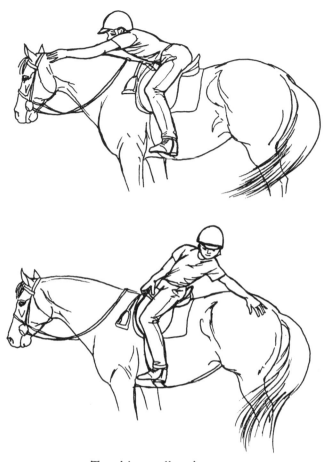

Touching poll and croup

2. Sit deep and tall in the saddle. Stretch one arm up over your head. Lean back, reach around behind you and pat your pony as far back on his croup as you can reach, near his tail. Your other arm stays in front of you. Then, sit up without using your hands to pull yourself up.

AROUND THE WORLD

This is good for balance and confidence, and besides, it's fun! You must have a helper to hold your pony and watch out for you while you are learning this exercise.

1. With feet out of stirrups (stirrups crossed over), swing your right leg over your pony's neck and sit sideways.
2. Then swing your left leg over his rump and sit backwards.
3. Swing your right leg over the rump and sit sideways.
4. Now swing your left leg over the neck and you're "home." Then try it the other way. How fast can you do it?

When you can go "around the world" using your hands, try it "no hands," with your arms folded. You can have "around the world" races (with hands or "no hands").

Around the world

LONGE LESSONS

For a longe lesson, your instructor controls your pony on a circle, using a longe line. You can work on your seat, balance and suppleness without having to control your pony. A longe lesson is a good time to practice exercises and to learn to sit better.

Your pony must be trained to work on a longe line. Your instructor should try out your pony to see if he is ready for longe lessons. He will need a longe line, a longe whip to give signals, side reins for control, boots or bandages to protect your pony's legs, and a special longe cavesson, which works on the pony's nose instead of his mouth. Your instructor will check the longeing equipment and longe your pony for a few minutes to get him ready before you start your lesson.

First, you must get used to the feeling of riding in a circle. You will not need the reins, so they are tied up out of the way. You may hold a neckstrap or the saddle. (Put your outside hand on the pommel and your inside hand behind you, on the cantle.) When you are comfortable at the walk, your instructor may ask you to drop your stirrups and cross them over. You can practice balance and suppling exercises until you can ride easily with "no hands" and without stirrups at a walk.

Next, your instructor will have you hold the neckstrap or the saddle while you try a slow trot. Holding the pommel with your outside hand helps you stay deep in the saddle; it also turns your

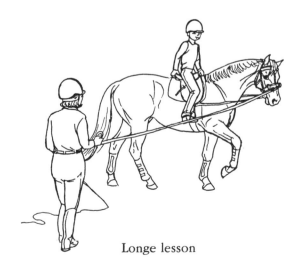

Longe lesson

55

shoulders to follow the track of the circle. As you get better at trotting, you can do exercises to help your seat and your balance. Eventually, you will be able to trot with no stirrups and "no hands." You can also practice posting the trot (with stirrups).

Longe lessons are hard work for a pony, because steady work on a circle is harder than ordinary riding. He should have a break, a chance to stretch his neck and a change of direction now and then, to rest his muscles. A longe lesson should not last too long (about twenty minutes is plenty).

RING FIGURES FOR BETTER CONTROL

When you first started to ride, you learned simple turns and changes of direction. Now you can ride with better control, making your pony follow the "track" you decide on. To do this, your eyes look ahead to pick out your track, and your aids (both legs and both hands) make sure he follows it. You must think ahead and look where you want your pony to go. It may help to set up cones, buckets or markers to show where to turn.

When you ride through a turn, remember to:

- Use your *eyes* to look where you want your pony to go.
- Use your *inside leg* to keep your pony moving and to keep him from cutting the corner.

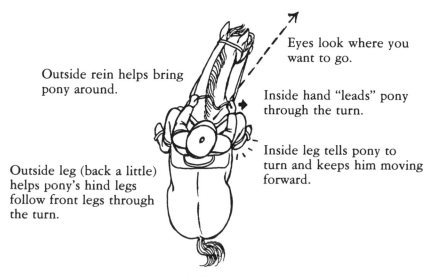

Outside rein helps bring pony around.

Eyes look where you want to go.

Inside hand "leads" pony through the turn.

Outside leg (back a little) helps pony's hind legs follow front legs through the turn.

Inside leg tells pony to turn and keeps him moving forward.

Aids for turning

56

- Use your *inside rein* to ask your pony to bend around the turn.
- Use your *outside rein* to help bring your pony around the turn.
- Keep your *outside leg* back a little, to keep your pony's hind legs from swinging out on the turn.

Here are some ways to practice turns.

Turns

To make smooth, even turns at each corner of the ring, you must turn your head and look through the turns. You can also turn across the ring or down the center of the ring. For turning practice, try setting up bending cones (three to five cones in a line about 25 feet apart). You can put cones or barrels in the corners of the ring to keep you on the track as you ride through the corners.

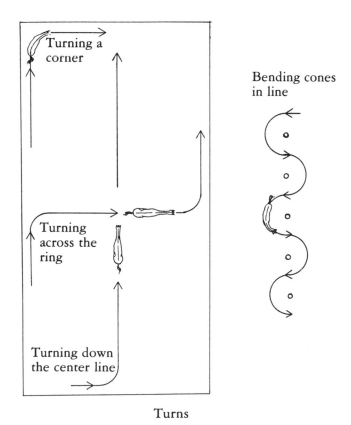

Turns

Circles

A circle must be round like an orange, not long like a bathtub or uneven like a pear. Make your circles big enough so your pony can keep moving forward easily (about 60 feet across is a good size). A small circle is harder for your pony.

Reverses

You can reverse by turning across the ring and then turning the other way when you reach the other side. Another way to reverse is to turn toward the inside of the ring, starting a circle, and then return to the rail. This kind of reverse is called a "half circle."

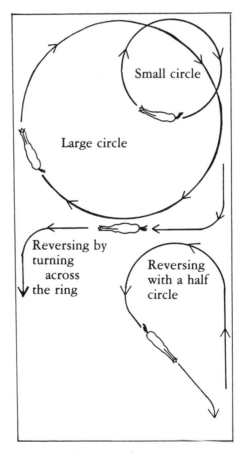

Small circle

Large circle

Reversing by turning across the ring

Reversing with a half circle

Circles and reverses

Top view of diagonals:
Left diagonal: L F and R H
Right diagonal: R F and L H

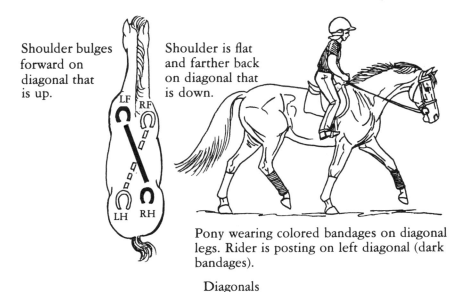

Shoulder bulges forward on diagonal that is up.

Shoulder is flat and farther back on diagonal that is down.

Pony wearing colored bandages on diagonal legs. Rider is posting on left diagonal (dark bandages).

Diagonals

LEARNING TO POST ON THE CORRECT DIAGONAL
What Is a Diagonal?

"Diagonal" means opposite corners. When a pony trots, his legs move in *diagonal* pairs. The left front and right hind legs move together; they are called the "left diagonal." The right front and left hind legs move together; they are called the "right diagonal."

It is easy to see the diagonals moving at a trot if your instructor puts different-colored bandages on each diagonal pair of your pony's legs.

What Is Posting on a Diagonal?

When you post or rise to the trot, you go up and down with one diagonal. When a pony is turning or going around a ring, you should post on the *outside* diagonal. This means that when you are riding to the *right,* you rise when the *left front* and *right hind* legs go up, and you sit when they go down. (When you turn *left,* you rise when the *right front* and *left hind* legs go up, and sit when they go down.)

Sit down when outside shoulder is down and back.

Rise when outside shoulder is forward and up.

Posting on the correct diagonal on a turn

If you watch a rider posting on a pony that is wearing different-colored bandages on each diagonal pair of legs, it is easy to see which legs he is going up and down with.

Why Should You Post on a Certain Diagonal?

It is easier for your pony to balance around a turn if you post on the outside diagonal. This means you rise and sit with the outside front leg and the inside hind leg.

The legs of the diagonal you are posting on work harder. You should change direction (and diagonals) every now and then to give your pony's muscles a rest.

How Can You Tell Which Diagonal You Are Posting On?

1. Start a steady posting trot along the rail.
2. As you *sit,* quickly glance down at the pony's *outside* shoulder. (Take a quick peek each time you sit, but don't ride along staring at the shoulder for a long time.)
3. If the outside shoulder is *back* when you sit, you are on the correct diagonal. If you find the shoulder is *forward* when you sit, you are on the wrong diagonal.

To help you check the shoulder, you can stick a piece of masking tape to the pony's hair at the bottom of the shoulder. It is easier to see if the tape is forward or back. Check the *outside* shoulder (next to the rail, not the one toward the center of the ring). It may help you remember if you say "Rise and fall with the leg near the wall."

As you get used to posting on the correct diagonal, you will be able to feel when you are on the correct diagonal and when you are on the wrong one.

How Do You Change Diagonals?

1. As you post to the trot, say "Up, down, Up, down" along with the rhythm of the trot.
2. To change diagonals, say "Up, down, Up, *down, down,* up." Sit down for one extra beat (two "downs") and then go on posting.
3. If you sit for two beats, you will change diagonals. If you sit for three beats, you will stay on the same diagonal.

When you change direction at the trot, you should change diagonals at the center of the ring. This prepares your pony to turn in the new direction.

LEARNING TO CANTER

As your seat, balance and control improve, you will be ready to learn to canter. The canter is a three-beat gait; it sounds like "one, two, three." It has a rocking motion like a merry-go-round, but it is a bit faster.

To canter safely, you must have good balance and control at a trot (both sitting trot and posting trot). You must know how to ask your pony to canter, how to ride the canter and how to come back to a trot and then a walk after cantering. You should learn to canter on a pony that is well trained and easy to canter.

Aids for Canter

When your pony starts to canter, it is called a "canter depart." To canter, you must:

1. Prepare to canter:
   - Sit deep and tall. Have your reins short enough to control your pony, but not tight or pulling back.
   - Wake up your pony with leg squeezes so that he wants

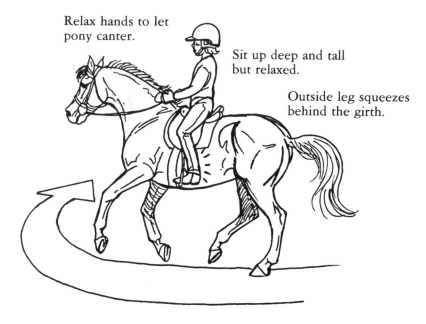

Relax hands to let pony canter.

Sit up deep and tall but relaxed.

Outside leg squeezes behind the girth.

Aids for a canter depart

to go faster, but keep him to a fast walk or a slow sitting trot. (A canter takes more energy, but if he trots fast or if you are posting, he won't be ready and will just trot faster instead of cantering.)

2. Give the signal for a canter depart:
   - Put your outside leg (the one next to the rail) back a couple of inches and squeeze or nudge his side. If your pony is lazy, you may have to use your leg quite firmly, and you may also have to cluck to your pony or say "Canter!"
   - Relax your hands to let him begin cantering.

Be careful not to pull back on the reins as he starts to canter. Keep your hands down on your pony's neck or hold a neckstrap.

Riding the Canter

As your pony canters, it feels like a rocking horse or a merry-go-round, but faster. To ride the canter, you must *sit down,* not stand up or bounce. It helps to sit·deep and tall and remember to breathe. You may even feel like you are leaning back a little, in order to keep your seat in the saddle. Relax as much as you can

Sitting down to the canter

and let your seat rock easily with your pony. Don't lean forward or stand up. This can put you off balance and might make your pony go too fast.

To come back to a trot and to a walk:

1. Take a deep breath and sit deep and tall.
2. Squeeze and relax your hands on the reins, as firmly as you have to, until your pony slows down and begins to trot. Use a quiet voice command, "Whoa," if you need to.
3. When your pony trots, post for a few steps and then sit deep and tall again, breathe and squeeze with your hands to ask him to walk.

Remember to thank your pony with a pat and a "Good boy!"

Leads at the Canter

What Is a Lead?   When a pony canters, his front and hind legs on one side reach out ahead of the other, like a person skipping. If his left legs are ahead, he is on the *left lead*. If his right legs are ahead, he is on the *right lead*.

It is easy to see which lead a pony is on if your instructor puts different-colored bandages on your pony's front legs. Watch to see which front leg reaches farther in front as he canters around a turn.

63

Why Should a Pony Canter on the Proper Lead? When a pony canters around a ring, or on a turn, he should be on the correct lead. His *inside* legs must be ahead, so he can balance safely around the turns. If his outside legs are ahead, he is on the wrong lead. (You can try this yourself if you skip with one leg in front of the other. It is easy to turn toward the leg that you are leading with, but if you turn the other way, your legs cross and you can't balance as well.)

How Can You Tell Which Lead Your Pony Is Cantering On? Your pony must be in a steady canter, and you must be sitting up deep and tall.

1. Take a quick peek at your pony's *inside* shoulder (the one toward the center of the ring). You may see the tip of his toe coming out in front of the shoulder. If you see his toe, he is on the correct lead.
2. Take a quick peek at *both* shoulders. When a pony is on the inside lead, the outside shoulder moves first and shorter, and the inside shoulder moves second and longer.

Caution: Just take a quick peek. Don't ride along with your head down looking at the shoulders or lean forward to look. That could put you off balance.

With more experience in the canter, you will be able to feel the difference between a correct lead and a wrong lead.

How Do You Ask Your Pony to Canter on the Correct Lead? When you give your pony the correct aids for a canter

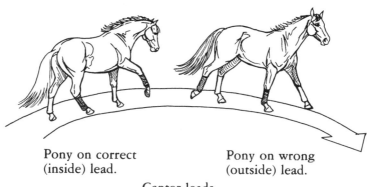

Pony on correct
(inside) lead.

Pony on wrong
(outside) lead.

Canter leads

depart, it tells him to take the correct lead. Most ponies are trained to take a left lead when you use your right leg a little behind the girth, and to take a right lead when you use your left leg behind the girth. Some ponies are trained to other signals. Your instructor will tell you if your pony needs other aids or signals.

If a pony can see that he is about to make a left turn, it makes sense to him to take the left lead. If he is thinking about turning right (perhaps because he wants to go back to the barn or toward other ponies), he may want to take a right lead. Giving him the correct canter aids just before a turn makes it easier to get the lead you want.

Some Tips About Cantering

- Remember that cantering is hard work for your pony, even if it's fun for you. Give him a break now and then, and don't overdo it.
- At first, canter only for short distances. Don't try to canter too long or too fast.
- If your pony gets into a fast trot, slow down and start over. He can't start a good canter from a fast trot.
- Let your seat relax and rock gently with your pony's canter. It may help to pretend that you have saddle soap on your seat and that you are polishing the saddle.

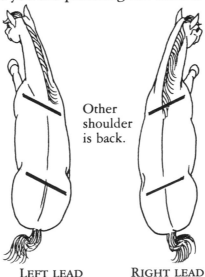

Front leg on lead side comes out in front of shoulder.

Leading shoulder is forward.

Other shoulder is back.

LEFT LEAD   RIGHT LEAD

How to identify the lead

65

- Keep your legs relaxed and your knees and ankles springy. If your legs get stiff, you will push against your stirrups and bounce.
- Go with your pony's balance around turns. Don't lean way over, but don't lean out to the outside, either.
- Canter only on good footing (not slippery) and on level ground or slightly uphill. Cantering downhill, around sharp turns or on slippery ground can get your pony off balance and is not safe.

BEGINNING JUMPING (D-2 LEVEL)

Jumping is just another part of riding, like learning to trot or canter. It should be safe, simple and fun. However, there are some things you must have or do in order to learn to jump.

- *Pony:* Your pony should be experienced and quiet over low jumps. Jumping is hard work, so he must be sound, in good condition, and his feet must be properly trimmed or shod. It is not a good idea to try to learn to jump on a green

What you need for safe jumping

An experienced helper. Never jump alone!

Enclosed area with good footing

Safe dress for riding (ASTM/SEI helmet, boots, etc. (Check your chin strap before jumping.)

All-purpose or jumping saddle in good condition. (Check your girth before you jump.)

Safe jumping equipment, set up properly

A quiet, well-trained jumping pony, suitable for the rider

Pony wears a neckstrap.

Always warm your pony up before jumping!

pony, as you can confuse each other. A pony that is lame, in poor condition or very young (under four years old) should not be jumped.

* *Place:* A ring or field should have good footing. It should be fairly level, not too hard or slippery, and not have holes or rocks.
* *Tack and dress:* You will need a general-purpose saddle or a jumping saddle. It should be the correct size, properly fitted and in good condition. A neckstrap is a good idea. Always wear safe riding clothes and boots, and your ASTM/ SEI-approved helmet with harness and chin strap securely fastened.
* *Jumps:* Poles should be at least 10 feet long and fairly thick (at least 3 inches). You can use jump standards, buckets or blocks to hold the poles. They should have no sharp points or edges, and no nails sticking out.

Commonsense Rules for Jumping

* Before you start jumping, you must have good balance and control at the trot. You should be able to walk and trot in jumping position with your heels down. It's a good idea to be able to canter safely before you start jumping.
* Always warm your pony up slowly before beginning jumping. Check your tack (especially your girth) before you jump.
* Don't jump your pony every day—every other day is plenty. Too much jumping pounds his feet and legs and can make him sore.
* Don't jump the same jump or course over and over. This can make your pony bored and sour, and he may get stubborn about jumping.
* Never jump alone. Someone should always be on hand in case of an accident.

Jumping Position

Review your jumping position:

* Your stirrups should be at jumping length (just touching the top of your ankle bone). This is usually about one hole shorter than your regular stirrup length.

Good basic jumping position for D-2 level

- Bend forward from your hips (not at your waist) just enough to let your shoulders come forward over your knees. Your seat should sink backward so that you stay close to the saddle and balanced over your feet.
- Your legs and feet must be under your body, with knees and ankles flexible and heels down. Your stirrup leathers should be vertical (straight up and down). The inside of your legs should touch the saddle and your pony's side, and your toes may turn out a little (but not not a lot!).
- Keep your back straight—not round, slumped, or hollow.
- Look ahead and keep your eyes up.

At first when you practice jumping position, you should hold a neckstrap or the mane, or rest your hands on your pony's neck. As your legs get stronger, you can do it "no hands." Never grab the reins to keep your balance—this hurts your pony's mouth.

Practice jumping position at a halt, walking, and at a slow trot. You can also review riding over ground poles in jumping position.

Jumping Basics

There are five jumping basics that you need every time you jump. They are Balance, Eyes, Sink, Release, and Finish.

Balance This means you must be in good balance with your pony. If you are too far forward ("ahead" of your pony) or too far back ("behind" your pony), you are out of balance and cannot stay "with" him when he jumps.

Eyes This means to look at your target, which keeps your pony straight and keeps you from looking down. Looking down will make you lose your balance.

Sink This means to sink your heels down and to let your seat sink back toward the saddle a little. This makes you more secure when you jump. It is the opposite of standing up.

When you jump, your "angles" (at your hips, knees and ankles)

Rider in balance, "with" pony

Out of balance, "left behind"

Out of balance, "ahead of pony"

Balance in jumping

69

close to absorb the thrust (or "push") of your pony's jump. If they are relaxed and springy, this is easy, but if they are stiff and tight, you may get bounced out of balance. Your angles should close automatically as your pony jumps. Don't try to guess when he will take off and make yourself stand up or lean forward. Instead, just wait for his jump, relax, and let your heels and seat sink.

Release This means that you must release your pony's mouth to let him stretch his neck and jump safely. To release, reach out and put both hands (holding the reins) on top of your pony's neck about 8 to 12 inches in front of the saddle. Hold the neckstrap or pinch the roots of the mane so your hands can't fly up and jerk

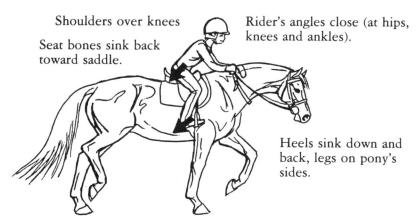

Shoulders over knees

Seat bones sink back toward saddle.

Rider's angles close (at hips, knees and ankles).

Heels sink down and back, legs on pony's sides.

Rider's angles closing in jumping position

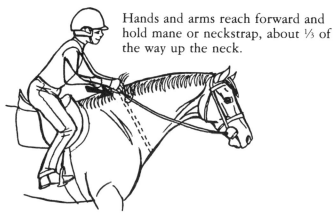

Hands and arms reach forward and hold mane or neckstrap, about ⅓ of the way up the neck.

Basic release, holding mane

70

his mouth. (This is called a "mane release." You will learn other releases later.)

You should release just as your pony jumps. Keep your hands on his neck until he finishes the jump, then pick them up gently.

You must release your pony every time he jumps. If you don't release, he will get a jerk in the mouth, and he will think he is being punished for jumping.

Finish This means that you must finish your job after a jump. You should sit up, look where you want to go, pick up your hands

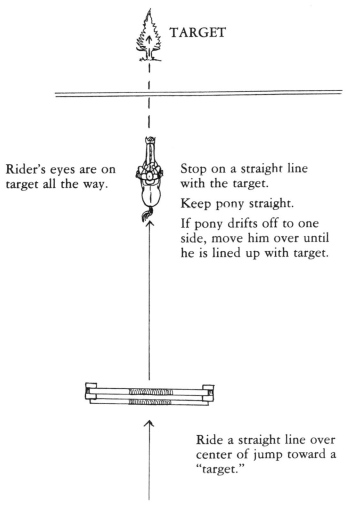

TARGET

Rider's eyes are on target all the way.

Stop on a straight line with the target.

Keep pony straight.

If pony drifts off to one side, move him over until he is lined up with target.

Ride a straight line over center of jump toward a "target."

Finishing by stopping on a line

and keep your pony under control. Sometimes you finish by stopping on a straight line after a jump, other times the finish may be a turn or getting ready for the next jump.

You can practice these basics over the "invisible jump," over a ground pole, and then work up to regular jumps. Most people have one or two basics that they have to work harder to remember. As you practice and the basics get easier, they will become habits. Eventually they should be so automatic that you don't have to think about them—you just do them. If you ever have a problem with your jumping, it will help to go back and review your basics.

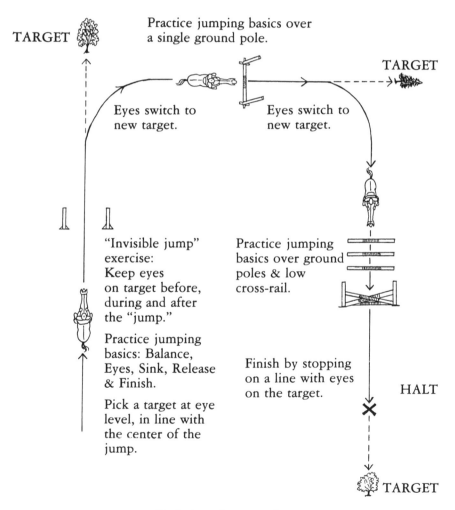

TARGET

Practice jumping basics over a single ground pole.

TARGET

Eyes switch to new target.

Eyes switch to new target.

"Invisible jump" exercise:
Keep eyes on target before, during and after the "jump."

Practice jumping basics over ground poles & low cross-rail.

Practice jumping basics: Balance, Eyes, Sink, Release & Finish.

Pick a target at eye level, in line with the center of the jump.

Finish by stopping on a line with eyes on the target.

HALT

TARGET

Basic jumping exercises

72

Simple Jumping

Jumps for Beginners It is easy to set up good, safe jumps if you follow a few simple rules.

- Cavaletti have supports attached to the end, like a little sawhorse. (A single one is called a "cavaletto.") They can be turned to make low (about 8 inches), medium (about 12 inches) or high cavaletti (about 18 inches). The kind of cavaletti with X-shaped ends should never be used because they have sharp points that can cause injuries. Cavaletti can be made with square ends instead, which are safer.
- Blocks (with poles) can be used in place of cavaletti. They can be turned to make different heights, used as jump standards, or used as "fillers" for larger jumps.
- Poles must be set so that they will fall if they are hit hard. Use jump cups or pegs, but don't use nails that stick out. Don't wedge poles so that they cannot fall. It is not safe to stack up fixed cavaletti to make a bigger jump.
- A ground line is a pole or a part of the jump that lies on

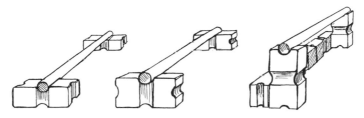

Plastic blocks can be turned or stacked to make jumps of different heights. They can also be used as filling material for larger jumps.

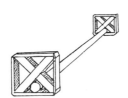

A cavaletto with supports safely enclosed. It can be turned for low, medium or high heights.

DANGER! This type of cavaletto can cause injury to pony or rider. DO NOT USE!

Blocks and cavaletti

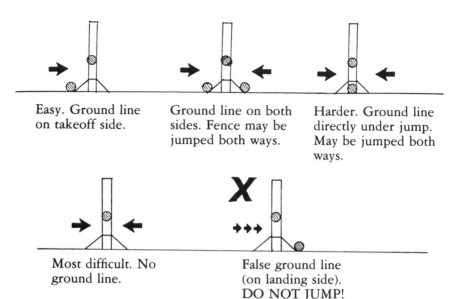

Easy. Ground line on takeoff side.

Ground line on both sides. Fence may be jumped both ways.

Harder. Ground line directly under jump. May be jumped both ways.

Most difficult. No ground line.

False ground line (on landing side).
DO NOT JUMP!

Ground lines

the ground at the bottom of a jump. It helps the pony judge how high a jump is and when to take off. It may be right under the jump or a little toward the takeoff side. Never jump a fence "backwards," with the ground line on the wrong side (the landing side). This is called a "false ground line." It can fool your pony and make him make a mistake. If you want to jump a fence in both directions, put a ground line on both sides.

- Cross-rails are made with two crossed rails, lower in the center. They should have a ground line on the takeoff side, or on both sides if they are to be jumped from both directions.

- Straight rails (also called "simple verticals") are made with a rail straight across. They should have a ground line on the takeoff side.

- Ground poles should be fixed so that they won't roll under a pony's feet if he knocks them.

- Small logs are good beginning jumps. They should be smooth with no sharp branches sticking out, and must have good ground on the takeoff and landing sides.

- All jumps should be set with enough space for a good approach and room afterward to turn easily or to stop. This

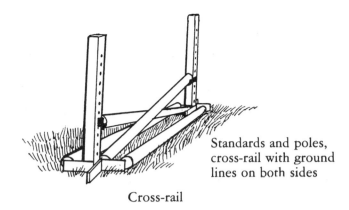

Standards and poles, cross-rail with ground lines on both sides

Cross-rail

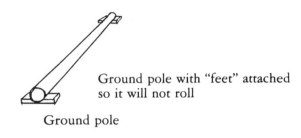

Ground pole with "feet" attached so it will not roll

Ground pole

requires at least 30 feet before and after a jump. More space makes it easier.

Riding Approaches Riding toward a jump is called "the approach." A good approach gets you and your pony ready for a good jump. A poor approach can cause mistakes.

- Before you approach a jump, your pony must be moving forward in the right gait (trot or canter), with good rhythm and balance. It's a good idea to make a large circle (at least 60 feet) to get him ready. Be sure you are in balance with him.
- Your pony must come into a jump with enough "impulsion" or energy to jump it. If he is lazy or not paying attention, he will not be ready to jump well and he might stop. Use your legs to keep him awake and ready to jump.
- As you ride toward the jump, plan where you will have to turn to line up with the middle. Pick a target in line with the middle of the jump and aim your eyes and your pony toward it.

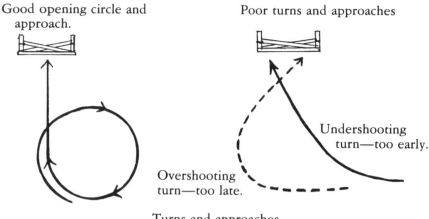

Good opening circle and approach.

Poor turns and approaches

Undershooting turn—too early.

Overshooting turn—too late.

Turns and approaches

- If you cut the corner and turn too soon, you may "undershoot." This brings you to the jump on a crooked line. Your pony might try to "run out" (go by the jump). If you turn too late, you may "overshoot" and come in crooked. If you forget to look ahead at your target, you may weave or zig-zag coming into the jump. Your pony will be confused and might stop or run out.

Single Jumps Start with a low-cross rail or perhaps a small log, only about 8 inches high in the center. When you can keep your balance and all your basics are working well, it can be raised a little. Practice over many small fences before you try bigger ones.

Trotting Grid (ground poles) Before a Cross-Rail The next step is to ride over a trotting grid of three to five ground poles, leading to a cross-rail. This helps your pony take off at the right place. It also helps you get ready for the jump. The ground poles must be spaced so that your pony can step in the middle of the spaces when he is trotting (about 4 feet apart for ponies, and up to 4 feet 6 inches apart for horses). The distance from the last ground pole to the jump should be twice the distance of the ground poles (8 to 9 feet).

Ride over the ground poles in jumping position and release at the first pole. Keep your jumping position (and your eyes on the target) until after the cross-rail.

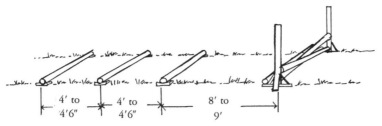

| 4' to 4'6" | 4' to 4'6" | 8' to 9' |

Distance from last ground pole to cross-rail is twice the distance between ground poles.

Spacing for ground poles and cross-rail

Lines of Fences When you can jump a single cross-rail well, you can learn to jump two in a line. The second jump should be about 48 feet away in a straight line. This gives you time to finish your first jump, keep your eyes on the target, and ride straight on over the second one. Remember to finish the line by stopping on a straight line or by turning smoothly under control.

It helps to make the second jump a ground rail at first, then build it up to a small cross-rail. This gives you practice in recovering your balance and control after the first jump in time to ride the second jump well.

For now, your jumping should be mostly at a trot while you practice your basics and control. You can ride the approach in a posting trot or a sitting trot, but get into jumping position just as your pony jumps. Don't try to stand up coming into the jumps. If your pony should break into a canter, slow him back down to a trot after the jump. This will help you stay in control.

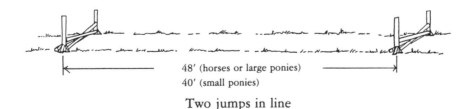

48' (horses or large ponies)
40' (small ponies)

Two jumps in line

Jumping a Simple Course When you put two or more lines of jumps together, it makes a course. The idea is to ride a jump course smoothly and with control, thinking ahead. To practice, you can set up a simple course of "invisible jumps" or poles on the ground. Later, you can raise them to cross-rails or regular jumps.

When you ride into the ring to jump a course, you should have your reins short enough for control, and your pony should be awake and listening to you. Start with a large circle before the first jump. Pick up a posting trot on the correct diagonal, and use the circle to get your pony in good balance and rhythm and lined up with the middle of the first jump. Keep your eyes on your target as you ride the first line of jumps, then look ahead through the turn and aim for the middle of the next jump. Remember to keep your eyes on your target for each line of jumps. When you finish the last jump, make another circle to bring your pony back to a walk smoothly and under control. Thank him with a pat!

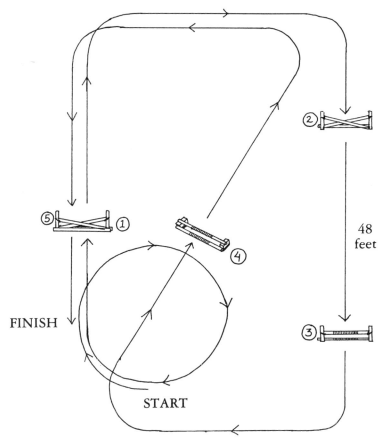

Simple course for D-2 level riders

RIDING IN THE OPEN (D-2 LEVEL)
Riding Outside the Ring

Riding outside can be the most fun of all, but you must be in good control of your pony. Most ponies like to go out, especially in a group, and some act more lively outside than they do in a ring. This makes it especially important to keep your pony paying attention to you and under control.

- Be sure you can stop your pony or slow down easily. Sit deep and tall, keep your shoulders back, and squeeze and relax on the reins.
- Don't let your pony eat grass while you are riding. This can teach him bad manners.
- The first time you ride outside, go with a good, sensible rider (your instructor is best) who has a quiet, well-behaved horse or pony. This sets a good example for your pony and makes it easier for you to have a good ride. Don't ride with people who want to go fast or who cannot control their ponies.
- If your pony should act nervous or see something that startles him, sit deep and tall and remember to breathe. This makes you feel calm and in control to him, and helps calm him down. Talk to him quietly and squeeze and relax on the reins to slow him down. If you tense up, lean forward or yell at him, he will get more nervous and be harder to control.

Riding Up and Down Hills

One of the nice things about riding outside is that you ride over different kinds of country, including fields, trails and hills. Going up and down hills is good for developing balance and strong muscles, in both you and your pony.

Riding Uphill When your pony climbs a hill, he needs to stretch his neck and his back, so you must lean forward in a half-seat or a jumping position. If the hill is long or steep, hold the mane so you don't pull on his mouth or sit back on him.

Riding Downhill When you ride downhill, it's important to stay in balance, with your feet under your center and your heels

Riding uphill

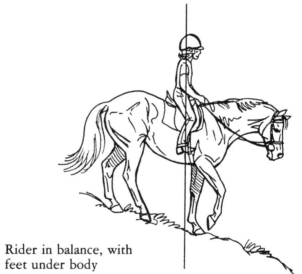

Rider in balance, with
feet under body

Riding downhill

down. On a gentle slope, you can sit slightly forward. On a steeper
hill, you should sit up deep and tall. Don't lean back or brace
your feet out ahead of you. This makes it harder for your pony
to use his back and his hind legs for balance, and for you to stay
in balance with him. Keep your eyes up and look ahead to keep
your pony straight.

Always ride your pony straight down a hill or slope, keeping
his hind legs in line with his front legs. If he is straight, he can
"sit down" a little and use his hind legs to help his balance. If you

try to take a slope at an angle or if he gets crooked, he is more likely to slip sideways. Let your pony stretch his neck to look where he is going, but make him slow down and take short steps, especially if the hill is steep.

It is safer for both you and your pony to walk down most hills.

Natural Obstacles

When you ride outside, you may want to go over small obstacles like logs. These should not be bigger than the obstacles you are jumping safely and easily in the ring. It's important to check the approach, takeoff and landing side of all obstacles outside. You wouldn't want to discover a hole or broken glass by accident.

Step-overs Some obstacles, like logs or tree roots across a trail or rocky places, are better to step over slowly than to jump. Walk your pony up to the obstacle and halt. Let him stretch his neck out and look at it. Then squeeze or nudge with your legs and ask him to walk on over it. You should be in a jumping position,

Riding a step-over obstacle

81

sitting close to your saddle with your heels down. Hold the mane or a neckstrap so that you won't pull on his mouth.

Low Jumps You jump low obstacles outside the same way you learned in the ring. Ride your pony straight forward over the middle of the jump, keeping your eyes up and ahead on your target. Use your legs to be sure he comes into the jump with enough energy to jump it, and hold the mane or neckstrap to avoid jerking his mouth.

For now, you should only jump obstacles no larger than those you are used to jumping—up to about 18 inches high.

Riding Outside in a Group

It is fun to ride with friends, but it is also important to follow safety rules when you ride together. Ponies in a group copy other ponies. If one shies, they all startle, and if one pony takes off, they all want to go. Some ponies do not like to be bumped or crowded, so you must give them space. This makes it very important for everyone to be considerate of other riders when you ride together. If one person doesn't think, he can make other people's ponies act up and spoil everyone else's ride.

Here are some rules for safety and courtesy when riding outside in a group:

- Keep a safe distance between your pony and others. Allow at least one pony space between your pony's nose and the next pony's tail. Be firm with your pony about not crowding the pony ahead of him.
- Don't hang back a long way behind the others. Your pony may decide to catch up and go faster than he should.
- When riding on a trail, stay in line. If you ride out to the side, your pony may want to catch up and pass or he may crowd the other riders. It is okay to ride side by side when the trail is wide. However, passing other ponies can make them excited and cause trouble, so ask the other rider if it's okay before you pass.
- If you want to go faster, ask the others if it is okay with them first. If you start trotting, other ponies will trot too, which can surprise another rider who is not ready.

Riding outside in a group is fun, but you must be a safe and courteous trail rider. *Photo: Susan Sexton.*

- If you see something that could be dangerous, like a hole, broken glass or wire, point to it as you pass it and warn the rider behind you. All warnings should be passed back to the last rider.
- If you need to stop quickly, warn the riders behind you by putting one hand up over your head, like a policeman. This means "Stop." If you see a rider ahead of you put his hand up, put your hand up too, then stop your pony in time to avoid crowding the ponies ahead of you.
- Pay attention to your pony. If he lays his ears back or swings his rump toward another pony, he may be about to kick. Tell him "No!" as you turn his head toward the other pony. This turns his rump away so he can't kick.

Be a Welcome Trail Rider Most riders today must ride on public land or on privately owned land if they want to ride on trails. This is only possible if land owners are willing to let riders use their land and trails. Good trail riders are careful and considerate of the land where they ride, and polite to land owners. Just one rude or careless rider can cause trouble for everyone. Sometimes public parks or private owners close their land to riders because riders have caused problems. Always remember that riding on someone else's land is a privilege. It's important to be a courteous and responsible trail rider to keep that privilege.

- Always ask permission before riding on someone's land. If you don't know who owns it, don't ride there. Trespassing (especially on horseback) makes land owners angry, and it is against the law.
- Stay off lawns, sidewalks and gardens and away from picnic areas, where nobody wants hoofprints or manure. If your pony drops manure near somebody's house, borrow a shovel and clean it up.
- When you ride in a field, stay along the edge, especially if the ground is soft. Don't ride through fields that are growing crops or hay. Hoofprints cut up the ground and cause damage.
- Leave gates the way you found them. Be careful to close

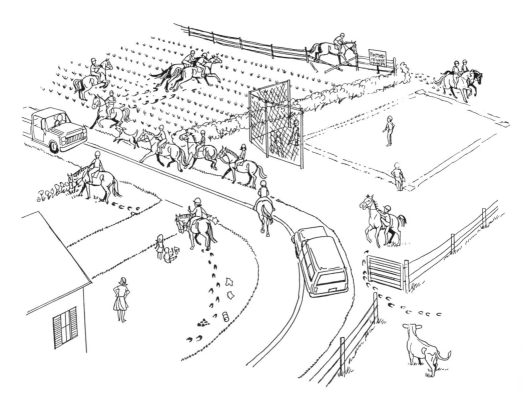

How many things can you find that these riders are doing wrong? Why are they wrong?

any gate you open. Be very careful not to let livestock get out. If you aren't sure a gate is meant to be left open, close it.

* Leave livestock alone, and be careful not to disturb them. If you take your dog along, be sure he doesn't chase or bother livestock. (It is safer for you and your dog and better for your riding to leave him at home.)
* Even if you have permission to ride on somebody's land, don't jump their jumps without special permission.
* Never leave litter behind you. If you see litter or trash, take it with you until you can throw it away in a trash can.
* Good trail riders don't hurt the environment. Stay on the trail instead of taking shortcuts in areas where hoofprints may start washouts and erosion. Stay out of especially fragile areas, where horses may cause lasting damage. Don't tie your pony where he can strip the bark from a tree, which may kill it. Don't break off branches unnecessarily, or pick wildflowers. Leave nature as beautiful as you found it!
* When you meet anyone else, whether they are on foot, on horseback, biking or whatever, stop and greet them politely. It might be the land owner, or his guests or friends. Whenever you meet someone who lets you ride on his land, be sure to thank him!

◆◆

USPC D-2 LEVEL RIDING TEST REQUIREMENTS

To pass the D-2 riding test, child should ride without a leading rein, demonstrating control, while maintaining a safe, correct position at the walk and trot, and should begin to develop the canter and jumping position. No need to canter over fences.

Riding on the Flat

1. Mount and dismount independently (using a mounting block if necessary).
2. Shorten and lengthen reins at the halt and walk.
3. Perform balancing and suppling exercises for the rider at the halt and walk.
4. Ride at the walk, performing simple turns and large circles.
5. Ride without stirrups at the walk.

6. Ride at the trot, posting on correct diagonal, performing simple turns and large circles.
7. Ride at the canter in both directions in an enclosed area; be aware of leads. Discuss performance with Examiner, indicating whether or not the pony was on the correct lead.

Riding Over Fences

8. Maintain jumping position at the trot on the flat and over ground poles.
9. In an enclosed area, ride a simple stadium jumping course of four to five obstacles, not to exceed 18 inches. Child will discuss with Examiner ways to improve ride.

Riding in the Open

10. Ride safely and considerately on public and private property, in a group, at the walk and trot.
11. Ride with control, up and down hills, at the walk and trot.
12. Jump simple natural obstacles, not to exceed 18 inches.

CHAPTER 4

D-3 Level:
Better Riding

Riding on the flat to D-3 Level standards means that you are able to ride well enough to progress to techniques and skills that will make you ride better and with greater ease. For example, you can learn to tighten your girth and adjust your stirrups while you are mounted. This takes less time than getting off to do it.

Before you start to fix your girth or stirrups, stop your pony and put your reins in one hand, short enough to control your pony. If you are with a group of riders, ask them to wait for you (on the trail), or move to the center of the ring out of the way.

Adjusting the Girth While Mounted

Keep your foot in the stirrup. Put your left leg up over the knee roll and lift the saddle flap. Take the end of the billet and pull up. It is easier to slip the buckle tongue into the next hole if you keep your finger on the tongue.

Check your girth about five minutes after you start to ride. It often gets looser as your pony warms up. Always check it before you jump. After a ride, let your girth out on or two holes while you cool your pony out.

Adjusting the Stirrups While Mounted

To adjust the stirrup leather, keep your feet in the irons but relax the pressure on the stirrup, and turn your knee out so you can reach the buckle. Pull on the end of the strap so that the buckle

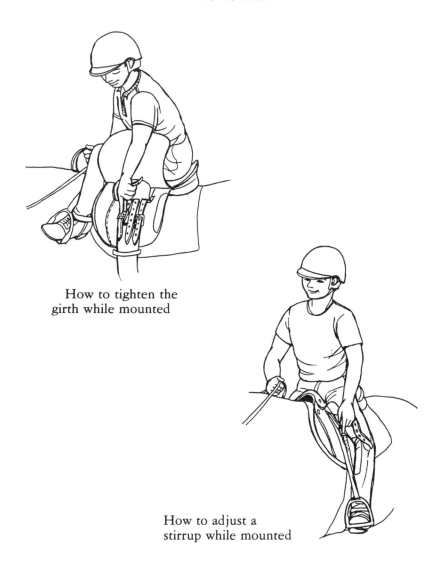

How to tighten the
girth while mounted

How to adjust a
stirrup while mounted

slides out where you can hold it. With your finger on the tongue
of the buckle, you can slide the buckle up toward the stirrup bar
(to shorten the leather), or down (to make the leather longer).
When you are finished, pull on the end of the leather to slide the
buckle up under the saddle skirt. Put the end of the stirrup leather
through the keeper.

To be safe, keep your feet in the irons and use only one hand
to fix your stirrups, while your other hand holds the reins. This
way, you still have your feet in the stirrups and control of your
pony if he should move while you are fixing your stirrups.

MORE BALANCE AND SUPPLING EXERCISES FOR RIDERS

You have already learned some basic suppling and balance exercises at the halt and the walk. Now you can add more, and even do some at the trot. A longe lesson is a good way to practice these exercises.

It's a good idea to practice the exercises you already know before you add these new ones. Remember to start slowly at first, and let your pony know that you won't hurt him when you do exercises. Here are some new exercises:

TOE TOUCHING AND OPPOSITE TOE TOUCHING

These make your waist supple and teach you to keep your legs in position while your upper body moves.

Toe Touching

Start with both hands straight up over your head. Bend down and touch both toes, then sit up straight again. Keep your feet and legs in position. (If you can't reach your toes, just touch your ankles, or as far down as you can reach.)

Touching Opposite Toe

Start with both arms straight out from your shoulders. Twist to the left, then bend down and touch your right hand to your left toe (or as far down as you can reach). Sit up again, then twist the other way and touch your left hand to your right toe. Try to keep your legs in place, and don't let your heels come up or your legs swing back when you bend down.

LYING DOWN AND SITTING UP, FORWARD AND BACKWARD

These make your muscles stronger, and teach your legs to stay in position even when your body and arms move.

Lying Forward and Sitting Up

Put your arms behind your back. With feet out of the stirrups (stirrups should be crossed over), lean forward until your chest touches your pony's neck. Try to sit up without using your hands. Keep your legs in position while you lean forward and sit up.

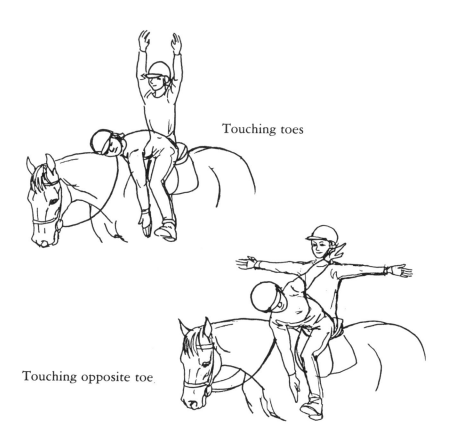

Touching toes

Touching opposite toe

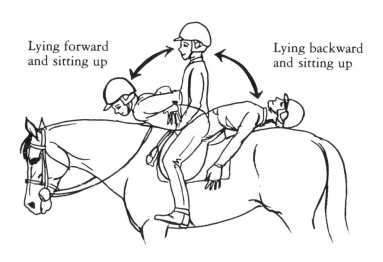

Lying forward
and sitting up

Lying backward
and sitting up

Lying Back and Sitting Up

With your feet out of the stirrups, lean back slowly until you are lying down on your pony's back. Let your arms hang by your sides. Try to sit up without using your hands, keeping your legs in good position.

STIRRUP STANDING AND "AIRPLANE" EXERCISES

These get your heels down and make your legs stronger. They also help your balance.

Stirrup Standing

With feet in the stirrups, lean slightly forward to find your balance, then stand up. Rest your hands on your pony's neck or hold a neckstrap. Let your knees relax, so your weight can go down past your knees into your feet, and let your heels sink down and back. Stay up while you count to five, then gently sink back down, leaving your heels down and your lower leg in position.

At first, do this exercise for five seconds or so at the halt, then at the walk and the trot. Then begin staying up longer—while you count to ten, twenty, or more. When your pony trots, you will feel him "bounce" your heels down with each step.

Remember that this is an *exercise,* not a position for regular riding or jumping. Don't get this exercise confused with half-seat or jumping position.

"Airplane" Exercise

This is a half-seat with "no hands," with your arms straight out from your shoulders. Don't stand up too high or lean too far forward. Just find the balance point where you can stay up without gripping with your knees. Start with two or three short "airplanes" at a halt; then work up to ten times. You can also practice "airplanes" at a walk and trot on the longe line.

SHOULDER CIRCLES AND DROPS

These loosen up your shoulder muscles and teach you how to keep your shoulders back and down. It helps to take a deep breath as you do them.

Stirrup stand

Airplane exercise

1. Move both shoulders in a circle: forward, up, back and down.
2. Lift both shoulders up toward your ears, then let them drop back and down behind your ribs.

Drop your shoulders whenever you need to sit up deep and tall or stop your pony. This keeps you from leaning forward and keeps your arms from getting pulled forward.

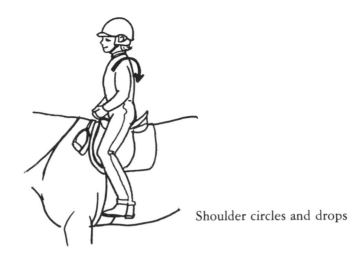

Shoulder circles and drops

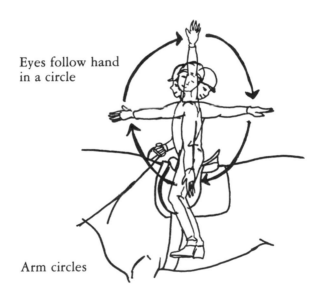

Eyes follow hand in a circle

Arm circles

ARM CIRCLES

These loosen up your neck, back and shoulders, and teach your legs to stay in position while your arms are moving. They also teach you to ride "automatically," without having to look at what you are doing.

Start with the reins in one hand. Stretch the other arm straight up over your head. Move it slowly in a big circle. Turn your head and watch your hand as it goes around. Be careful not to pull on the reins with your other hand. Circle your arm in both directions, then switch and do it with the other arm.

You can do this exercise on a longe line, while somebody leads your pony, or while you ride with the reins in one hand.

FINDING YOUR CENTER FOR BALANCE AND CONTROL

Your "center" is your balance and control point. When you can feel your center is in the right place, it makes it easier to sit deep and tall and to keep your balance. It also helps your pony to pay attention to your balance and your aids.

To find your center, put one hand over your belly, just below your bellybutton. Put the other hand on the back of your seat, behind it. Your center "floats" between your two hands. If you are a little bit tense or if you are leaning forward, it may be too far forward. Take a deep breath and think of your center floating back until it finds the middle. When it does, you may get a feeling that it sinks down. This helps your seat feel deeper and more relaxed and secure.

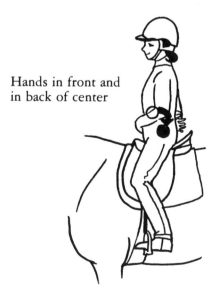

Hands in front and in back of center

Finding your center

Once you have learned how to take a deep breath and find your center, you can use this any time you need to relax, sit deeper or get your balance back. It helps to let your center sink down when you want to halt or make a transition down to a slower gait. It also can help you sit the trot and canter without bouncing.

"TEETER-TOTTER" EXERCISE FOR BALANCE

This exercise helps you find your best balance sitting in the saddle, and to know when you are out of balance forward or backward. It gets you balanced correctly on your seat bones. This exercise should be done at the halt.

With your feet out of the stirrups, find your center and sit deep

Teeter-totter exercise for balance

and tall in the middle of your saddle. Tip your body forward from your seat bones, keeping your back long and straight and your head and neck in line with your back. Then tip backward. Tip forward and backward several times, a little bit less each time (this is the "teeter-totter"). Notice how it feels when you are too far forward and too far back. Let your "teeters" get smaller and smaller, until you end up sitting balanced, straight up and down, with your feet hanging down under your body.

SWIVEL EXERCISE FOR TURNING

This exercise teaches you to keep your balance instead of leaning forward or sideways when you turn. It makes it easier for your pony to turn better, and gives you better control.

At a halt, with feet in the stirrups, take a deep breath and find your center. Put one hand on your belly and the other hand behind your seat.

Sit deep and tall and turn your body a little bit, deep inside between your hands, at the bottom of your center. Imagine a barber pole or a candy cane with spiral stripes running up through your center and out the top of your head, spiraling in the direction

Swivel turns

you are turning. Then come back to the center and turn the other way. You should make several short "swivels," not try to hold one for a long time.

When you turn like this, you will feel that you sit up deep and tall and that your body "swivels" instead of leaning forward or sideways. Your shoulders and chest turn, and your eyes can see where you are going.

Once you have tried this at a halt, do it at a walk. You may find that your pony listens so well to your "swivels" that he turns with almost no rein aids. This is fun to practice around a line of bending cones. When you can do it in the walk, you can also practice it in turns at the trot.

EMERGENCY DISMOUNTS

An emergency dismount is the fastest safe way to get off a pony. You could use it an emergency or any time you need to get off quickly, or just for fun and practice. Here's how:

1. Take *both* feet out of the stirrups.
2. Put both hands on your pony's withers, lean forward and swing your legs back and up, to clear the saddle and the pony's rump.
3. As you swing off, turn so that your side is next to the saddle (not your stomach). If you don't, you could lose your balance and sit down when you land.
4. Land with your knees bent, holding the reins in one hand.

When you practice emergency dismounts, have somebody stand by to help you at first. As you get better, try faster dismounts. When you can do emergency dismounts easily at a halt, you can practice them at a walk.

CAUTION: Don't try to jump off your pony if things go wrong, just because you have learned emergency dismounts. It is usually best to try to stay on and get back in control. Emergency dismounts are for dismounting quickly on purpose, or to land on your feet in case you begin to fall off.

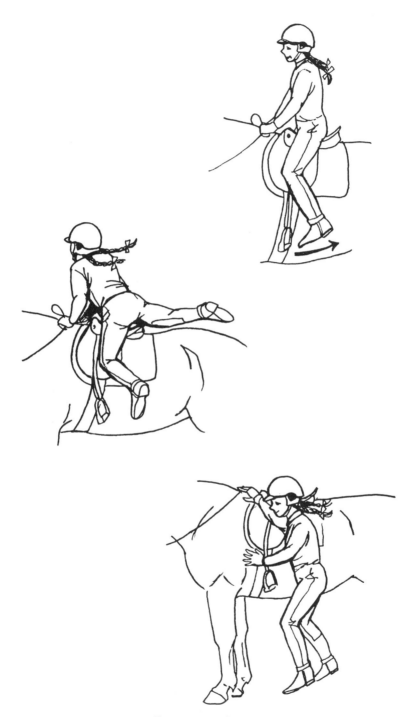

Emergency dismount

FALLS

If you ride very much, sooner or later you may take a spill. Most falls are about like tipping over on a bicycle—no fun, but not serious. Sometimes you just slip off and land on your feet. If you should fall, try to remember to fold up your arms and legs, fall as relaxed as you can, and don't try to hang on to the reins. Falling like this means you are less likely to get hurt.

If a rider falls and you are there to help, don't move the rider. Keep him or her lying still until you are sure there is no injury or until further help arrives.

RIDING WITHOUT STIRRUPS AT THE SITTING TROT

To ride a sitting trot well, you must be in balance, relaxed and supple. (Your pony should trot slowly and smoothly. If he trots too fast, you will have a hard time sitting the trot.) Practice the suppling and balance exercises (especially finding your center and the teeter-totter exercise) to help you get ready to sit the trot.

The best way to learn to ride the sitting trot is in a longe lesson. Cross over your stirrups and find your balance in the center of the saddle. Hold the pommel of the saddle with your outside hand and the cantle with your inside hand. Let your legs relax and hang down under your seat. Your instructor can start your pony into a slow, easy trot while you breathe, relax and let your seat go with the motion. If you feel bouncy, use your hands to pull your seat down into the saddle. Don't grip with your legs or tighten your muscles. This makes you bounce and can make your pony go faster. The more you breathe deeply, relax and keep your balance, the easier it is to let your seat go with your pony's trot.

At first, ride the sitting trot for just a little way, then come back to the walk. As you get better at it, you can relax your hold on the saddle and trot longer. Eventually, you will be able to trot "no hands." When you are comfortable at a sitting trot without holding on, you are ready to take your reins and learn to keep your pony in a slow, steady sitting trot yourself. You can start out with the reins in one hand and the other hand on the pommel of the saddle, but be careful not to pull on the reins if you need to catch your balance.

Riding a sitting trot without stirrups in a longe lesson

LEARNING TO REIN-BACK (BACKING UP)

The rein-back, or backing up, is not easy for a pony, so you must be careful when you ask him to do it. One step backward is enough at first.

To ask your pony to rein-back (or back up), sit up deep and tall. Your reins must be short enough for you to feel his mouth, and your legs must be against his sides. Give him a short squeeze or two with your legs to wake him up and make him think of moving, then squeeze your fingers on the reins to keep him from moving forward. As he begins to step backward, relax your legs and hands to say "That's right, thank you." After he has made one step backward, use your legs to make him walk forward again.

Be gentle and patient when you ask your pony to rein-back. If you pull long and hard on the reins, or kick to go forward while pulling backward, he will get confused and upset. You must give him a clear idea of what you want him to do, then give him time to understand and to do it right. For now, only ask for one step backwards, not several steps in a row.

20-METER CIRCLES

Circles are good practice for you and your pony. They help you learn good control, and they help your pony with his balance and make him supple and easier to ride. For now, your circles should be quite big. Small circles make it too hard for your pony to keep going and to balance well.

A 20-meter circle is a circle that is 20 meters, or 66 feet, across. It fits perfectly into a dressage ring, which is 20 meters wide. This is a good size circle for practice, and it also gets you ready for Pony Club dressage tests.

To learn to ride a 20-meter circle, it helps to mark out a space the right size with cones or other markers. If you set four cones on a square, 20 meters or 66 feet apart, your circle will fit perfectly inside.

A circle should be round, like an orange, not flat on one side or uneven, like a pear. To make a round circle, try looking one quarter of the circle ahead. When you are at one cone, look ahead to the next one. This will keep your circle the right size and even— not wide on one side and short on the other.

The aids that you use to ride a circle are your legs, seat and hands. Your inside leg (the one toward the inside of the circle)

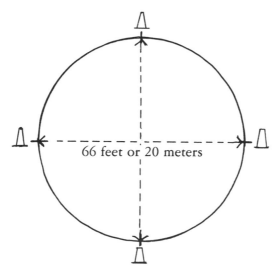

66 feet or 20 meters

20-meter circle with cones set as quarter markers.

stays in its regular position, close to the girth. It tells your pony to keep moving and not to cut in. Your outside leg should be just a little bit farther back. It tells your pony's hind legs to stay on the track of the circle and not to swing out. Your seat tells him to keep turning by "swiveling." (If you lean sideways instead of swiveling, he may cut in and make the circle too small.) Your hands help to keep him on the track. The inside rein asks him to look in the right direction, and the outside rein tells him not to go too fast or make the circle too wide. Your eyes are also important. They should look ahead on the circle, where you are going. Looking somewhere else (especially looking down) makes it hard to ride a circle.

Start at the walk, riding 20-meter circles in both directions. (You will find that it is easier for your pony to make a good circle in one direction than the other. Ponies are righthanded or left-handed just like people.) Then practice circles at the sitting trot and the posting trot. In the posting trot, remember to post on the correct diagonal (the outside diagonal), because this makes it easier for your pony to balance well on a circle. Finally, you can canter on a 20-meter circle. When you canter, your pony should be on the correct lead (the inside lead) because it is quite uncom-

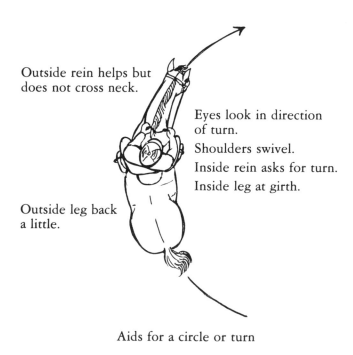

Outside rein helps but does not cross neck.

Eyes look in direction of turn.

Shoulders swivel.

Inside rein asks for turn.

Inside leg at girth.

Outside leg back a little.

Aids for a circle or turn

fortable to be on the wrong lead on a circle this size. Check your pony's lead. If he is on the wrong lead, come back to the walk and try again.

SIMPLE RING FIGURES

Ring figures are good for practicing control, and they help your pony to become more supple and easier to turn. You will need to know simple ring figures for riding lessons and for Pony Club dressage tests.

It is easier to learn to ride ring figures if you practice in a dressage arena or a riding ring with dressage letters. The letters give you a place to begin and end your ring figures, and help you judge whether your figures are the right size. Your practice ring should be twice as long as it is wide. A small dressage arena is 20 meters (66 feet) wide and 40 meters (132 feet) long, and the dressage letters are always in the same places. (A larger dressage arena, 20 meters by 60 meters, is used for some competitions.) You can set up dressage letters in your riding ring by painting them on the fence or on the wall, or by setting up buckets or plastic cones with the dressage letters painted on them. If you use dressage letters when you are practicing ring figures and ordinary flat work, it will be easier to learn dressage tests for your Pony Club ratings and for competitions.

The illustration on page 104 shows a small dressage arena with the basic dressage letters.

Circle

You have already learned about 20-meter circles. You can also make smaller circles (but not so small that your pony has trouble keeping his balance). Remember that all circles should be round and even, not flat on one side or with a "bulge."

Half Circle

A half circle is one way to reverse or turn around. To ride a half circle, pick a spot along the rail (like a letter or a marker), and begin to ride a circle. When you have made half a circle, ride back to the rail on a diagonal line (a slanting line). A half circle looks something like an ice-cream cone. You make the round part (the "ice cream") first, then the "cone."

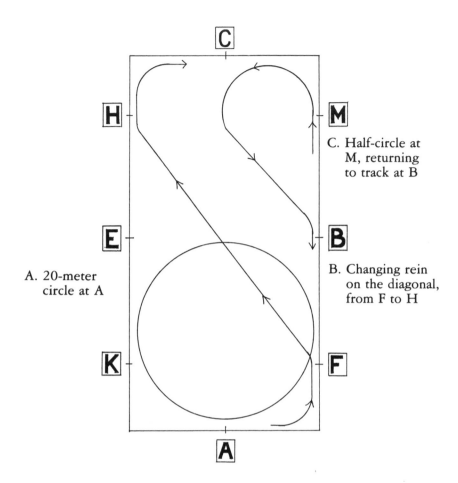

C. Half-circle at
M, returning
to track at B

B. Changing rein
on the diagonal,
from F to H

A. 20-meter
circle at A

Ring figures using dressage letters

Changing the Rein

This means changing directions. (When you are riding with your right hand toward the center, you are riding "on the right rein.") When you change directions, you "change the rein." The most common way of changing the rein is "changing the rein on the diagonal." Here's how:

1. Make sure you are on the track of the ring, close to the rail.
2. Ride through the "short side" (the end of the ring) to the corner marker.
3. At the corner marker, turn and ride toward the opposite

corner maker. Look at the marker to "aim" your pony straight.

4. When you reach the rail at the next corner marker, stay on the track.

If you are posting to the trot, remember to change your diagonal in the center whenever you change directions.

INCREASING AND DECREASING SPEED AT THE TROT

Increasing and decreasing your pony's speed is called "rating."

* To increase speed at the trot, use short squeezes or nudges with your legs in rhythm with the trot. If you are posting, use your legs when you sit, and relax them when you rise. Your hands must relax just enough to tell your pony he may go faster, but don't let your reins get too long and sloppy.
* To decrease speed at the trot, squeeze your fingers shut on the reins each time you sit, and relax them as you rise. Your legs should be ready to keep your pony trotting, so that he doesn't break down to a walk.

Passing other riders and being passed (at the trot) will give you practice in rating, or speed control. You will have to use your legs firmly to get your pony's attention and to make him trot fast enough to pass another pony. (For safety, pass wide—at least one pony length away.) When it is your turn to be passed, slow your pony's trot down and keep his head turned a little bit toward the pony that is passing him, to prevent him from kicking.

UNDERSTANDING THE BASIC AIDS

The "aids" are the means by which you communicate with your pony and control him. The "natural aids" are the aids that are part of you: your hands, legs, seat, and voice; "artificial aids" are things that help out the natural aids, like crops and spurs.

Your aids are like a language that lets you talk with your pony by touch. When you use your aids very softly, it is like a whisper. Strong aids are more like a shout. Always start out with soft, light aids. If your pony does not pay attention, then you can use stronger aids. (Wouldn't you hate it if somebody yelled at you, when you could hear them just as well if they spoke quietly?)

Any natural aid (hands, legs or seat) can be "active," "passive," or a "preventing" aid. An "active aid" is an aid that is asking your pony to do something (for example, a leg that is squeezing to ask him to move). A "passive aid" is ready, but is not asking (for example, a leg that is against the pony's side but relaxed, not squeezing). A "preventing aid" is one that tells a pony *not* to do something (for example, a short squeeze on the reins that says "No" when a pony wants to go faster).

Simple Leg Aids

There are three different leg aids:

1. *Both legs* (used in short squeezes or nudges)—ask the pony to move forward or increase his speed.
2. *One leg in normal position near the girth*—asks the pony to move forward and bend or turn in that direction (left leg for left turn). It can also be used as a preventing aid, to tell the pony not to cut corners.
3. *One leg a little behind the girth* (about 4 inches)—asks the pony to move his hindquarters sideways. It can also be used

Both legs close to the girth: go forward.

One leg close to the girth: bend and turn.

One leg behind the girth: move hind legs sideways.

Simple leg aids

as a preventing aid to tell the pony not to swing his hind legs sideways.

Simple Rein Aids

1. *Both hands squeeze and relax, straight back*—asks the pony to slow down or stop. Can be a preventing aid to tell the pony not to move forward.
2. *One hand moves slightly out to one side*—asks the pony to turn in a wide turn without slowing down. This is called a "leading rein" because it "leads" the pony into a turn.
3. *One hand squeezes and relaxes, straight back*—asks the pony to turn in that direction, in a tighter turn. This is called a "direct rein."
4. *One hand presses inward, against the pony's neck*—a preventing aid that asks the pony to stop going sideways. It is called a "neck rein" because it presses against the pony's neck.

When you use rein aids, remember to squeeze and relax your fingers and hands. Don't pull your hands backward. Give rein aids in short squeezes, not long, hard pulls.

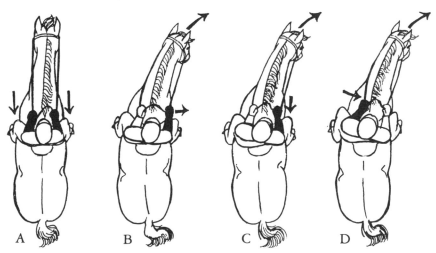

A. Both hands squeeze backward: slow down or stop.
B. Leading rein—one hand moves outward: turning.
C. Direct rein—one hand squeezes backward: turning.
D. Neck rein—one hand moves inward toward neck (but not crossing neck): outside rein to help turn.

Simple rein aids

Simple Seat or Weight Aids

1. *Sitting up deep and tall*—tells your pony to pay attention, to slow down or stop, or to fix his balance. Always do this when you need to stop or slow down.
2. *"Swiveling"* (turning your body a little, deep in your seat) —tells your pony to turn the way you "swivel." (It also turns your seat bones, so your pony feels it through his back.)
3. *Aiming your eyes where you want your pony to go*—tells your pony to go straight or to turn, depending on where you are looking. This works because your head is quite heavy (about thirteen pounds), so your pony can feel your head turn

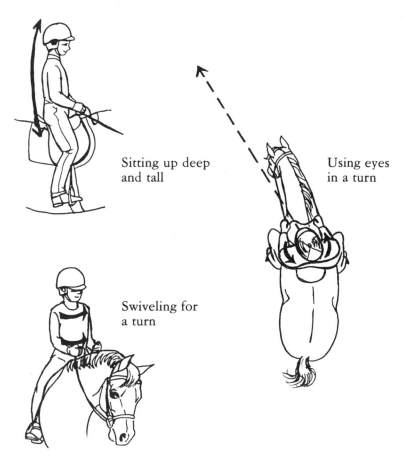

Sitting up deep and tall

Using eyes in a turn

Swiveling for a turn

Simple seat aids

when you turn your eyes. Don't look down, or your pony will feel your head wobble. This tips your weight forward and upsets your balance, and he might stop.

You have to use the right aids or your pony won't understand what you want. When you use your aids together, they must help each other, not work against each other. "Clashing your aids" means using two aids against each other by mistake (like pulling to stop while kicking to go forward). This makes ponies confused, upset and stubborn. When a pony doesn't do what you want him to, it is usually because he does not understand your aids.

Aids must be used on purpose, not by accident. If you accidentally pull on the reins, your pony will think you mean he should stop. If your legs bump his sides, he might think you mean to go faster. Pulling, kicking or giving aids by accident can get a pony mixed up and very cross. After a while, he may become hard to ride. That is why it is so important to learn to ride with your legs, seat and hands in good position, and to develop an independent seat.

RIDING OVER FENCES (D-3 LEVEL)
Some Important Things About Jumping

- Jumping is fun for you but hard work for your pony, especially when you are cantering. Don't jump the same jumps too many times or jump too long. This can make him tired, bored and sour, and he will not want to jump at all. Don't jump every day because it is hard on your pony's legs. Every other day is usually enough.
- Always warm up before jumping (fifteen minutes of walking and trotting, with a short canter or two). Cool your pony out thoroughly afterward, and rub his legs down. This helps you notice any small bumps, cuts or injuries right away.
- Always check your tack before jumping, even if you checked it when you mounted up. Check the girth. Make sure your stirrups are at jumping length, and tighten the chin strap on your helmet.
- Build safe fences, with ground lines on the takeoff side.

How a pony jumps

APPROACH   TAKEOFF   FLIGHT

What a rider does during each phase of the jump
Approach: eyes up, use legs, let pony use his head and neck to see and
    judge the jump.
Takeoff: Jumping position (shoulders over knees), angles close, hands
    release, eyes up, heels down.
Flight: stay in balance, hands maintain release, eyes up, heels down.

Don't jump fences in the wrong direction, with a false
ground line. Check the footing. Don't jump when it is too
slippery or very hard (like concrete).

• You should have lots of experience over all kinds of low,
  simple fences before you jump higher ones. This is not
  only safer for you and your pony, but it helps you build
  confidence and good jumping habits.

• Always keep a safe jumping distance (at least five or six
  pony lengths) when you are jumping behind another pony.

• Don't jump a pony that you can't control, especially cross-
  country. This is very dangerous for both you and the pony.
  If you are having trouble with control, or with any part of
  your jumping, get help from your instructor.

• Never jump alone. Someone should always be on hand in
  case of an accident.

Types of Releases

Whenever your pony jumps, you must give him a "release." This
means that your hands let him stretch out his head and neck so
he can jump. If you don't release him, he will get jerked in the
mouth when he tries to jump. This could make him jump badly
or even stop jumping.

There are several kinds of releases. Of the four that are ex-

110

LANDING   RECOVERY

Landing: sink into heels, balance over feet, eyes up, hands maintain
  release.
Recovery: eyes up, hands following, stay in balance with heels down, use
  legs to ride on.

plained, the first is the most basic and the automatic release is the
most advanced. You should only try the next release when you
can do the first one very well, and so on.

Basic Release This release, also called "mane release," is for riders
just beginning to jump. It is also used when things go wrong, to
keep from pulling the pony's mouth. For a basic release, keep the
reins in your hands but open your thumb and first fingers. Reach
forward about 12 inches up the pony's neck, pinch the roots of
the mane with both hands, and close your fingers. Hold the mane
firmly until your pony has finished jumping. (Instead of the mane,
you may use a neckstrap buckled around your pony's neck about
12 inches in front of the saddle.) After the jump, pick your hands
up gently and bring them back where they belong for normal
control.

Crest Release This is the next step after the basic release. Reach
forward about 12 inches up the pony's neck. Put both hands
together on top of the neck and press down firmly against his
crest. (If you don't press hard enough, your hands might fly up
and jerk his mouth.) Keep your hands pressed on his crest until
he has finished the jump.

Short Release This is a crest release that does not reach as far,
so it gives you more control. Reach forward toward the bit only

111

about 4 or 5 inches, until your knuckles press against the pony's neck closer to the saddle. This release doesn't let your pony stretch his neck as far as the last two releases, so it is used for vertical jumps and jumps where you need quick control afterward. It should not be used over spread jumps.

Automatic Release This release is also called "following through the air" or "jumping on contact." For this release, your hands keep contact with your pony's mouth and stay off the neck. As your pony stretches his neck forward, he draws your hands through the air, making your arms stretch just as much as his head and neck stretch out. You have light contact with his mouth during the jump and while he is landing, so this release gives you the

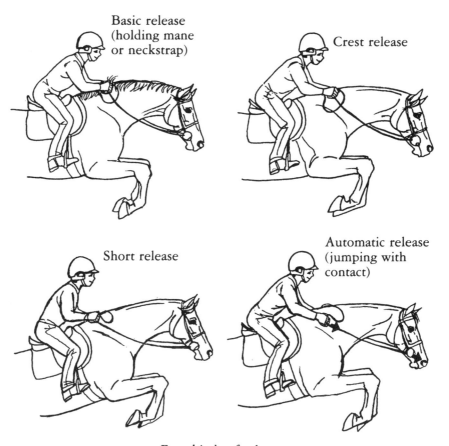

Basic release
(holding mane
or neckstrap)

Crest release

Short release

Automatic release
(jumping with
contact)

Four kinds of release

Excellent jumping form for D level. This rider is in balance with her pony, with eyes up, heels down, seat close to the saddle and shoulders just over her knees. *Photo: Micki Dobson.*

This rider shows a good basic release, which lets her pony stretch his neck over the jump. However, she is standing up too far forward and her heels have slipped up and back, which could make her insecure. *Photo: Micki Dobson.*

most control. (CAUTION: this is an advanced release, to be used only by riders who can do the last three releases perfectly. If you try to jump on contact and don't do it quite right, any mistakes you make will pull on your pony's mouth and may spoil his jumping.)

"Dropping" the Pony This is a mistake some riders make when they are trying to release. "Dropping" means suddenly dropping contact with the pony's mouth (loosening the reins) at just the wrong time, right before a jump, instead of releasing correctly just as he takes off. Often the rider looks down or leans forward, too. This surprises a pony just as he is getting ready to jump. He might make a bad jump, or he might even stop. If it happens often enough, he will not trust his rider about jumping. To keep from dropping your pony, keep your eyes up and wait to release until you feel him lift for the takeoff.

Trotting Grids, Cavaletti and Cross-Rails

You have already practiced riding over single ground poles and simple cross-rails. Now you can begin riding over several (three to five) ground poles or low cavaletti (also called a "trotting grid") with a cross-rail at the end. This helps your balance, suppleness and jumping position. It also teaches your pony to balance himself better, to pick up his feet, and to take off at the right spot.

Cavaletti or trotting grids must be set at just the right distances, to fit your pony's strides. You should have help from an instructor or an experienced person who can adjust the poles so they are safe and right for your pony. The ground poles or low cavaletti should be 3 to 4 feet apart (3 feet for small ponies, 4 feet 6 inches for horses). The distance from the last cavaletto to the cross-rail is exactly twice the cavaletti distance (6 feet to 8 feet). This gives your pony just the right amount of room to take off.

When you ride over cavaletti and cross-rails, approach in a steady posting trot with plenty of energy. At the first pole, take a jumping position (shoulders over knees, heels down, seat close to saddle)—stay in jumping position until your pony has landed after the cross-rail. Let the extra bounce of the cavaletti make your knees and ankles springy, so your heels will sink down and your seat stays close to the saddle. Remember to give your pony a release at the jump, and keep your eyes up.

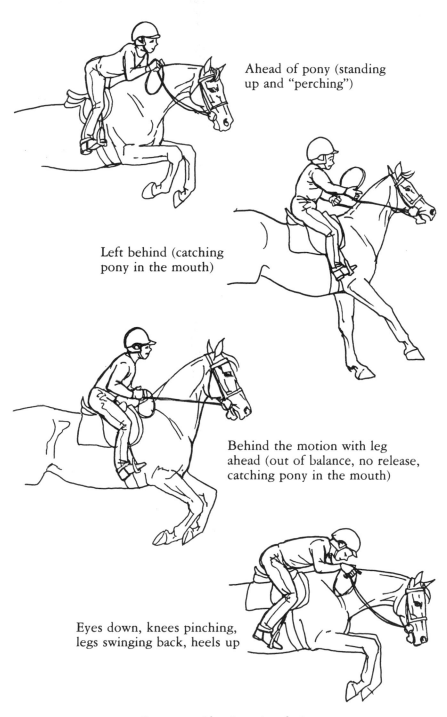

Ahead of pony (standing up and "perching")

Left behind (catching pony in the mouth)

Behind the motion with leg ahead (out of balance, no release, catching pony in the mouth)

Eyes down, knees pinching, legs swinging back, heels up

Common rider jumping faults

Trotting grid with cross-rail

Ground poles spaced 4′ to 4′6″ apart. 8′ to 9′ from last ground pole to
  cross-rail
Ground poles should be spaced so pony steps in the middle.
Distance to the jump is twice the ground pole distance.
Rider is in jumping position over the ground poles and cross-rail.

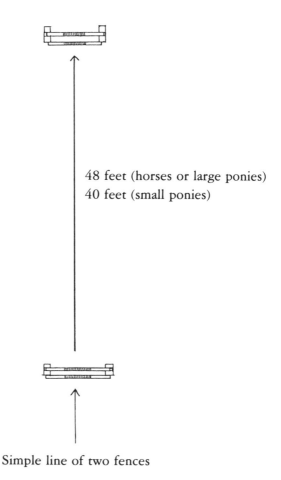

48 feet (horses or large ponies)
40 feet (small ponies)

Simple line of two fences

Jumping at the Canter

When you and your pony have plenty of experience jumping at the trot, you can learn to jump at the canter. The easiest way to do this is in stages. You can set up two cross-rails 48 feet apart (40 feet for small ponies). Trot the first cross-rail, and give an extra leg squeeze and a cluck during the jump. This will encourage your pony to land cantering. When he does, just relax and ride the canter (sitting in the saddle) straight to the next cross-rail. It may help to count "one, two, three, four," and so on, with his canter strides. Keep your eyes up and heels down, and you will canter on over the second cross-rail.

When you can trot into the first cross-rail and canter the second, you can canter into the first jump. Start with a 20-meter circle at the trot, and pick up your canter (on the correct lead) about halfway around your circle. Canter straight to the jump, keeping

Cantering between jumps. This rider shows good balance and control at the canter, with her eyes up and her heels down. (However, her seat could be closer to the saddle.) *Photo: Micki Dobson.*

117

your eyes up and counting to keep the rhythm of his strides. (For now, the number of strides doesn't matter as much as staying in rhythm with his canter.) Later, you can canter two fences in a line.

Jumping Simple Courses (Maximum Height 2′6″)

When you can canter over two fences in a line, making good approaches and turns before and after the jumps, you can put lines of jumps together to make a course. The jumps should be quite simple (no higher than you are used to, or 2′6″ at the maximum), and you should jump each fence by itself, for schooling, before you jump a course. (Later, when you are competing, you will have to jump a course without practicing over it first.)

The jumps should be set at good cantering distances (48 feet,

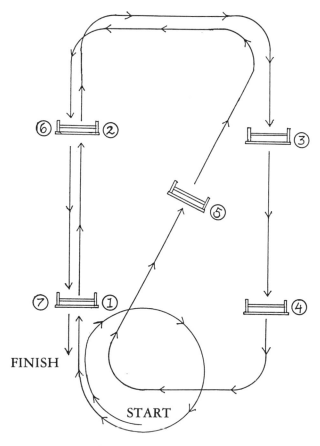

Simple course for D-3 level riders (maximum height 2′6″)

60 feet or 72 feet for horses; 40 feet, 51 feet or 61 feet for small ponies). Be sure that there is room to make a good circle and approach to the first fence, and room to turn easily after each line. The fences and distances should be checked by your instructor or an experienced helper, to make sure they are safe and right for your pony.

Ride smart: plan how you will ride your course! Think about where you will make your opening circle, and where to start your approach to the first fence. Pick out a "target" to look at to keep you lined up straight over the middle of each line of jumps. Walk through each turn and plan where you should turn to make a good approach to the next jump. Think about where you will need to use more leg to keep your pony going, and where he might want to go too fast (like going back to the gate!), or cut a corner. When you have made your riding plan, you can mount up and ride the course just the way you have planned it. Afterward, think about how you did. Did your plan work? Was there anything you could do to ride it better the next time?

Pony Jumping Problems

Disobediences (Refusals and Runouts)   When a pony disobeys at a jump, you must do two things: first, handle the refusal or runout properly. Second, figure out why he stopped or ran out and how to keep him from doing it again. If he refuses more than once, it can get to be a habit.

WHY THE PONY MIGHT REFUSE OR RUN OUT:

WHAT TO DO:

1. Rider error: you didn't bring him in straight, didn't use your legs, dropped him, or pulled his mouth.

1. Ride a better approach: use your legs, eyes and release correctly.

2. Jump is too big or unfamiliar, or the ground is slippery.

2. Lower the jump; let the pony look at it; don't jump on bad footing.

3. The pony got off balance, or got to such a bad takeoff spot that he didn't think he could jump safely.

3. Try again, riding a better approach (especially better balanced).

4. The pony is lame or sore.

4. Have the veterinarian check him. Don't jump a lame pony!

5. You are not really sure you want to jump. Ponies can tell!

5. Take time to build up confidence over easier jumps.

6. The pony is green (inexperienced) or has lost confidence in jumping because of a bad experience.

6. Work slowly over very small jumps to build up the pony's confidence. Good riding is very important.

Handling a Refusal (Stopping) First, keep your eyes up and keep your balance. Sit up and stay in control. Next, bring your pony right to the center of the jump. Let him have a good look at it, but don't let him turn away from it or jump it from a standstill. Keep him there while you squeeze your legs and cluck once or twice, to get him to think "Forward!" (A lazy or stubborn pony might need a tap of a stick right behind your leg, too.) Then turn around, go back and try again, using your legs firmly and adding a cluck to remind him to go forward. (CAUTION: If your pony is afraid of a jump, you may need to make it lower before you try it again. It may also help to follow another pony over it the first time.)

Handling a Runout When a pony runs out, it is not quite the same as a stop. First you must get control again, then correct the runout. Sit up deep and tall and stop your pony, then *think* before you turn him around. You must turn him opposite from the way he ran out (if he ran out to the right, turn him left). This is important to correct his runout. Next, ride him back to the center of the jump and make him look straight over the middle of it. You may need to use your leg and cluck or tap with a stick to make him think "Forward over the middle!" When you turn around to repeat the jump, turn the way that will correct his runout ideas (if he ran out right, turn left). When you approach the fence again, keep your eyes on your "target" over the middle of the jump, and use your legs firmly, but don't come too fast. Be ready to steer sideways if he starts to run out again. Put your crop in the hand on the side he ran out toward. It can help to keep him from running out that way again.

120

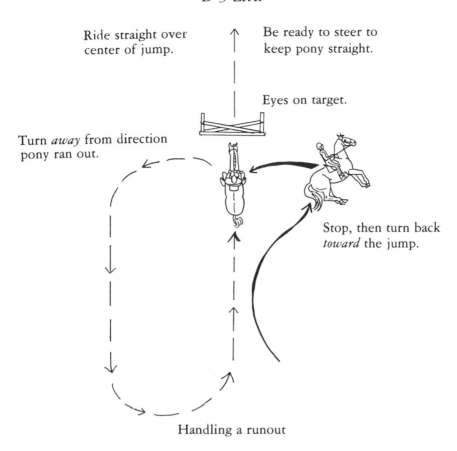

Ride straight over center of jump.

Be ready to steer to keep pony straight.

Eyes on target.

Turn *away* from direction pony ran out.

Stop, then turn back *toward* the jump.

Handling a runout

Rushing Jumps A pony that rushes too fast at his jumps is hard to ride and may not jump safely. It takes an experienced rider to control a rusher and teach him to jump better. This is not the kind of pony for a beginning jumping rider.

WHY THE PONY MAY RUSH:
1. He is too fresh and "full of beans." He may have had too much grain and too little exercise.
2. He is nervous about jumping (he may be green or have had bad experiences).

WHAT TO DO:
1. Longe or exercise him until he settles down. Don't overfeed him.

2. Work slowly over ground poles, cavaletti and low jumps. A good, patient and experienced rider is very important.

3. You use too much leg, hang on the pony's mouth or clash your aids.

3. You need help to improve your riding.

4. You are tense and nervous, and the pony catches your nervousness.

4. You must calm down, breathe, go back to easier jumps to build up confidence.

5. The pony is experienced and "strong"; "takes over" when jumping.

5. The pony needs an experienced rider. He needs good flat work to make him easier to control. Circles or cavaletti before jumps may help.

Jumping Simple Cross-Country Fences (maximum 2'6")

Jumping cross-country fences is a lot like jumping in the ring, but there are some differences. Many ponies act more lively and want to move on more freely when they jump outside. This makes for good, bold jumping, but you must have control. Practice stopping and slowing down until your pony will "come back" when you ask him to. Some ponies may need a stronger bit for jumping outside the ring.

Another difference is that cross-country fences are solid—they do not knock down like ring jumps. This seems scary to some riders, but it actually makes for better jumping. Ponies can see and judge a solid fence (like a log, coop or brush pile) more easily than a jump made of poles. They usually jump bigger, with more power, and more freely over solid fences. When you jump solid fences, you don't ride differently than over other jumps. Just be "positive" (sure and strong); you don't want to take away your pony's confidence with a half-hearted approach. The way to build your own confidence (and your pony's confidence) about solid fences is to start by jumping very low, easy ones at first. Always check the footing on takeoff and landing first to be sure it is safe to jump.

If your pony is not sure he wants to jump a cross-country fence, give him a chance to stand and take a good look at it. Ride several 20-meter circles in front of the fence at a trot, giving him a look at the jump each time he comes around the circle. When he feels like he will go forward calmly, follow another pony over the jump.

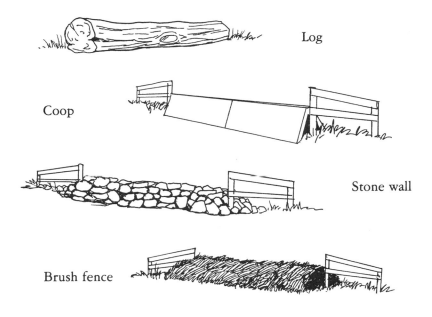

Some simple cross-country fences

Be careful to look up, keep your heels down and release properly, so you won't be surprised if he jumps big and catch him in the mouth.

When you follow another rider over a jump, you must keep a safe distance. This is *at least* five or six pony lengths back; sometimes more. The rider ahead of you should have landed and recovered before your pony gets to the jump. You should be far enough back so that you could stop your pony if the rider ahead had a refusal or a fall. Riding too close is dangerous—for you, your pony and the rider ahead.

RIDING IN THE OPEN (D-3 LEVEL)
Control in the Open, Alone and in a Group

Many ponies act more lively and want to go forward more when they are outside the ring, especially when they are with a group of ponies. Good control is important for safety, to keep your pony from being a nuisance to others and so you can enjoy your riding. Some ponies need a stronger bit when they are being ridden outside.

Ponies in a group obey their "herd instinct." This goes back to the time when all ponies lived in wild herds. Herd instinct tells ponies that they are safest in the middle of a group, and that they should do whatever the herd does. If one pony startles or takes off, the others will want to, too. If a pony gets left behind the herd, he may get very upset until he can catch up with his friends. Some ponies get stubborn if you try to make them leave the group.

When you ride in a group, you will have to work against herd instinct by making your pony keep a safe distance from the other ponies (at least one pony length). He may want to crowd closer, but he (or you) could get kicked. No one in a group should take off in a faster gait without asking the others if it is all right with them. If the whole group starts racing, passing each other or going too fast, some ponies will get excited and become very hard to control. This is dangerous! A group should not ride off and leave one pony and his rider alone, especially if the rider is busy mounting or trying to close a gate. The pony may get upset and try to catch up too fast. When you ride with a group, don't try to hold

Trotting and cantering outside in a group requires good control and good sense, because ponies may get excited. If one pony takes off, the others will want to go, too. *Photo: Neena Ewing.*

your pony back and keep him so far behind the group that he gets upset, or he may get very hard to control. Ask the group to slow down and wait for you, or catch up with them and then keep a safe distance.

When you ride a pony outside by himself, he may act as if his barn is his herd. He may be slow and stubborn about going away from the stable area, and may want to hurry back home. A pony that will not leave the barn, or that rushes back to the barn, is called "barn sour." This can be caused by letting a pony run back to his barn, which quickly becomes a bad habit. If your pony acts barn sour, you will need help from your instructor to teach him to be easier to control. If you always make him walk the last mile back to the stable area, you can keep this problem from getting started.

Here are some ways to help control your pony in a group outside:

Pulley Rein This is a strong rein aid for emergency control. It should only be used when your pony does not pay attention to ordinary aids to stop or slow down, or if he tries to take off or buck.

1. Sit up deep and tall, with your heels down. Look up!
2. With your reins quite short, set one hand firmly on the top of your pony's neck. The rein should be tight.
3. With the other hand, lift up sharply as you rock your shoulders back. Use a short, sharp lift, not long pull. If he doesn't behave for one pulley rein, use several, one after the other. Don't use a pulley rein any harder than you need to, but be as strong as you have to, to get control.

Circling If you are trotting or cantering in the open and your pony gets "strong" and hard to stop, turn him in a large circle. (Even if he won't stop, he will usually turn quite easily.) Gradually make the circle smaller, and he will have to slow down and then stop.

If you have to circle to get control, be careful to do it on good footing and where it is level or slightly uphill. Turning too sharply, going downhill, or turning on slippery footing can make your control problem worse.

Pulley rein

Riding over a shallow ditch

Riding through Shallow Water

When you are riding outside, you may need to cross a stream. You should start by crossing shallow streams with gently sloping banks. Don't start out trying to cross difficult places like deep water, boggy places or streams with steep banks at first.

When you approach a stream, keep your pony moving forward and straight. Use your legs firmly to keep him moving. If he stops, don't let him turn away—make him stand facing the stream until he

126

is ready to go forward. Try following another pony through the water (about one pony length behind him). When he is in the water, you can let him drink, but use your legs to move him onright away if he starts to paw or bend his knees. (Some ponies like to lie down in water, and they usually paw or bend their knees first!)

Riding Shallow, Natural Ditches

When you first start riding over ditches, pick an easy, shallow ditch, one with gently sloping banks. (It should not be a steep ditch or one with "revetted" banks—banks that are straight and faced with wood or stone. Those will come later.)

Keep your pony straight and keep your eyes up. Use your legs firmly to keep him moving forward. The best way to ride over a ditch the first time is to follow an experienced pony at a short but safe distance (about two pony lengths), at a fast walk or a slow trot. Keep your seat in the saddle and your heels down, and be ready to take a jumping position in case your pony jumps. Don't look down or "drop" your pony (by loosening the reins suddenly). This surprises him and might make him stop.

◆◆

USPC D-3 LEVEL RIDING TEST REQUIREMENTS

To pass the D-3 riding test, child should ride with control, maintaining a reasonably secure position at the walk, trot and canter, while developing balance and a steady position over fences.

Riding on the Flat

1. Demonstrate an emergency dismount at the halt and walk.
2. Adjust stirrups and girth while mounted at the halt.
3. Perform balancing and suppling exercises (for rider) at the walk and trot.
4. Ride without stirrups at the sitting trot.
5. Demonstrate a simple step back.
6. Perform 20-meter circles in both directions, at the walk, sitting trot and posting trot with correct diagonals, and at the canter with correct leads.
7. Demonstrate increase and decrease of speed at the trot by passing other riders on the rail and taking the lead.
8. Child will discuss performance with Examiner, including

whether the circles were round and the natural aids were used correctly.

Riding Over Fences

9. Trot over ground poles, followed by a cross-rail.
10. Jump a simple stadium course, height not to exceed 2'6". (Five to seven jumping efforts; some obstacles may be jumped in both directions.) Child will discuss performance with Examiner, including reasons for any disobediences.

Riding in the Open

11. Ride safely with a group at the walk and trot, over varied terrain, through shallow water and small ditches, as they occur in natural terrain (ditches to be unrevetted).
12. Jump simple cross-country obstacles, not to exceed 2'6". (Five to seven jumping efforts; some obstacles may be jumped in both directions. Not a cross-country course.)
13. Child will discuss ways to control a pony in the open.
14. Child will discuss performance with Examiner.

◆◆

PART 3

PONY CARE
AND
MANAGEMENT

CHAPTER 5

Handling, Leading and Tying Your Pony

When you are in charge of a pony, whether he is your own pony or one you are riding or handling, you must know how to handle him right. Proper handling keeps you, other people and the pony safe, and prevents accidents. It also makes it easier for the pony to understand what you want him to do and to behave with good "pony manners."

PONY HANDLING

The first thing to know about ponies is that they scare easily. When all ponies were wild, they had to be quick to spot anything strange or dangerous in order to run away from it. Ponies still use their eyes, ears and noses to notice anything new, and if they are surprised or startled, the first thing they want to do is run. If a pony is startled or scared and can't get away, he might kick to defend himself.

A pony's eyes are on the sides of his head, so he can see all around him. However, he has two "blind spots"—behind his rump and right in front of his nose. If you come up on him in his blind spots without warning (for instance, if you walk up behind his rump or pop up under his nose), he can be startled and might try to get away or kick before he knows who you are.

When you are around ponies, move slowly and speak quietly. Loud noises and sudden movements upset a pony. He can also

How a pony sees

Both eyes

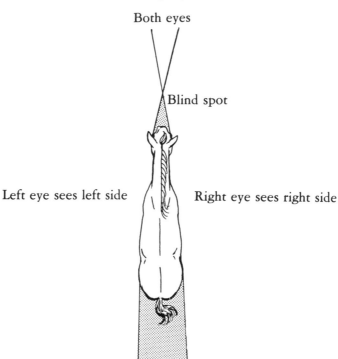

Blind spot

Left eye sees left side   Right eye sees right side

Blind spot

get excited if he is in a strange place, or if something happens that he isn't used to. If your pony acts nervous, pat him and talk quietly to him to calm him down.

Approaching a Pony

When you go up to a pony, speak kindly to him so that he knows you are there. Go toward his shoulder instead of straight toward his face or behind him. To make friends, let him sniff your hand; that is how he learns who you are. He will like it better if you stroke his neck or shoulder than if you try to pat his nose or face.

If a pony is tied to a fence or in a tie stall, you may have to approach from the rear. (It is always safer to approach from the front if you can.) Never come right up behind him, because he might be dozing or not paying attention. Speak to him first, and wait until he turns his head and looks at you, so he knows you are there. Then put your hand on his hip (gently but firmly—don't tickle) and give him a voice command like "Tony, step over." As he steps over, you can walk up to his shoulder.

Approaching a pony safely from the front

Approaching a pony safely from behind

Some Rules for Safe Pony Handling

- Don't run, shout or make loud noises around ponies. It upsets them and can scare them.
- Remember that some things that seem ordinary to people can scare ponies, especially if sudden movement is involved. Things like balloons, umbrellas, bouncing balls or even a person on a bicycle can look like monsters to a pony if he isn't used to them.

133

- Watch out for your pony's feet. He doesn't aways look where he steps, and he may step on your feet by accident if you are careless. Anyone working around ponies should wear strong shoes that give some protection—never sandals, sneakers, or bare feet. (The current *USPC Horse Management Handbook* describes approved footwear.)[1]
- Stay away from the rear end of a pony unless you are working on him. He could switch his tail at a fly and whip it across your face, or kick at a fly and hurt you accidentally. It is safer to be near the front than the rear.
- When you are handling a pony around people who are inexperienced with ponies (especially small children), you have to be extra careful and show them how to behave safely. Be polite, but be firm about safety rules for the safety of everyone.

Putting on a Halter

When a pony is loose in a stall, he may not be wearing a halter. If he is well trained, he should turn his head toward you when you call him and stand quietly while you put the halter on. (You should have help getting your pony out until you know him well enough to handle him by yourself.) To halter a pony, stand by his left shoulder, facing forward. Put the lead rope around his neck, near the ears, to keep him still while you put the halter on. Hold the halter with the buckle in your left hand and the crownpiece in your right. The pony's nose goes in the middle. Slip the noseband onto his nose and reach under his neck with your right hand; pass the crownpiece over his poll and buckle it behind his ears. Your lead rope should be snapped to the chin ring (the center ring) of the halter unless it is necessary to attach it in a special way for extra control.

Catching a Pony in a Field

Catching a gentle pony in a field is much like haltering him in a box stall. Call his name and walk slowly toward his shoulder, not

[1] *The USPC Horse Management Handbook* contains additional information on clothing, equipment, horse transportation and horse management, especially in connection with rallies and other Pony Club events. It is available from the U.S. Pony Clubs, 4071 Ironworks Pike, Lexington, KY 40511.

How to put on a halter

toward his face or his hindquarters. Wait until he looks at you, so he knows you are there, then walk up and pat him quietly on the neck. Put the lead rope around his neck right behind his ears to hold him still while you halter him. If he is alone in the field, you can give him a treat for being caught. This may help teach him to come when you call him. (**CAUTION**: Don't take treats or a bucket of feed into a pasture where there are other ponies. They may crowd around you and get pushy, which is not safe.)

If your pony starts to walk away before you get up to him, don't chase him—stop and wait. When he stops, call his name and hold out your hand. Offer him a treat or a little grain. However, don't give him his treat until he has been caught and haltered.

Some ponies become hard to catch because they know that being caught always means they have to work. If you go out often and catch your pony just to give him a treat and a pat, then let him go, he may learn that being caught means nice things, not just work. If your pony is still too hard to catch, ask your instructor for advice.

Leading a Pony

When you lead or hold a pony, you should *always* use a lead rope or lead shank, unless he is bridled. Never try to lead a pony, even for a short distance, by holding on to the halter without a lead rope. If he should act up, you might have to let go or you could

135

be dragged. You could get hurt and your pony can learn a bad habit.

There are two ways to hold the lead rope with your leading hand:

First method Hold the lead rope in your fist with your thumb on top, about 6 inches from the halter ring. To stop or turn your pony, bend your wrist and give a brief tug backward or sideways.

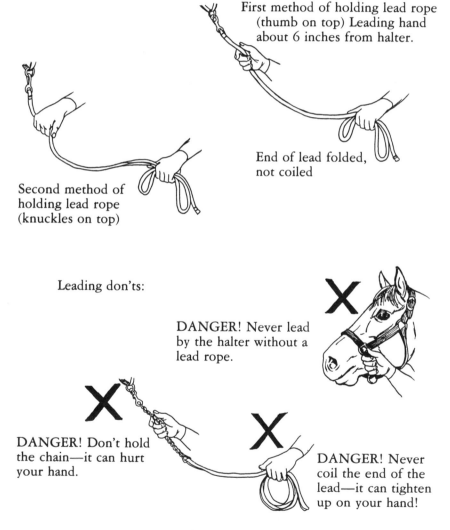

First method of holding lead rope (thumb on top) Leading hand about 6 inches from halter.

End of lead folded, not coiled

Second method of holding lead rope (knuckles on top)

Leading don'ts:

DANGER! Never lead by the halter without a lead rope.

DANGER! Don't hold the chain—it can hurt your hand.

DANGER! Never coil the end of the lead—it can tighten up on your hand!

Holding the lead rope

Leading position

Second method Hold the lead rope with your knuckles on top, about 6 inches from the halter ring. This method may give you more control if your pony is hard to lead. However, be careful not to let your hand and arm hang on the lead rope with a steady pull.

Hold the lead rope about 6 inches from the halter ring with the hand that is next to the pony (your right hand, if you are on his left side). If you are using a chain-end lead shank, hold the strap, not the chain. (The chain can hurt if it gets pulled through your hand.) The other hand should hold the rest of the lead rope, folded up so it won't drag on the ground. It must *never* be looped around your hand—if a pony should spook or take off, the loops could tighten up around your hand. *Never* let yourself get caught in a lead rope or tie it to yourself in any way—that is dangerous!

When you want your pony to move, you must be in a leading position. That means you are beside his neck, facing the front. If you get out ahead of him, you can't see him or control him well, and if you turn around and face him, he may stop and pull back. Say his name and give him a voice command, like "Tony, walk on." Push your leading hand forward, under his chin, to give him a gentle signal to move forward.

◆◆◆

USPC D-1 TEST

Approach pony, put on halter, lead and turn correctly and safely.

◆◆◆

To stop a pony or make him stand still, give him a voice command, like "Tony, whoa," and stop walking. Close your fist on
the lead rope and hold your hand still. When he feels the pressure
of the halter, he should stop. If he doesn't stop, give a short tug
and release down and backward. If he tries to pull away instead
of standing still, use short tugs and releases down and backward
or sideways. Long pulls do not work—he will just pull harder on
you.

When you lead a pony out of his stall or field, turn him away
from you. It is safer to turn a pony away from you whenever you
can, instead of pulling him toward you. This keeps him from
accidentally stepping on your toes. To make him turn, push your
right arm out to the side, leading his chin away from you.

When you lead a pony in a straight line at a trot, it is called

Safe way to turn a pony—away from leader

◆•◆

USPC D-2 TEST

Do walk—halt—walk transitions in hand.

◆•◆

"jogging him out." This is sometimes done to check for lameness. To get your pony to trot, cluck to him or give a quiet voice command, like "Tony, trot." Push your leading hand forward, under his chin, and start to jog. Don't get out ahead of him and pull—that will make him hang back and get stubborn. When he begins to trot, aim straight ahead at something and jog beside him in a straight line. When you want to walk, give a quiet voice command like "Tony, walk," and slow down to a walk yourself. Close your fingers on the reins or lead rope, then relax them as he comes back to a walk.

◆•◆

USPC D-3 TEST

Do walk—trot—walk—halt transitions in hand.

◆•◆

Training for Better Leading

Some ponies need training to move forward properly when they are led. To teach your pony to move out freely at a walk or a trot, you can use a long stiff training whip (about 4 feet long). Put the pony beside a fence, so that he will have to go straight. When leading from the left side, hold the lead rope or rein in your right hand, and the end in your left. Carry the whip in your left hand, with the tip trailing on the ground behind you. With your pony walking, give him a quiet voice command to trot, and push your lead hand forward as you start to jog. If he does not trot, tap him once on his hindquarters by flicking the whip sideways behind you. Tap just hard enough to make him trot, not enough to scare him or make him leap forward. You must tap him within one second of giving the trot command, or he will not

Using whip to teach pony to trot on command

understand. When he trots, be careful not to pull back on him. Jog with him and praise him right away. Bring him back to a walk and try again. If he trots on command, praise him and don't use the whip. If he is lazy, tap him just enough to get him to trot and then praise him. You can use the same method to teach a pony to walk out freely from a halt instead of hanging back.

Another way is to have a helper follow the pony, giving him a little tap with a whip on the hind leg if he hangs back or doesn't respond to your command. The helper must be calm and quiet, and must not tap too hard or scare the pony. You want the pony to pay attention to his leader, not to be afraid of your helper. The helper must also be careful not to get within kicking distance.

A well-trained pony can be led from either side. You should practice leading your pony from the right side as well as the left, so that he gets used to seeing you on that side. When leading

◆◆

USPC D-3 TEST

Lead correctly, moving pony forward with a whip or assistance if necessary.

◆◆

◆◆

USPC D-3 TEST

Lead pony safely from both sides.

◆◆

from the right, hold the rein or lead rope in your left hand about 6 inches from the bit or halter, and carry the end of the reins or lead rope folded up in your right hand. Since most people are more used to handling ponies from the left side, it may take some practice before you can lead as well from the right side as you can from the left.

Tying a Pony

It is very important to tie your pony safely, because he could get loose or be hurt if he is tied in the wrong way. A well-trained pony stands quietly when he is tied up. However, if a pony gets frightened when he is tied up, even a well-trained pony may pull back very hard. This can be unsafe for him and for anyone around him, especially if he is not tied properly. If your pony is nervous or hard to handle about being tied up, ask your instructor for help, and don't try to tie him up on your own until he is trained better.

A pony must always be tied up with a halter and tie rope, *never* with a bridle. If he pulls back against his bridle, the bit will hurt his mouth and the bridle or reins may break. Never fasten a tie rope to your pony's bit, or loop his reins over something to tie him up.

Always tie your pony in a safe place. Tie him to a solid object that cannot be pulled loose, broken off or moved even by the strongest horse. (For example, tie him to a solid fence post, not to a board that could be pulled off the fence.) Be sure there is nothing close by that he could get hurt on or catch his foot in if he should paw, like a wire fence or a nail sticking out of a post. Be sure that there is enough space around him for you to work safely.

Use a good tie rope that will not slip or jam. A cotton, Dacron or hemp rope is good. Watch out for nylon—nylon ropes can slip loose and flat nylon lead shanks may jam so that they are very

Pony tied safely

Tied to solid object, using a safety string
Tied with halter and tie rope, with quick-release knot
Tied at height of withers, with about 18 inches from knot to halter
Tied in a safe place

hard to untie. Never tie a pony with a chain lead shank—this is only for leading, not for tying. A leather lead shank may break if a pony pulls back, and a pony must *never* be tied with a chain over his nose or under his chin. If he pulls back, he could be injured.

A pony should be tied at about the level of his back. If he is tied lower down, he can injure his neck if he pulls back. He should be tied so that he can turn his head and look around, but not with enough slack to get his foot or his head caught in the rope. About 18 inches from the knot to the snap of the rope is usually a good safe length for tying. If the snap of the rope reaches to the ground, the rope is too long—the pony could catch his front leg in it.

For safety, you should use a "safety string" when you tie up a pony. This is a loop of baling twine that is tied around the post or ring—you tie the lead rope to it. It is strong enough to hold your pony for ordinary tying, but it would break if he should get scared and pull back really hard. (If this should happen, the tie rope could get pulled so tight that you would not be able to untie it.) It is better to have to catch your pony than to have him get seriously hurt.

A "panic snap" or "breakaway snap" is a special snap that can

Safety devices for tying

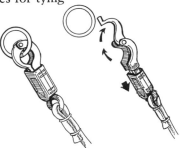

Safety string: a loop of twine that will hold for ordinary tying, but will break loose in an emergency.

Panic snap: a special snap that can be released quickly even during a strong pull.

1. Never tie by a bridle! Pony can break reins and hurt his mouth.

2. Never tie with a chain end lead shank! It can hurt your pony, and the knot may jam tight.

3. Never tie too long and too low! Pony can get his foot over the rope and get hurt.

Don'ts in tying

143

How to tie a quick-release knot

Use a safety string (a loop of twine tied through the ring or around the post).

Step 1: Put end of rope through string loop.

Step 2: Wrap end once around rope, making a circle.

Step 3: Slip doubled end through circle.

Step 4: Make knot snug. (To release, pull on rope end.)

To keep pony from untying himself, tuck rope end through loop.

be used on a tie rope or cross-ties. It is made so that you can release a pony even when the rope is being pulled tight.

When you tie a pony, always use a "quick-release knot." This kind of knot lets you pull on one end and untie a pony quickly if you have to. Other kinds of knots could jam so tight that you cannot get them loose, or they may slip and let go by accident. To tie a quick-release knot, follow these steps:

1. Tie a safety string around the post or through the tie ring.
2. Pass the end of the rope through the safety string.
3. Make a circle around the tie rope.
4. Push the doubled end of the rope through the circle and pull it snug. To release the rope, pull on the long end.
5. If your pony might chew on the rope end and release himself, tuck it back through the loop.

USPC D-2 TEST

Lead pony in and out of a stall safely; tie up in appropriate place with a quick-release knot.

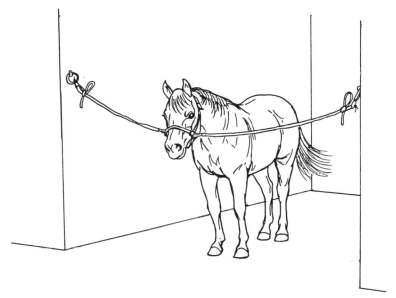

Pony on safe cross-ties, with safety strings

Another way of tying a pony is to "cross-tie" him with two tie ropes, or "cross-ties." One runs from each side of his halter to a ring on the wall with a quick-release knot and a breakable safety string or a panic snap. The cross-ties should not be too high (about the height of the pony's back). This is a good way to have a pony stand still while you groom him.

Cross-ties are often used in a stable aisle, where other people may be working. If your pony is cross-tied and someone needs to lead another pony past, unsnap the cross-ties and move him over. Never try to go under cross-ties when you are leading a pony. Don't leave a pony alone on cross-ties—if something should happen to make him pull back, he could get into trouble.

GETTING READY TO RIDE

Before you ride, you will need to halter your pony, tie him up safely, groom him clean and pick out his feet, and tack him up (put his saddle and bridle on). It saves time if you go and get your tack, your grooming tools, your riding helmet and anything else you need before you get your pony out.

It is easier to carry your tack if you set it up properly first. *Photo: Ruth Harvie.*

How to Carry Tack

It is easier to carry tack if you set it up properly first. The stirrups should be run up, and the girth should be unbuckled and laid across the seat of the saddle, with the ends tucked through the stirrup irons. The saddle pad should be over the top of the saddle. Your bridle and reins can hang on your shoulder, so you have both hands free to pick up and carry your saddle.

A saddle should be set down on a saddle rack, or something like a fence rail. Be careful not to put it on something that will scratch the leather underneath. If you must set it on the ground, set it on the front end, with the cantle leaning against a wall. Put

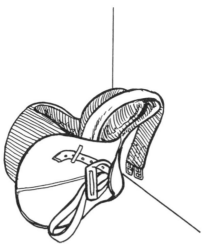

How to set a saddle on the ground.

the girth between the cantle and the wall, to keep the cantle from getting scratched. The pad should be on top of the saddle, out of the dirt. The bridle should be hung up by the top (the crownpiece), or carefully laid across the saddle.

Don't let the girth or reins drag on the ground when carrying your tack. They will get dirty, and you or your pony could step on them and trip. Your tack should not be left where your pony could knock it down, step on it or chew it.

Your Pony Must Be Clean

To get your pony clean for riding, you will need a currycomb and a stiff brush (a dandy brush), and sometimes other grooming tools. You will also need a hoof pick to pick out his feet. (See pages 170–173 for how to groom and pages 204–205 for how to pick out a pony's feet.)

Before tacking up, make sure your pony is brushed clean, especially his back, girth, elbows, head and any place the tack will touch him. If there is dirt, dried sweat or burrs under his tack, he could get a sore. Run your bare hand over those places—they should feel soft and smooth. If you feel dirt, dried sweat or a rough spot, be sure you get it clean and smooth before you tack up. The saddle pad and girth must also be clean, smooth and dry, or they could make him sore.

147

Tacking Up

Your pony should be tied up with a halter. A pony should *never* be tied up by his bridle or left with a bridle on even for a minute. He could step on his reins or catch his bridle on something. It makes sense to saddle him first and only bridle him when you are ready to ride. You can leave him tied safely with his saddle on for a few minutes, while you get your hat or do something else, but after he is bridled, you can't leave him.

Saddling a Pony The saddle pad goes on first. Put it on a little forward, in front of the withers, and slide it back into the right place (over the withers and back), so that the hair is smooth underneath. The front of the saddle pad should be about 2 or 3 inches in front of the saddle. If you get the saddle or pad too far back, start over. Don't push a saddle or saddle pad forward, as this roughs up the hair underneath.

Some people leave the saddle pad attached to the billets all the time. This saves time when saddling, but you must be sure the saddle pad is clean and properly attached. The pad should be taken off to wash it and to let it dry after riding.

Set the saddle gently on the saddle pad. The saddle should sit in the "hollow" below the pony's withers. If it is too far back, the girth won't reach around him. If it is too far forward, it will tip up in front and may pinch the pony's shoulders. Pull the front of the pad up into the gullet of the saddle—this makes an air space over the pony's back and keeps the pad from slipping backward.

Go to the pony's right side (off side) and fasten the saddle pad. The tab should slip over one of the billets. The buckle guard goes below the saddle pad tab. Buckle the girth to the first and last billets, about halfway up. Pull the buckle guard down over the girth buckles. While you are on the right side, check to see that everything is smooth and in the right place.

Go back to the pony's left side (near side) and fasten the saddle pad tab the same way you did on the right. Bring the girth under, taking care to keep it smooth and straight, not twisted. Buckle the girth to the first and last billets. It should be snug enough to keep the saddle from slipping, but not tight yet.

Steps in saddling

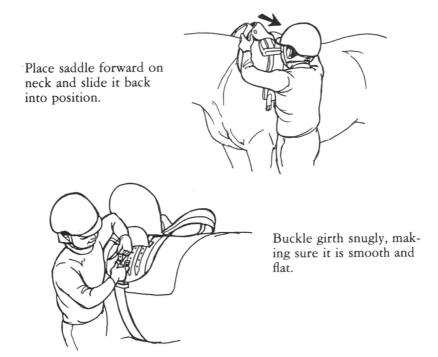

Place saddle forward on neck and slide it back into position.

Buckle girth snugly, making sure it is smooth and flat.

Tightening the Girth Some ponies "blow up," meaning they take a big breath while you are tightening the girth, then let it out later, so the girth will be loose. This usually comes from having the girth pulled up very tight and hard, which makes them uncomfortable. Never hit or kick a pony to make him let out his breath. This can make him hate being saddled, and it might teach him to bite or kick instead of just blowing up. Instead, take up the girth a little, then untie him and turn him around in a circle. He will forget to hold his breath, and you can tighten the girth a bit more. If you girth him up smoothly and gently, he may learn that you won't hurt him and he may get easier to saddle. Be patient and gentle with your pony when you are tacking him up.

For riding, the girth must be snug enough to keep the saddle safely in place, but no tighter than necessary. Very tight girths are uncomfortable and can cause saddle sores. However, a girth that is too loose can let your saddle slip, which is dangerous. Check the girth by slipping your fingers under it just below the saddle flap. It should feel snug, but not so tight that you can't get your fingers inside.

After you have tightened your girth, pick up your pony's front foot and pull his leg forward. This stretches the skin around his elbow, so that it won't get pinched under the girth. Remember to stretch the other leg, too.

If you will not be riding for a while, leave the girth one or two holes loose, so your pony will be more comfortable. However, *never* leave a saddle on a pony with the girth undone or so loose that the saddle could slip off his back. If he moved suddenly, this could cause an accident.

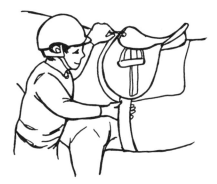

How to check the girth

Stretching a foreleg

Running Up Stirrups

For safety's sake, English stirrups *must always be run up whenever the rider is out of the saddle.* This keeps them from catching on things, banging into the pony, or hitting you. If a pony should bite at a fly on his side, he could catch his teeth on a loose-hanging stirrup iron and get hurt.

To Run Up the Stirrup Hold the top strap of the stirrup leather. Take the iron and turn it a little, then slide it up the *bottom* strap (the one next to the saddle) until it touches the stirrup bar. Next, pull the stirrup leathers down through the iron so that it lies flat. Always run your stirrups up as soon as you dismount, and any time you see them hanging down on a saddle that is not being ridden.

To Pull Down the Stirrup Put your hand on the bottom of the stirrup iron and turn it a little, so it will slide more easily. Then pull it down to the bottom of the stirrup leather.

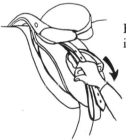

How to pull stirrup irons down.

How to run stirrups up:

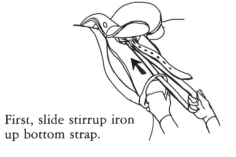

First, slide stirrup iron up bottom strap.

Then, put all stirrup leathers down through stirrup iron.

Bridling a Pony

Before you put the bridle on, make sure the noseband and throat-lash are unbuckled and all parts of the bridle are straight. Unbuckle the halter, slip it off the pony's nose, and re-buckle it around his neck. This keeps him tied up while you are bridling him. (If your halter has a throat snap, it is *not* safe to unsnap the halter and slide it off over his head. This leaves the pony loose for a few seconds, and he could get away from you with nothing on his head.)

First, put the reins over the pony's head, so they won't drop on the ground where you or the pony could step on them. Stand close to your pony's neck on his left side, facing the front. If his head is low enough, you can put your right arm over his head and hold the top of the bridle (crownpiece) in your right hand. The bit rests on your left fingers. Bring the bit up to his mouth and gently squeeze the side of his lip with your thumb. As he opens his mouth, your right hand pulls on the top of the bridle, sliding the bit up into his mouth. Your fingers never go into his teeth. Once the bit is in, slip the crownpiece gently over one ear and then the other. Be careful not to twist his ears or hurt his face with the bridle.

Next, buckle the throatlash under his throat—not too tight. Buckle the noseband inside the bridle so that it is snug but not too tight. You should be able to slip a finger under all parts of the bridle, and a fist should fit between the throatlash and the pony's cheek. Finally, run your fingers underneath the browband and crownpiece to be sure the bridle fits comfortably, and pull the forelock out so that is free of the bridle.

If your pony is high-headed or if you are short, you may not be able to get your arm up over his head. Instead, put your right arm around your pony's face with your hand on his nose, as if you were giving him a hug. Hold the sides of the bridle (the cheekpieces) together in your right hand on top of his face, while your left hand offers him the bit and gently squeezes his lip. When he takes the bit, hold the bridle up with your right hand. You may have to put the crownpiece over his left ear first.

If your pony is hard to bridle, you should have help with bridling until he learns to put his head down and is easy to bridle, or until

Halter around pony's
neck before bridling

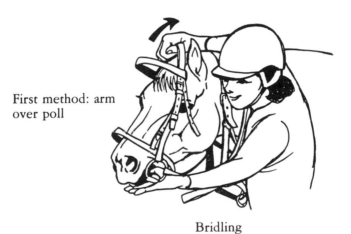

First method: arm
over poll

Bridling

Second method: arm
around under head

Bridling

Young children need help and supervision when bridling a pony. *Photo: Neena Ewing.*

you get better at it. If you keep having trouble bridling him by yourself, he may learn to hate bridling because it is uncomfortable for him. This can make a pony "head shy," or hard to handle around the head.

Leading a Pony When Tacked Up

When you lead a pony that is tacked up, handle him with the bridle reins. The stirrups should be run up and the reins should be taken over his head. Standing on the left side beside his neck, hold the reins with your right hand about 6 inches from the bit. Your left hand holds the end of the reins, folded up so they won't drag on the ground. You lead the pony the same way you do with a lead rope, but remember that the reins are attached to the bit

◆◆

USPC D-2 TEST

Lead pony correctly in bridle and tacked up.

◆◆

Stirrups run up, correct rein hold.

Leading pony while tacked up

in the pony's mouth, so be gentle. Never let the reins drop on the ground. If a pony steps on a rein, he may give his mouth a bad jerk, and he could break his bridle. Don't let a pony eat grass when he is bridled, or he will soon get into the habit of stopping to eat grass whenever he wants to.

CARE AFTER RIDING

After a ride, you must untack your pony and put him away cool, clean and comfortable. You should also take care of your tack and leave the stable area neat and clean. You can always tell good horse-persons by the way they take care of their ponies after riding.

Cooling Out

At the end of a ride, walk your pony around to let him relax and cool out. You can ride him quietly at a walk, or get off and lead him. When you dismount, the first thing to do is to run your stirrups up (see above). Next, loosen the girth one or two holes so your pony can be comfortable. This should be done as soon as you dismount, before you lead your pony back to his stall or wherever you untack him.

Untacking

You should unbridle first. Buckle the crownpiece of the halter around your pony's neck, so he will be tied by the halter and lead rope while you take his bridle off. Unbuckle the noseband and throatlash first (if your bridle has a curb chain, unfasten the curb chain on the left side). Slip the crownpiece and reins gently over his ears, and be careful not to let the bit bang his teeth as it comes out. Unbuckle the halter and slip it over his nose in the normal way, then buckle it up again. Hang your bridle up on a peg or a fence post. Don't drop it on the ground. The bit should be rinsed off as soon as possible.

To unsaddle, unbuckle the girth on the left side. Put your hand under the saddle, pad and all, and lift it up and toward you. Catch the girth as it comes over the pony's back, and put it over the seat of the saddle. When you set the saddle down, you should undo the girth on the right side and take the saddle pad off. (Undo the tabs from the billets.) Hang the wet saddle pad up separately to dry, or put it upside down over the saddle. Don't leave a saddle sitting on a wet saddle pad—the pad will mat down and stay damp. Your girth and saddle should be cleaned as soon as possible.

Caring for Your Pony After Riding

After you untack your pony, you should make him comfortable. (If your pony has worked hard and is hot and sweaty, he will need special cooling out care. See page 163 for how to cool out a hot pony.) If he has damp or sweaty places (like the "saddle mark" and girth area), he should be rubbed with a towel and brushed

* * *

USPC D-1 TEST
Tack up and untack a pony with assistance.

* * *

USPC D-2 TEST
Tack up and untack independently.

* * *

until his coat is smooth. Pick out his feet and check for stones or loose shoes.

If your pony is kept in a stall, he should be put away clean, dry and comfortable, and he should have a fresh bucket of water. If he is kept outside, he can be turned out in his field. Ponies often like to roll after they have been ridden. This is their natural way of grooming themselves and scratching itchy places.

Turning a Pony Out

To safely let a pony loose in his stall or in a pasture, lead him through the gate and turn him around so that he is facing the gate. Close the gate behind you before you let him go. Make him stand for a moment, then quietly unbuckle his halter and slip it off. Never chase a pony or encourage him to take off and run when you let him go. This teaches him bad manners, and he may learn to pull away before you are ready.

For safety, the halter should be removed whenever a pony is loose in a stall or in a pasture. A pony can catch a halter on a fence, on something that sticks out or even on his shoe. If his head is caught he will struggle and may be badly hurt if the halter does not break. If you must leave a halter on your pony, it should be a "safety halter" that has a breakable leather crownpiece or a special safety release that will let go if he should get caught.

How to turn a pony out safely

Notes to Adults on Tacking and Untacking

It is important for children to have help and supervision when tacking up and untacking, until they are old enough, big enough and competent to manage on their own. For your child's safety, it is essential that the saddle and bridle be put on correctly every time he rides.

Teach your child to be gentle, deliberate and patient when tacking up, and avoid all rough methods. Even with kind and gentle horses and ponies, rough or awkward handling during tacking up can upset and annoy the animal. This often leads ponies to develop tricks and defenses that can make them harder to tack up and become unsafe.

Whenever you put on or take off a halter, you should unbuckle it. Don't unsnap the throatlash and slip it over the pony's ears. This can irritate the pony's ears and make him head shy, and it gives you less control.

Finishing Up

After you have taken care of your pony, you should leave your tack and the stable area neat and clean. The tack should be cleaned after every ride. If you don't have time to do a thorough cleaning, at least rinse off the bit and dry it with a towel, and wipe the sweat and dirt off the saddle, bridle and girth with a damp sponge. Hang the damp saddle pad up to dry, and cover the saddle with a towel or dust cover to keep it clean.

Your grooming tools should be cleaned and put away in your grooming kit, and you should sweep or rake the aisle and pick up any manure or trash before you leave. Hang up your pony's halter and rope where it belongs—on his stall or next to the gate of his field.

CHAPTER 6

Pony Care and Management

Because our continent is so large and different regions have different climates, there are different ways of keeping and managing ponies in North America. You might have to handle cold winters in the North, hot and humid weather in the South, dry heat and wind in the Southwest, or other conditions where you live. Keeping a pony on a western ranch, a horse farm, a boarding stable or your own backyard are all different ways of keeping a pony, but they can be equally good. There is no single "correct" American method of stable management. However, there are some things that are basic to all good pony care and management, wherever you live.

You will need advice from experts who know about special aspects of pony care and management where you live. Your veterinarian is a good expert to call on. So is your instructor or District Commissioner. Your county Cooperative Extension office has pamphlets (usually free or inexpensive) on horse and pony management, feeding, health, pastures and plants, and building stables and fences.

At Pony Club D Level, you will learn about basic pony care and should begin to do as much daily care as you can. However, you will need to know more about pony care and management before you are ready to take over the care of a pony on your own. An experienced horse person should supervise your pony's care and management, show you how to care for your pony and help you with any problems.

STABLE, PASTURE OR BOTH?

There are three ways to keep a pony: stabled, in a pasture, or a combination (stabled part of the time and in pasture part of the time). Each has good points and drawbacks. Keeping a pony stabled means more daily work, because you will have to do chores (feeding, stall cleaning, turnout, grooming and so on) and make sure your pony is exercised every day, whether you ride or not. It may also cost more to build or rent a stall and to supply bedding. However, your pony is always there when you want to ride him, and he can be kept cleaner.

A pastured pony lives a more natural life. He can graze and exercise when he wants to, and he is less likely to be too frisky or develop bad habits ("stable vices") from being closed in and bored. However, he will still need daily visits for feeding, care and pasture maintenance, and he may be hard to catch or covered with mud when you want to ride. Pasturing also requires more land, good fencing and a shed or shelter, and you will have to provide hay whenever there is not enough good grass. If you have a stable that opens onto a pasture or paddock, you may be able to let your pony go in and out as he pleases, feed and water him inside, and keep him in his stall when you want him inside.

Boarding Your Pony

Many people keep their ponies in a boarding stable because they do not have a good place to keep them at home. In a boarding stable you pay for the rent of the stall, use of the facilities (like riding rings, trails and tack room), feed and bedding, and for having your pony fed and watered for you. Some boarding stables offer complete care, including stall cleaning, daily turnout, grooming and other services. Others charge less if the owner helps with the daily care of his pony. In Pony Club, you are expected to take over as much of the care of your pony as possible, so you should be prepared to go to the stable every day and do some work for your pony, whether you ride or not. If you board your pony, your parents and an experienced horse person (like your instructor) should visit the stable with you, to see if it offers good care and stable management. It must be a safe and friendly place for you and your pony.

EXERCISE

All horses and ponies need exercise for their health and happiness. They developed over millions of years as free-roaming creatures. Keeping a pony in a stall without exercise is one of the worst things you could do to him. A pony must be physically fit before you can do hard work without causing injury. If he stands around all week, he will be soft and unfit. It is unfair to him and can hurt him if you work him too hard on the weekend. If you can, try to ride your pony at least a little bit every day, and make sure he has plenty of time turned out in a pasture or paddock or gets some other kind of exercise when you can't ride.

Warming Up

Every time you ride a pony, he needs to be warmed up slowly. Start out by walking for the first fifteen minutes. While you are walking, you can practice halts, turns and circles or other exercises, or enjoy a short trail ride. After fifteen minutes, your pony can begin trotting and later cantering. This is important to get his heart pumping strongly and his muscles loosened up and ready to work. If you started right out with hard work, he could pull a muscle and go lame.

Exercise or Work

Your pony's daily work might include ordinary riding, lessons, trail rides, Pony Club working rallies (mounted meetings) or other activities like competitions or special events. To keep him fit enough for ordinary riding, he should be ridden at least three times a week (five or six days a week is better). If your pony is "soft" (not physically fit for ordinary work), you will have to build him up slowly by exercising him a little every day and gradually increasing his work. To do this, you will need help and advice from your veterinarian and from an experienced horse person, who can tell you what your pony needs to get fit and how much work it is safe to do with him. This is important, as your pony can be injured or get sick if you don't condition him properly. (*The Pony Club C Manual* will cover conditioning in more detail.)

There are several ways to exercise a pony when you can't ride him for some reason. If he is turned out in a pasture, he can exercise himself. Turning a pony out for an hour or more before you ride can let him get rid of his extra energy, so he will be less frisky when you ride him. Longeing is another way to exercise a pony, but this *must* be done by an experienced horse-person who can longe safely and correctly. (Pony Club recommends that longeing be done only by experienced members at the C-3 Level or higher, not by D Level members.) If a pony cannot be ridden or turned out (for instance, if he is lame or if the footing is not usable for riding or turnout), you can lead him in hand for half an hour or so.

COOLING OUT A PONY AFTER WORK

When a pony works hard he gets hot and sweaty, just as you do when you run and play hard. He *must* be cooled out properly, or he may get chills, muscle cramps or even colic (a bellyache). He should always be put away cool, dry, clean and comfortable after a ride. Cooling out is one of the most important things you can do for your pony.

Basic Cooling Out

Every ride should end by walking your pony for at least ten to fifteen minutes to gradually let his body come back to normal, which helps prevent sore muscles and other injuries. You can ride at a relaxed walk, or dismount and lead him around. (Remember to run up your stirrups and loosen the girth a hole or two when you dismount.) How is his breathing—is he puffing and are his nostrils open wide? Notice how hot and sweaty he feels on his neck and chest, and if the small veins are sticking out under his skin. He is not completely cooled until all of these are back to normal, and he should keep walking slowly until he is completely cooled out.

USPC D-1 TEST

Know one reason for cooling out a pony after exercise.

You should lead your pony around to cool him out after hard work. *Photo: Micki Dobson.*

Water During Cooling Out When a pony works or sweats (even a little), he loses water and needs to drink enough to replace it. However, a hot, sweaty pony must *never* be allowed to gulp cold water. This can cause a serious illness, such as colic or founder (a condition that can cripple a pony's feet). He should have one or two swallows of lukewarm (not cold) water every few minutes while he is walking to cool out. A good way to do this is to set out a bucket of water and walk your pony in a large circle nearby. Each time you go by the bucket, you can let your pony stop and take a couple of swallows. By the time he is completely cooled out and dry, he should have had all the water he wants, a little at a time.

Covering a Pony While Cooling Out A pony that is very hot should be allowed to cool down to a normal temperature before

Walking pony under a cooler

he is covered (but he should be kept walking while he cools). Covering him too soon keeps him too hot for too long and is not good for him. You will have to check his temperature often as you walk him, so you will notice when he has come back to normal. (If you aren't sure whether he is still hot, ask an experienced horse-person to check him.) If the weather is cool or windy, he should be covered with a "cooler" (a big square blanket for cooling out), so he won't get a chill while his coat is still damp. An "anti-sweat sheet" is a special cover that looks like a fish net. It helps a pony with a wet coat stay warm while he dries.

Don't cover a hot pony in warm weather. This can make him overheat and keep him from cooling down normally. Don't put a heavy winter blanket on a hot, sweaty pony in cold weather. He may stay too hot under the blanket and will get the blanket lining wet, which will make it damp and clammy for a long time. If he needs a cover while he is wet, use a cooler or an anti-sweat sheet instead. The blanket should be put on later, after he is dry.

Sponging and Scraping a Wet Pony If a pony is quite wet, you can use a sweat scraper to squeeze most of the water out of his coat. Rubbing the damp places with a towel or with a handful of dry straw will help them start drying. Scrape him quickly, then get him walking right away. (In cool weather, cover him if he has cooled down to a normal temperature.)

In hot weather, a pony may need to be sponged off to remove sweat and dirt and help him cool off. Use lukewarm water, not

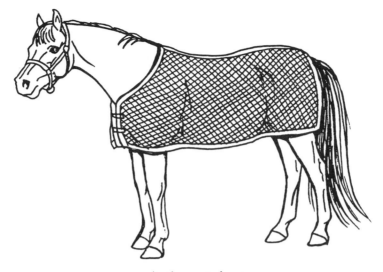

Anti-sweat sheet

Using a sweat scraper

cold water. With a big sponge, wash away the sweat and dirt, then scrape his neck and body with a sweat scraper. You can rub his head, legs and other wet places with a towel to get them started drying. After sponging and scraping, walk the pony until he is dry.

When a pony has wet mud on his legs and belly, it works best to let it dry and then brush it away. If you brush wet, muddy legs you may scrape mud into his skin and start chapped skin or "mud cracks." In cool weather, don't use water to clean mud off his legs—this can also cause chapped skin and painful mud cracks. In warm weather, you can wash his legs off with water, but be sure to dry them thoroughly afterwards.

165

◆◆◆

USPC D-2 TEST

Describe ways to know if a pony is properly cooled out.

◆◆◆

Signs that a pony is properly cooled out:

- His temperature is normal and his chest feels cool and dry (the same as his normal skin), and he is cool and dry everywhere else.
- His breathing is normal—he is not puffing and his nostrils are not wide open.
- The small veins of his face and neck are back to normal—not sticking out.

A pony should always be left clean, dry and comfortable after riding. His feet should be picked out, and any sweat marks or mud should be brushed or sponged off. He should have had all the water he wants (a little at a time, every few minutes while he was walking), to replace the water he lost through work, sweating and during cooling out. If you turn your pony out in a pasture or pen after riding, he may enjoy a roll, which allows him to scratch his itchy places and makes him feel good.

CARE AFTER HARD WORK

When a pony has done especially hard work (like galloping), he may be very hot and tired. He needs special care and attention right away. As soon as you dismount, run up your stirrups and loosen your girth, but leave the saddle in place while you walk him. (You can lift the back of the saddle and pad for a moment to let air get to his back.) If he is very hot, don't cover him until his temperature has come back to normal.

After your pony has walked for about ten minutes, stop and check his temperature. If he has cooled down to normal, untack him and quickly scrape his sweaty places. (In warm weather, he can be quickly sponged off and then scraped.) Pick out his feet and check for stones and loose or missing shoes. You should also feel each leg and check for cuts, heat or swelling. Don't keep the pony standing still for long or let him get chilled while you untack or check his legs. If it is cold or windy, cover him, and get him walking again right away. Later, when he is cool and dry, you can check his legs more thoroughly and go over the rest of him while you are brushing him off.

In very hot and humid weather, a pony may not cool down to a normal temperature quickly enough. He may need to be sponged with water or even have ice applied. An experienced horse-person must help you with this, as you could harm your pony if he is not cooled out properly.

A pony that has worked hard should be offered a few sips of lukewarm water (not cold water) every few minutes while he walks and cools out. It's important for him to drink all the water he needs (but a little at a time) to replace the fluids he lost during hard work, through sweating and while cooling out. When he is cool and dry, he can be given hay and water, but he should not be fed grain until he has been back to normal for at least an hour. When you do feed him grain, it should be a small amount (about half as much as usual). He can have the rest of his grain about two hours later. He should be checked over thoroughly for cuts, swellings or other injuries. All sweat marks should be brushed away before you leave him to rest in his stall or turn him out in his pasture to relax and graze.

You should check him often for about two hours to see if his temperature has gone up or if he is breaking out in a sweat again. If he is damp and sweaty, or if his ears feel cold and clammy, put on an anti-sweat sheet and rub him dry with a towel or several

USPC D-3 TEST

Know the care of a pony after strenuous work, including:

- Cooling out.
- Inspection of legs.
- Watering and feeding.

NOTES TO ADULTS ON WARMING UP AND COOLING OUT

It is essential for pony's health and well-being that he is properly warmed up and cooled out each time he is ridden. Sometimes children neglect this because they are in a hurry to get on with the fun of riding, or because they are pressed for time when ending a ride and taking care of the pony. Children must be supervised by adults until they are sufficiently experienced and responsible, and even then adults should supervise.

---

handfuls of dry straw. Rubbing and pulling his ears gently will also help. If the weather is very hot and humid, a pony may break out in a sweat again because it is too hot in his stall. Take him outside and walk him until he is cool and dry. (If this should happen, check his temperature carefully and get expert help.)

The next day, your pony should be led out and jogged to check for lameness or stiffness, and his legs should be checked again for heat, swelling or injuries.

GROOMING YOUR PONY
Reasons for Grooming

There are several reasons to groom your pony:

- To clean him and make him look nice and feel comfortable.
- To check him over carefully for injuries or skin problems.
- To prevent sores from dirt under the tack when you ride him.
- To condition his skin and make his coat shine.
- To promote good circulation of the blood.

Your pony should be groomed or at least checked over every day, whether he is ridden or not. He must be cleaned before he is saddled to prevent dirt from causing saddle and girth sores, and he should be brushed smooth after he has been ridden. The best time to groom a pony thoroughly is after he has been ridden, when his skin is warm. However, for Pony Club working rallies (mounted meetings), Competitive Rallies and other special events, you are expected to have your pony clean and thoroughly groomed for inspection before riding. Your care and grooming of your pony before and after riding are both evaluated in Stable Management inspections.

Grooming Tools

Your grooming tools should be kept together in a grooming kit. The basic grooming tools include:

- *Currycomb* (rubber or plastic): for loosening caked mud and dirt and rubbing the pony's skin. It should be flexible, not too hard and sharp. (*Metal currycombs* should only be used for cleaning the body brush. They are too sharp to use on a pony's skin.)
- *Dandy brush* or *stiff brush:* for removing heavy dirt and

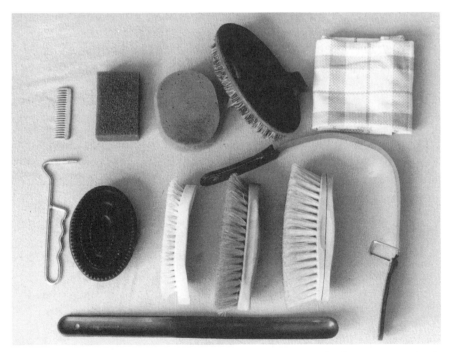

Contents of grooming kit: Top, left to right: mane comb, face sponge, dock sponge, body brush, and rub rag. Center, left to right: hoof pick, rubber curry comb, plastic scrub brush (substitute for water brush), dandy brush, water brush, shedding blade. Bottom: sweat scraper. *Photo: Ruth Harvie.*

dried mud. Good for long coats and pastured ponies.

- *Body brush* or *soft brush:* has short bristles set close together, to remove dirt, dust and scurf (dried sweat and dandruff) from the coat and skin. Best tool to get a pony really clean!
- *Hoof pick:* For picking out the feet.
- *Hoof brush:* Small stiff bush for cleaning the feet (a scrub brush works well). Some hoof picks have a hoof brush at one end.
- *Sponges:* Two smaller ones, for cleaning eyes, nose, lips and dock. Use different colors or shapes for face and dock sponges, so they won't get mixed up. A larger sponge is used for washing the pony.
- *Mane comb* or *hairbrush:* for untangling the mane and tail (after picking out tangles with your fingers). (Metal mane combs are not recommended, because they break off too many hairs.)
- *Stable rubber* or *towel:* for removing stains, or for a final polish after grooming. Also good for rubbing out sweat marks.
- *Water brush:* for wetting down the mane and tail and scrubbing away stains. (This can be a plastic scrub brush from the grocery store, or a special brush made for this purpose.)

There are some other things you may want to keep in your grooming kit, like disposable cotton balls for cleaning the eyes and nose, a Styrofoam scraper block for removing bot-fly eggs, hoof dressing and a brush to paint it on with, "cactus cloth" (a special grooming cloth for removing stains) and fly repellent.

How to Groom a Pony

1. Before you start to groom your pony, he should be tied up correctly in a safe place. (See page 142 for instructions on safe tying.) Don't try to groom a pony when he is loose in a stall or not wearing a halter. If he tries to turn around or get away, you will have no control.
2. Pick out his feet with the hoof pick. (For instructions on picking up the feet safely, see page 200.) Use the hoof pick from heel to toe, so you won't accidentally dig it into the frog (the softer center part of the hoof). Clean the cleft of the frog (the groove down the middle), and the spaces on

each side of the frog. Use a hoof brush to brush the foot clean, so you can check it thoroughly. Check that each shoe is tight and the clinches (the bent-over ends of the nails) are smooth.

3. Use the rubber or plastic currycomb to rub the skin in circles or side to side, starting at the top of the neck and working back and down. Go easy on sensitive places. This tool breaks up caked mud, loosens scurf, and rubs and stimulates the skin, but it can be too harsh for some ponies. Don't use a currycomb on the head, lower legs or anyplace that is especially sensitive.

Using currycomb: rub side to side or in a circle.

Using dandy brush: short, firm strokes the way the hair grows.

Using body brush: short, firm strokes the way the hair grows.

Clean body brush every few strokes by scraping it over currycomb.

Steps in grooming a pony

171

4. Starting at the top of the neck, brush the coat with the dandy brush, in the direction the hair grows. Use short, snappy strokes to get down to the skin and flick the dirt out. The dandy brush takes away the larger bits of dirt loosened by the currycomb. You can use this brush on the body, neck and legs, and on the head if your pony doesn't mind. If your pony is very sensitive or if he has been clipped, the dandy brush may be too harsh for him.

5. The body brush is used to clean away dirt, dust and scurf from the skin. Use short, firm strokes the way the hair grows, with firm pressure to get between the hairs, right down to the skin. After every few strokes, clean the body brush by scraping it across the teeth of a metal currycomb, or use the dandy brush to clean it. This way, the dirt goes into the brush and then out into the air, not back on the pony. You can use the body brush all over your pony's body, head and legs. It is the best brush for getting the coat really clean and shiny. Because it is soft, it can be used on clipped ponies or those with sensitive skin.

6. The mane and tail should be carefully picked free from tangles, taking just a few hairs at a time so you don't break off or pull out hairs. Part the hair and use the body brush to clean the skin and the roots of the hair, one section at a time. To be safe when you work on the tail, stand to one side, not right behind the pony.

7. A stable rubber or folded towel is used to bring out the shine of the coat. Bear down and rub firmly across and with the direction the hair grows. Firm rubbing warms up the skin and spreads the skin oils over the hair, making the coat sleek and shiny.

8. Use a damp sponge or a disposable cotton ball to clean the eyelids, nostrils and muzzle. You can also gently clean inside the ears. Use another sponge to clean underneath the tail and around the sheath or the udder.

9. If your pony still has manure or grass stains after you finish grooming, these can be removed by rubbing the spots with a damp towel, by a shampooing them or by rubbing them out with a cactus cloth.

More grooming

Stand to one side while working on pony's tail.

Wipe eyelids, lips and muzzle with damp sponge. Use another sponge to clean the dock.

10. You may paint hoof dressing around the coronet and across the heels of the feet. For everyday grooming, it is not necessary to cover the whole hoof with hoof dressing. For special occasions like Formal Inspections, you can paint the oil over the whole hoof wall and coronet band. Be sure to wipe away all the excess oil with a paper towel, so there is no sticky extra dressing left on the hoof or the heels.
11. For a final touch, wet your water brush and dampen the roots of the mane, and brush it neatly over to the right side of the neck. You can also dampen and brush down the hairs at the top of the dock.

Grooming a Pastured Pony

A pony who lives outdoors usually has healthy skin and hair and does not need to be groomed daily, except to get him clean for riding and for special occasions. He should be checked over and have his feet picked out every day, whether he is ridden or not, and his eyes, nose and dock should be cleaned. In some parts of

Brush the coat with the dandy brush in the direction the hair grows. (You may need help with grooming.) *Photo: Neena Ewing.*

the country, he should be checked for ticks, especially in his mane and tail. Besides that, he will only need currying and brushing with the dandy brush to make his coat smooth. The body brush will not do much good on a pony that rolls every day, and you do not want to remove the natural grease and scurf from his coat, as it protects him from getting wet and cold. After riding, sweat marks should be brushed out or rubbed out with a towel.

Controlling Flies

When horse flies, mosquitoes or other biting insects are a problem, you may need to use a fly repellent to keep your pony comfortable. Fly repellents (fly sprays, wipes and fly strips) have strong chemicals, so always use them according to directions. Don't use them near your pony's eyes or get fly spray in his feed or water. Always wash your hands after using fly spray.

Other things you can do to keep biting flies away from your pony include using a fly bonnet, which covers his ears and face, and a face net (made of fine mesh), which keep flies out of his eyes but still lets him see. If the flies are very bad, it may help to let him stay in his stall or in the shade during the day and turn him out at night.

Fly protection

Face net

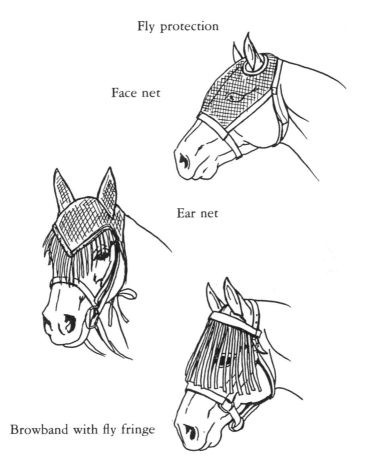

Ear net

Browband with fly fringe

* *

USPC D-1 TEST

Groom with brush and currycomb; pick out feet with assistance.

* *

USPC D-2 TEST

Groom, pick out feet (with assistance if needed).

* *

USPC D-2 TEST

Name five grooming tools and explain how to use them.

* *

STALL CLEANING AND BEDDING

If your pony is kept in a stall, you will have to use some kind of bedding to keep his stall clean and dry and to give him a cushion to stand on and lie down on. It is very hard on his legs to stand on a hard surface like boards or concrete without enough bedding, and he can get sores on his legs if he lies down on a hard surface. There are many kinds of bedding, including straw, wood shavings and sawdust. The kind of bedding you choose will probably depend on what is easy to get and affordable where you live.

In some parts of the country, ponies are kept in outdoor pens. An outside pen should have a roof over part of it, for shelter from the sun. Most pens have sand or dirt footing, so bedding is not usually necessary. Hay and grain should not be fed directly on a sandy surface, because ponies may swallow sand along with their feed, which can cause "sand colic," a serious stomach upset. The pen should have hay and grain feeders to keep feed off the ground.

Your pony's stall or pen must be kept clean, or it will become wet, smelly and unhealthy. The stall or pen should be cleaned thoroughly at least once a day. (It is easier and safer to clean a stall while the pony is out.) When you clean a stall, you take out the manure and wet bedding, but any good bedding should be saved.

Steps in Stall Cleaning

1. First, pick up all the manure and soiled bedding from the surface and throw it into a wheelbarrow or muck basket. If you use straw for bedding, a pitchfork works best. If your stall is bedded with shavings, sawdust or shredded paper, a "stall picker" with tines set close together makes it easier to pick manure out of the bedding.
2. Next, sort through the bedding with fork or picker, turning it over and throwing out the wet and soiled bedding and manure. Separate the good bedding and pile it in a clean spot, against the walls of the stall. Be sure to find and clean out the wet spots.
3. If the pony will be out for several hours, you can dust the wet spots with lime and leave the floor bare. This lets the floor dry out and air.

◆◆

USPC D-3 TEST
Clean and bed a stall. Know reasons for each step.

◆◆

4. Before you put the pony back in his stall, you should "re-bed" it. Add just enough fresh bedding to replace what you took out, and mix it with the bedding you saved. Don't waste bedding, but use enough to give your pony a dry, comfortable cushion to stand on and lie on. Spread it evenly over the floor, and bank it up higher against the stall walls and in the corners. This helps keep your pony from getting cast (stuck) if he rolls in his stall.

5. When you are cleaning a stall, notice anything that needs repairs or could hurt your pony (like splinters or nails sticking out), and take care of it right away. The feed tub should be cleaned, and the water bucket rinsed out and filled with fresh water.

6. "Picking out" a stall means doing a quick pickup of manure instead of a thorough cleaning. If you pick out your pony's stall later in the day (besides cleaning it thoroughly), it will stay cleaner and save you work. It also saves bedding.

Stable Cleanliness and Manure Disposal

A neat and clean stable area is safer and healthier, has fewer flies and is nicer for you, your pony and your neighbors. Flies breed in manure, wet and rotting hay and bedding, and spilled grain. Besides keeping your pony's stall clean, remember to sweep or rake tack and feed rooms, barn aisles and the area around your stable every day. Muck baskets, forks, and rakes should be hung up safely out of the way (with tines facing the wall), so the aisle is clear and safe. Put trash in a trash container, and remember to recycle!

Manure and soiled bedding should be piled neatly at a distance from the stable, so you will not have flies and odors around the stable. It can be composted and used as garden fertilizer, or it's possible to arrange with a farmer or a manure removal company to have it hauled away. A manure pile generates heat, so it should not be piled against a wooden building.

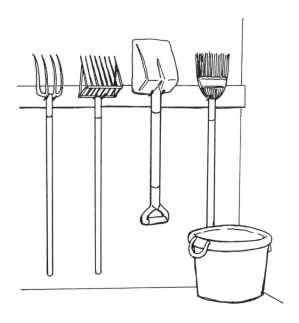

Stall cleaning tools. Left to right: pitchfork, stall picker, scoop shovel, broom, and muck basket. Always hang tools with points turned toward the wall.

Cleaning a stall

USPC D-3 TEST

Know use of hay net and dangers of improper use.

Using a Hay Net

A hay net is used to carry hay and to feed it to a pony. It is a bag made of rope or plastic twine, with one end that opens and closes with a drawstring. It is useful when you want to give hay to a pony who is tied to a trailer or in some other place where it is not good to feed hay on the ground.

To fill a hay net, open it up wide and stack several flakes of hay in it, then pull it up over the hay and close it by pulling the drawstrings.

Hay nets must be tied safely or they can cause accidents. If a hay net is tied incorrectly, it will hang too low as it is emptied and the pony may paw at it. He could get his foot caught in it and be hurt. Don't tie a hay net to the same ring a pony is tied to. If he should pull back and pull the ring loose, the hay net would be attached to his halter rope and could scare him.

To tie a hay net safely, hang it at about eye level. Pass the rope through a ring or over a board and run it back through one of

Put strings through ring or around board.

Run strings through bottom loop.

Pull strings up and tie in back with quick-release knot.

How to hang up a hay net safely

the hay net sections at the bottom. Tie it with a quick-release knot, so you can get it loose easily when it is empty. (See page 144 to learn how to tie a quick-release knot.)

STABLE VICES

Stable vices are habits some ponies learn, usually out of nervousness or boredom. Ponies that are kept in stalls or pens most of the time often have them. They are not good for the pony and sometimes can cause health problems or damage to his stall. They sometimes become such strong habits that they are very hard to stop. Keeping your pony happy and interested in what goes on around him can help to prevent stable vices. Let him look out a window, see other horses, have "stall toys" like a rubber ball and especially, if possible, give him plenty of time in the pasture.

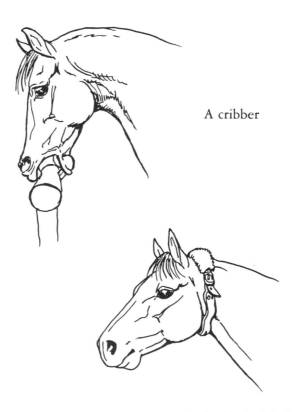

A cribber

Cribbing strap worn to prevent cribbing (padded with fleece)

Ponies with stable vices are usually showing that they are unhappy. Prevention works better than punishment.

Here are some stable vices and ways to prevent or deal with them.

Cribbing

The pony grabs a solid object with his teeth and arches his neck while he swallows air. Some cribbers suck so much air that they colic, or become thin and run down. A cribbing strap buckled tightly around the throat can be used to stop a pony from cribbing, but it does not cure the habit.

When a pony wears a cribbing strap, it must be taken off for an hour or two every day, to let the skin underneath dry out and to keep sores from forming under the strap.

Wood Chewing

The pony chews on wood but does not suck in air. He can damage his stall or fences, or anything made of wood. A pony that chews wood may have a vitamin or mineral deficiency or may lack salt. He may also chew wood if he is hungry and is not getting enough hay, or if he is bored because he is kept in a stall or pen all the

U-shaped stall screen to prevent weaving

time. If your pony gets plenty of hay, vitamins and minerals and salt, is getting turned out enough and still chews wood, you can paint the wood with a bad-tasting coating that is made to discourage wood chewing. (Be sure that anything you paint on his stall is safe for ponies.)

Stall Kicking

Some ponies kick the walls of their stall when they are anxious to be fed, jealous of their neighbors or upset. Some just seem to like to make noise. Hanging a rubber stall mat over the kicking area sometimes helps, as it cuts down on the noise and prevents the pony from injuring himself.

Pawing

Some ponies paw when they are excited or waiting to be fed, digging holes in their stall floors. Some do it for attention. Putting down a rubber stall mat may stop the pony from digging holes, even if he still paws.

Weaving

The pony sways from side to side, swinging his head and shifting from one foot to the other. This habit is usually seen in nervous ponies. A stall screen with a U-shape lets a pony look out but makes it hard for him to weave.

CHAPTER 7

Feeding, Watering and Condition

Your pony must be fed and watered properly every day in order to be comfortable and stay in good condition. This is one of the most important responsibilities for anyone who owns or takes care of a pony. As a Pony Club rider, you should learn how to feed and water your pony safely and know what your pony is fed, his feeding schedule and some basic rules for feeding ponies. You also need to know what is considered good condition and to notice if your pony is getting too fat or too thin. However, the complete care and feeding of a pony take more knowledge and experience than you can get from this book. If you own a pony, you must have help from your instructor or another experienced horse-person in learning how to feed and take care of your pony.

FEEDING AND WATERING

There are three ways to keep a pony: (1) stabled, (2) in pasture or (3) stabled part of the time and in pasture part of the time. A stabled pony is given all his feed and water in his stall. A pony living in pasture may get most or part of his feed from eating grass, but this depends on the kind of pasture he lives in and the level of work expected of him. If the pasture does not have enough good grass (for instance, if it is too bare, weedy or covered with snow), the pony will need extra feed.

Your Pony's Digestion

Horses and ponies have developed over thousands of years as grazing animals. Their stomachs are small, so their digestion works best when they eat small amounts often. (In nature, wild horses and ponies graze and move almost constantly.) They cannot handle a lot of food all at once, especially on an empty stomach. They need natural roughage (bulky food like grass or hay), and plenty of water for good digestion.

A pony's digestion can get upset if he is not fed properly, and this can be serious. He can get colic (a bellyache), or founder (a condition that can cripple his feet). This is why it is so important to follow proper feeding practices.

Feeding Schedule

A pony should be fed on a regular schedule—at the same times every day. Ponies get used to regular feeding times. If they are not fed on time, they get upset and can even become ill.

Ponies need to eat small meals several times a day, never one big meal all at once. A stabled pony must be fed at least twice a day (three times a day is better). Some pastured ponies are only fed grain or extra hay once a day (depending on how much extra food they need and how they are managed), but they can graze as much as they need to.

Write down your pony's feeding schedule—what times he is fed and how much he gets for each feeding.

MY PONY'S DAILY FEEDING SCHEDULE

Morning

Time: ____ How much hay: ____ How much grain: ____
Other: _____

Noon (optional)
Time: ____ Hay: ____ Grain: ____ Other: _____

Afternoon
Time: ____ Hay: ____ Grain: ____ Other: _____

Night (optional)
Time: ____ Hay: ____ Grain: ____ Other: _____

What Ponies Need to Eat

Ponies need five basic kinds of nutrition: roughage, concentrates, succulents, water and salt.

Roughage Roughage means bulky food, like grass, hay, and some special feeds like beet pulp and range cubes. A pony must have plenty of roughage for good digestion. Some kinds of roughage are:

- *Grass:* The most natural food for ponies. Different kinds of grasses grow in different parts of the country.
- *Hay:* The most common source of roughage. There are many kinds, including timothy, clover, bermuda, oat hay and alfalfa. Alfalfa is the richest kind of hay.
- *Other roughages:* These include range cubes, hay pellets and sugar beet pulp.

Concentrates Concentrates are foods that have more food value concentrated in a smaller amount. For ponies, concentrates include grain, mixed feeds and pellets, and supplements.

Ponies need concentrates when they require more nutrition than they can get from the hay or pasture grass they eat. Hard work, getting fit, putting on weight, a young pony that is still growing, an old pony or a mare that is nursing a foal are all reasons why a pony might need concentrates. However, if any of these reasons don't exist, then a pony may need very little grain or no grain at all, especially if he has plenty of good grass or hay. It is important not to overfeed grain, as it can make a pony sick, colic, lame, too fat, or too frisky and hard to handle.

Some kinds of concentrates are:

- *Grain:* Oats, corn, barley and bran are the most common.
- *Mixed feed and feed pellets:* These are made by mixing different grains. Some are ground up and pressed into grain pellets.
- *Supplements:* Vitamin and mineral supplements (usually powders or pellets) are sometimes added to the feed in small amounts when a pony needs extra nutrition.

Succulents Succulents are juicy foods like fresh grass or carrots.

Water Like all animals, a pony must have plenty of fresh, clean water. It keeps him healthy and helps him to digest his food.

Salt Ponies need salt to keep the proper chemical balance in their bodies. They lose salt when they sweat, especially in hot weather, but they need salt at all times because they usually cannot get enough salt from their natural food. It can be given loose or as a salt block.

CAUTION: *Never* **feed grass clippings to a pony. They wilt quickly and can cause serious colic, which can result in death. Even fresh, unwilted grass clippings can contain lawn-care chemicals that can poison a pony.**

Pony owners may not always use the same kinds of feed, because different kinds of feed are grown in different parts of the country. You will have to find out which kinds of roughage and concentrates are available where you live, and which are the best for you to feed your pony. Ask for advice from an experienced horse person like your instructor, veterinarian, local feed stores and hay dealers, or your Cooperative Extension office.

Giving Treats and Tidbits

Ponies love treats like carrots and apples. It is nice to give your pony a tidbit when he has done well or after you ride him, but he must have good manners. Some ponies get so greedy for treats that they nip or get pushy. These ponies should not be given treats by hand. Instead, you can put treats in their feed bucket. Treats must be good for ponies to eat (not candy or junk food!) and it

---

USPC D-2 TEST

Know own pony's feeding schedule.

USPC D-3 TEST

Know what roughage and concentrates are.

How to give a pony a tidbit safely

is better not to feed sugar to ponies because it often makes them nippy. Carrots or apples are better, but they should be sliced up so they can't get stuck in a pony's throat.

To give a pony a tidbit safely, put it on your hand and keep your hand flat as you hold it up to the pony's lips. Don't hold it with your fingers. The pony might get your fingers with the treat by mistake. If you offer it and then jerk your hand away, he might think you are teasing him and try to grab it.

Feeding Hay, Water, Grain and Salt

Water Water comes first. A pony should have water available all the time, so he can drink whenever he needs to. The only time he should not have all the water he wants is when he is hot and sweaty. Then he must be cooled out before he is allowed to drink all he wants. A pony needs eight to twelve gallons of water a day or even more. It is especially important to make sure he drinks plenty of water in cold weather. Ponies can easily get dehydrated (lacking enough water for good health) during cold weather, when they may not drink enough, especially if the water is too cold.

◆◆

USPC D-1 TEST

Know how to give a pony a tidbit safely.

◆◆

This can lead to impaction colic (a kind of colic caused by food blocking the intestines).

Ponies only like to drink fresh, clean water. If the water is dirty, a pony may not drink enough. This can make him thin and run down, or even sick. To keep your pony's water clean, empty his bucket, scrub it with a brush and rinse it out each day before you fill it with fresh water. Water tanks in pastures must be kept clean, too. They should be scrubbed out when they are dirty, or at least once a week.

In cold weather, you must be sure that your pony's water is not frozen over so that he cannot drink. You may have to break the ice in the water tank or dump the ice out of his bucket before you re-fill it, at least twice a day. Sometimes a special water bucket heater or stock tank heater may help.

Remember to water your pony often when you are at a show, a rally or any Pony Club event.

Pony Clubbers water their ponies during a rally. (Make sure your pony always has plenty of fresh, clean water.) *Photo: Neena Ewing.*

Hay Hay comes in bales, which can weigh from forty pounds to over seventy-five pounds. When you open a bale, fold up the strings or wire and put them in a trash bin or a bag for recycling. If they are left lying around, they can cause accidents. A bale comes apart in sections, or "flakes," about 3 to 4 inches thick. Depending on his size and the kind of hay, a pony might get one or two flakes of hay at a feeding. Your adviser (an experienced horse person, instructor or veterinarian) should show you how much hay to feed your pony. Weigh an average-size flake of hay (use a feed scale or baby scale), so you know how many pounds of hay your pony gets for each feeding and each day.

Write down the amount of hay for each feeding on your pony's feed chart.

Always check each flake of hay for dust and mold. Good hay smells sweet, like newly cut grass. Moldy hay smells musty and may have white or gray patches. Moldy or dusty hay can give your pony a cough or make him sick, so if you find any, put it aside and do not feed it to your pony.

If your pony wastes a lot of hay, cut down on the amount, but check the leftover hay to be sure it is good hay that he is leaving. Some people like to shake out the hay into a loose pile, which makes it easier to check for mold and for the pony to eat. This is fine for some kinds of hay (like grass hays) but not a good idea for hay like alfalfa, as many of the leaves and small pieces will be lost.

Hay can be fed in a hay feeder or manger, in a hay net or on the ground. A hay feeder should not be so high that dust and seeds can fall into the pony's eyes and nose as he eats. A low trough makes a good hay feeder for pens and pastures, as it keeps hay off the ground and cuts down on wasted hay. If you use a hay net, it must be tied safely and hung high enough so that a pony cannot get his leg caught in it. (See page 179 for more about

USPC D-3 TEST

Know amount of roughage in own pony's diet.

hay nets and how to hang them safely.) Feeding hay on the ground is the easiest and the most natural way for a pony to eat, but some hay will be wasted, and the pony may pick up internal parasites or "worms" because the hay gets manure in it. If you feed hay on the ground, put it in a corner of the stall or a dry place in the pen or pasture. Hay must not be fed on sandy ground because ponies swallow sand along with the hay, which causes a stomach problem called "sand colic."

When you feed hay to a pastured pony, it should be fed in a dry open area, away from fences, gates, corners or anything a pony could get hurt on. If there is more than one pony, put out extra piles of hay and space them at least three or four pony lengths apart (about 30 to 40 feet). This gives each pony a chance to get some hay, even if he gets chased away from one pile.

Grain Grain is a concentrated feed. It can make a pony sick if he gets too much all at once. Ponies love grain and will eat as much as they can get. It is *very important* to keep grain safely locked up in a grain bin, so your pony can't get into it if he should get loose from his stall or pasture. If he does get into the grain bin, he may eat until he gets colic or founder, and he could even die. Always remember to close up the feed room securely before you leave.

Your adviser will have to help you decide how much grain your pony needs, and whether he needs any vitamins or other supplements. You can measure out his grain in a feed scoop or a coffee can, then weigh it on a feed scale or baby scale. Write down on your feed chart how many pounds and what kind of grain your pony gets for each feeding. Also write down any special supplements and how much he gets, if you use them.

Grain should be fed after your pony has had water and been given his hay, and after he has been completely cooled out if he has been ridden. Use a feed tub or bucket that is smooth, with

◆◆

USPC D-3 TEST

Know amount of concentrates in own pony's ration.

◆◆

no sharp edges. The feed tub can be placed on the ground, but your pony may waste a lot of grain this way. It is better to hang the tub at about the height of his shoulder.

The grain should be measured into a container or bucket with any vitamins or supplements mixed in, then dumped into the feed tub. Never mix old stale leftover feed with fresh feed. Feed tubs and buckets should be kept clean, especially in hot weather, when sticky feed tubs attract flies.

When you feed grain to a pastured pony, he should have a feed tub or grain feeder to eat from. If there is more than one pony, it is better to put the ponies in their own stalls to eat their grain (if you have stalls), or tie them up until all are finished. If you feed grain to a group of loose ponies, they will fight over it and some ponies may not get their share.

Insist on good manners from your pony when you feed him. Teach him to step back and wait while you put his grain in his feed tub. However, don't tease him or make him upset by making him wait longer than necessary. If you give him his hay first, he will not be so hungry and is apt to behave better.

Salt Salt is important for your pony's good health and condition, especially in hot weather. Salt comes in blocks, which may be plain salt (white), or with iodine or trace minerals added (red or blue). A pony should have a salt block in his stall, either attached to the wall in a salt block holder or kept in his feed tub, or you could feed loose salt in a small tub instead. He should also have a larger salt block in the pasture, placed on a salt holder to keep it off the ground. A pony should be free to lick as much salt as he needs, whenever he wants to.

Pasture Grass

Grass is the most natural food for ponies. However, all grass is not equally good to eat. If a pasture does not have enough good

◆◆◆

USPC D-1 TEST

Know how to give hay, water and grain to pony safely.

◆◆◆

grass (if it is bare and overgrazed, weedy or covered with snow), a pony cannot get enough good feed and will need extra feed (like hay and perhaps grain) to stay in good condition. A pony will get thin and can starve on a poor pasture.

In the spring, the new grass grows fast and has a lot of water in it. This can upset a pony's digestion and can cause laminitis, or founder, a painful condition that can cripple a pony's feet. Very rich pastures are not good for ponies (especially small ponies). A pony can become overweight on a rich pasture, and may suffer from founder. In the spring, or if your pasture is too rich for your pony, you may have to limit his time in the pasture each day.

Different kinds of grass (such as bluegrass, clover, orchardgrass and bermuda grass) grow in different areas. You will need to find out which grasses grow in your pasture, and whether it has enough good grass for proper nutrition. There are also some poisonous plants to watch out for. Your adviser, veterinarian or the Cooperative Extension office can teach you about pasture grasses and plants in your area that are poisonous to ponies.

Remember—never feed your pony grass clippings! They can make him very ill and even cause his death.

Some Rules for Good Feeding

- Feed small amounts often, not one big meal all at once. Ponies have small stomachs, and this helps them digest their food more easily.
- Feed plenty of roughage (hay or grass, but never grass clippings). This is necessary for a pony's digestion.
- Feed according to a pony's size, condition, temperament and the work he does. If a pony works hard, he will need more feed (especially grain). If he works less, his grain should be cut back. If he has a day off or stops working, his grain should be reduced or cut out entirely. If you cut back on his grain, give him some extra hay to make up the difference.
- All changes in feed should be made gradually over ten days to two weeks. It takes that long for a pony's digestion to change over to handle a new kind of food. You can cut grain back quickly, but it should be added more slowly.
- Feed on a regular schedule every day. Don't be late!

◆◆

USPC D-2 TEST

Know basic rules for safe feeding.

◆◆

- Feed only clean, good-quality hay and grain. Dusty, spoiled or poor feed won't give your pony good nutrition and can make him sick. Keep feed tubs, hay feeders and water buckets clean.
- Clean, fresh water must be available at all times, except when a pony is hot and sweaty. Water tanks and buckets must be kept clear of ice in the winter.
- Salt should be available at all times, in a salt block or loose. It is usually best to use the kind of salt that has minerals added.
- Do not ride your pony when his stomach is full—it may give him indigestion. He should have an hour to digest his grain before working hard. A pony must be completely cooled out after work before being fed grain, or he may colic.
- Learn how your pony normally eats. If he doesn't eat the way he usually does (for instance, if he doesn't want to eat, eats very slowly, spills grain out of his mouth or slobbers), he might be sick. If ponies are kept together in a pasture, be sure that each is getting enough to eat and that no one is chased away from his feed by other ponies.

Things to Do to Learn About Feeding and Nutrition

1. Visit a feed store with your Pony Club (call ahead and ask if it's okay). They can show you different kinds of feed and how they are processed and mixed. You could ask for a small sample (baby food jar) of each kind of grain to learn what it looks like. Ask: How can you tell good grain from bad? What is the most economical feed to buy?
2. Ask a horse nutrition expert (from your county agriculture extension service, or from a feed company) to come and talk to your Pony Club about feeds and nutrition.
3. Visit a farm that grows hay. Ask the farmer to show you

different kinds of hay and the difference between good and poor hay. He can tell you about the kinds of plants that make good hay, when it should be cut and baled, what makes hay get dusty, moldy or weather damaged, and how to store your hay properly. Collect samples of different kinds and grades of hay.

4. Organize your feed room. Get large trash bins to hold grain and label them (they should close tightly to keep mice out). Put up shelves to hold such items as buckets, scoops and

NOTES TO ADULTS ABOUT FEEDING, WATERING AND NUTRITION

Feeding a pony properly is one of the most important responsibilities of an owner. A pony is completely dependent on his owners for his feed, well-being and even his life. You must know about the pony's basic condition and feeding requirements and be sure that your child is doing a good job of feeding and watering him regularly. You will also have to be responsible for providing a regular and consistent source of feed. Working with your child on planning the pony's ration, buying and storing feed and supervising daily feeding chores is a good way to teach him or her about the responsibility that comes with owning an animal.

If your pony is boarded out and somebody else takes over the feeding chores, it is still important for you and your child to know how the pony is fed and to help with the process as much as possible. This makes it easier to make sensible decisions about your pony's feeding, care and work, and to avoid trouble caused by improper feeding.

This book does not go into enough detail about feeding and pony care to teach a child or a novice pony owner enough to take full charge of feeding and caring for a pony. You will need an experienced horse-person as an adviser—preferably your veterinarian, along with your child's instructor. It is best to consult your veterinarian about the nutritional needs of your child's pony, especially if the pony appears ill or not in the best condition, or if you are dealing with a young, growing pony, a mare with a foal or an older pony.

supplements. Sweep the feed room clean. Put a lock on the door so your pony can't get in! It is easier to do chores in a neat stable, and you will be proud of the way your feed room looks.

WEIGHT AND CONDITION

Condition means the state of a pony's health and fitness. A healthy pony is normal and not sick. A "fit" pony is a healthy pony whose muscles, heart and lungs have been built up or conditioned for work. A pony could be healthy but "soft" or "unfit" and therefore not be ready to do hard work. It is unkind to work a pony too hard for his level of fitness, and this can hurt him or make him sick.

There is a range of condition, from very thin to very fat. A healthy pony is somewhere in the middle. It is important to know your pony's condition and to notice if he is putting on weight or losing weight. Ask your veterinarian about your pony's condition and how to improve it.

Kinds of Condition

Very Poor Condition   The pony is terribly thin and appears to be starving. His ribs show, his backbone sticks up and his muscles are wasted. He may be sick or starved and is probably infested

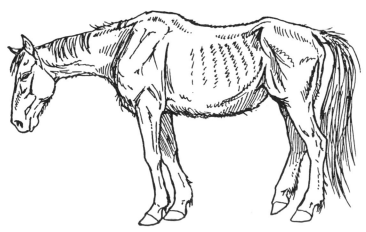

Very poor condition

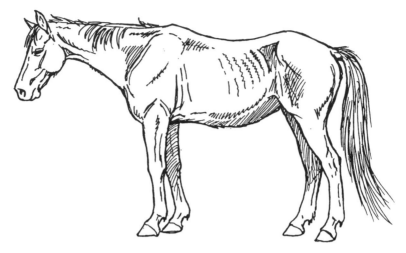

Thin or poor condition

with worms. He is weak and depressed and cannot be ridden until he is in better condition, which may take many weeks.

Poor or Thin Condition The pony is thin, with little fat between the muscles and skin. His ribs show and can be felt easily. His muscles look thin, with hollows in his flanks and hindquarters. His withers are thin and sharp, and he can get saddle sores easily. He is likely to be depressed and dull, and he is probably infested with worms. In the winter, ponies may be thin under their long coats, but you might not notice it unless you feel their ribs.

Good or Fit Condition The pony is neither thin nor fat. His muscles are well developed and his skin is loose and flexible. His coat is shiny and he looks and feels good. Some fit horses (like racehorses) are light in flesh, with a tucked-up belly and a rib or two showing. Show horses may be slightly fat, showing dapples and a "bloom," or special shine, on their coats.

◆◆

USPC D-2 TEST

Know basic condition of own pony.

◆◆

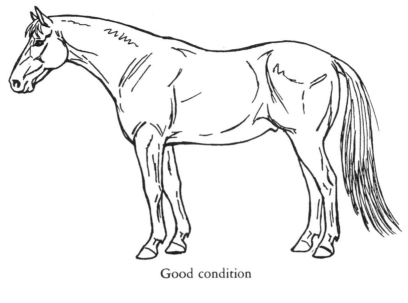

Good condition

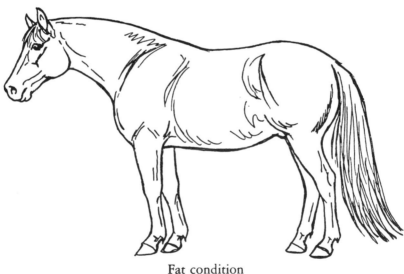

Fat condition

Fat Condition The pony is round and fat over his back, the top of his neck, and his hindquarters and rump. His ribs are covered with a layer of fat and there is a crease down his back. His belly is large and his hindquarters look round instead of muscled. He sweats easily and cannot work hard without puffing. He needs to go on a diet and get fit before he can do hard work, and he may be in danger of foundering.

Very fat or obese condition

Very Fat or Obese Condition The pony has heavy fat deposits on his neck, shoulders, back, ribs and hindquarters. His withers may be hidden in fat, his belly is large and his muscles may feel soft and jiggly. He sweats and tires easily and cannot do even slow work without puffing. He is in danger of foundering and urgently needs to lose weight before he can do even ordinary work safely.

NOTES TO ADULTS ON WEIGHT AND CONDITION

Children need the help of a knowledgeable adult in evaluating the pony's fitness and condition and correcting any problems. This is essential for the health, well-being and humane treatment of the pony. Your veterinarian, your child's instructor or the District Commissioner can give you an honest appraisal of your pony's condition and suggest feeding, exercise and other measures to get him fit for Pony Club riding. A child that comes to a mounted meeting or rally or any Pony Club event with a very thin, very fat or unfit pony may not be allowed to ride. The child will need help in understanding what his pony needs and why he must limit his riding.

CHAPTER 8

Your Pony's Feet and Shoeing

Nothing is more important to your pony than good, sound feet. If his feet are not properly cared for he will be uncomfortable, may go lame or stumble, and you will not be able to ride him. Good hoof care includes picking out and checking your pony's feet every day, conditioning the feet, and having a farrier (a horse-shoer) trim or shoe his feet on a regular schedule.

CLEANING AND CHECKING THE FEET

Your pony's feet should be picked out every day, whether you ride him or not. A pony may pick up a stone in his hoof or step on a nail, which can get stuck in his foot. If you didn't pick out his feet and missed it, his foot could be hurt and he could go lame. Puncture wounds, which are caused by stepping on something sharp, can be quite serious. If you should find a nail or a wound in your pony's foot, or if he goes lame, call your veterinarian right away.

Another reason for picking out feet is cleanliness. If a pony's feet are left packed full of dirt and manure for too long, or if he stands in a wet, dirty stall or pen that is not cleaned often enough, he can get an infection called "thrush." This is caused by a fungus that lives in wet, dirty feet. Thrush attacks the frog (the soft center part of the foot) and makes it rot; it has a very bad odor. Picking

Good hoof care includes picking out and checking your pony's feet every day. *Photo: Neena Ewing.*

out your pony's feet daily and keeping his stall clean is the best way to prevent thrush.

Finally, picking out the feet lets you check your pony's shoes, if he wears shoes, and the condition of his feet. You should notice a loose shoe or a bent nail, or if his feet are growing too long or starting to crack. This means he needs attention from the farrier.

How to Pick Up a Pony's Foot

Your pony should be trained to pick up his feet when you ask him to. (If he is difficult about picking up his feet, an experienced horse person must help you handle his feet safely and train him

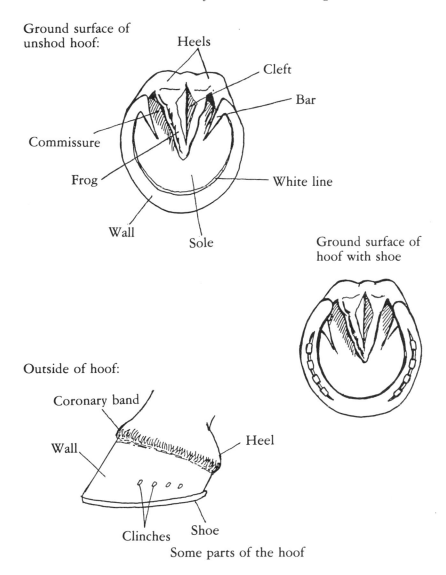

Ground surface of
unshod hoof:

Heels

Cleft

Bar

Commissure

Frog

White line

Wall

Sole

Ground surface of
hoof with shoe

Outside of hoof:

Coronary band

Wall

Heel

Clinches   Shoe

Some parts of the hoof

to pick them up easily.) You must handle his feet properly to be safe, and to make it easy for him do as you ask. At first, you should have help in handling and cleaning your pony's feet.

To pick up a front foot:

1. Stand beside the pony's front leg, facing the tail.
2. Run your hand down his leg to the back tendons. Squeeze with your fingers and say "Pick up."

201

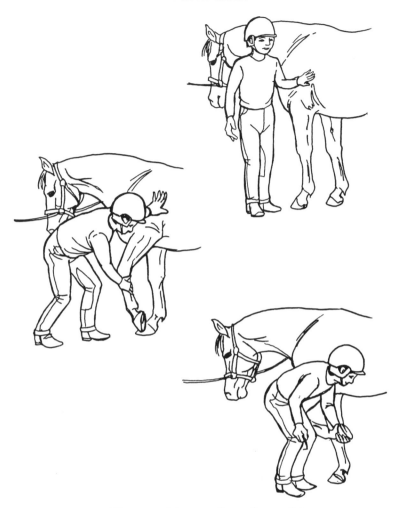

How to pick up a front foot safely

3. When he lifts the foot, hold it by the hoof (not by the pastern).
4. When you are finished, set the foot down gently.

To pick up a hind foot safely:

1. Stand beside the pony's hindquarters, facing backwards.
2. Put your hand on the hindquarters and slide it down the outside of the hind leg to the back tendons. Squeeze and pull forward gently and say "Pick up."

How to pick up a hind foot safely

3. When he lifts his foot, it comes forward first. Use your hand to guide the leg back until it is a little behind him.
4. Bend your knees and slide your thigh behind the pony's hind foot. Hold the hoof, not the pastern. (If you hold the leg this way, a pony can't kick you—he would have to push you out of the way instead.)

There are other ways to pick up a pony's feet, but this is the method recommended for D Level Pony Clubbers.

Your pony will pick up his feet more easily if you always use the same signal to ask him to lift his foot. When you are finished with his foot, set it down gently—don't drop it. If he puts his foot

203

◆◆

USPC D-1 TEST

Give one reason to pick out feet.

◆◆

USPC D-2 TEST

Know reasons for daily foot care.

◆◆

down before you are finished, make him pick it up again right away. Be careful where you put your own feet—your pony will not look out for them when he sets his foot down!

For safety, don't put your arm around the inside of the hind leg from the front. If the pony should snatch his hind leg up quickly, he could catch your arm. Don't pull his hind leg out to the side or hold it up too high. This hurts his leg and makes it hard for him to balance. It will make him want to take his leg away from you.

How to Clean the Feet

You will need a hoof pick and a stiff brush. (The kind of hoof pick with a brush on the end is a help.) Pick up your pony's foot and hold it by the hoof, not the pastern. Dig the point of the hoof pick into the dirt at the back of the foot, beside the frog. If you can get the pick under the packed dirt, it will come out quicker and easier than if you scrape a little at a time. Always pick from

How to pick out a hoof

the heel toward the toe. If you pick from toe to heel, you could poke the hoof pick into the frog by accident.

Clean all the dirt from the sole of the foot, the spaces beside the frog and the "cleft" (the groove in the center of the frog). Use the brush to clean away loose dirt, so that you can see all the parts of the hoof.

Remember to sweep up the dirt you pick out of your pony's feet when you are finished.

HOOF CONDITION

The condition of your pony's feet can change, depending on his health and the conditions he lives in. If he lives in a dry, dusty place, his feet may become dry and hard and they sometimes crack. You can help by applying hoof dressing around the coronet and across the heels. (It is not necessary or helpful to paint the whole foot.) It may also help to let him spend more time in damp grass, so his feet will absorb moisture naturally. If your pony lives in wet, swampy conditions all the time, his feet may become too soft. They may break off easily, and his shoes may not stay on. You will need to keep him in drier conditions to help his feet get tougher.

HOOF GROWTH, TRIMMING AND SHOEING

A pony's hoofs grow all the time, like your fingernails—about ¼ inch each month. Some ponies' feet wear down faster than they grow, because of the work they do and the hard or sandy ground over which they are ridden. They need shoes to protect their feet and keep them from becoming sore. Other ponies' feet grow faster than they wear down. They get long feet, which puts strain on their legs and can make them stumble. These ponies need to have their feet trimmed to keep them at a normal length. Some ponies' feet grow unevenly, so that their feet are out of balance, which makes it hard for them to move well. It is unkind and unsafe to let a pony's feet get too long, cracked and sore or badly out of balance, and he cannot be ridden that way.

Ponies that are shod need to have their shoes "reset" every six to eight weeks. This means removing the shoes and trimming away the extra hoof, then replacing them. When shoes get old and worn out, new shoes are needed.

Your pony should have his feet checked by a farrier (a horse-shoer) every six to eight weeks, whether he is ridden or not, to see if he needs his feet trimmed or his shoes reset. (Some ponies with special foot problems need to be checked every four or five weeks.) A farrier is an expert on trimming and balancing ponies' feet. He should check your pony's feet regularly, even if there is not much hoof growth. He can tell if your pony's feet are in good condition, and if they are balanced correctly, so that your pony can move without strain on his legs. If you aren't sure whether your pony needs shoes, ask your farrier.

Signs that a Pony Needs Shoeing or Trimming

The first sign that a pony needs shoeing or trimming is long feet. Often the toes grow longer than the heels. This can make a pony trip and stumble, and it puts extra strain on his tendons. If your pony wears shoes, there are some other signs to look for. As the

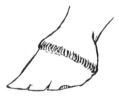

Long toe, low heel, cracked and broken hoof

Long toe, clinches risen, shoe too far forward

Shoe overgrown by foot, bent and missing nails, shoe loose

Signs of a foot needing trimming or shoeing

206

◆◆◆

USPC D-2 TEST

Give two reasons why the farrier regularly checks a pony.

◆◆◆

USPC D-3 TEST

Describe the obvious signs of a foot needing shoeing or trimming.

◆◆◆

hoof grows longer, the shoe seems to sit farther down the foot, away from the heels. This can cause the end of the shoe to press on the space between the bars and the wall, making a painful bruise called a "corn." The wall of the foot may start to grow over the edge of the shoe, and the clinches (the ends of the nails) will stand up from the wall of the foot instead of lying down smooth and tight. Some nails may loosen up or even fall out. Finally, the shoe may become loose. You can hear it click as the pony walks on a hard surface, and you may be able to move the shoe with your fingers. If you do not have the pony reshod, he may lose the shoe.

CHAPTER 9

Health Care and Veterinary Knowledge

When you own or ride a pony, you need to know when he is feeling well and when he is sick or lame, and how to keep him healthy. Every pony owner should have an "equine veterinarian" (an animal doctor who treats horses and ponies). The veterinarian should check out a new pony before you and your parents buy him to make sure he is sound and healthy. (This is called a "pre-purchase exam.") He should also give your pony a checkup at least once a year to make sure he is healthy. If your pony gets hurt or sick, if he goes lame, or if you notice another problem (like being too thin or too fat, having a skin rash or a cough, or not eating), you should call your veterinarian. The veterinarian can also give you good advice on worming, feeding, inoculations ("shots") and other ways to keep your pony healthy.

WHEN TO CALL THE VETERINARIAN

As you learn about ponies, it is important to know what you can take care of yourself and when to call the veterinarian. It is good to follow these rules:

- If a pony is in distress (won't eat, looks very sick or badly hurt), or you think it is an emergency, don't wait. Call the veterinarian right away.
- If you know there is a problem, but you don't know what

it is or how to help your pony, your veterinarian is the best person to call.

- If you aren't sure whether you should call a veterinarian or not, but you don't think it is an emergency, call your instructor for advice. Don't just wait to see if it will get worse!

Signs of a Healthy Pony

A healthy pony that feels well is alert and contented. His eyes are clear and bright, he breathes normally, and he is interested in what is going on. His coat is shiny and his skin is loose and supple. He may lie down and stretch out for a while, but he will get up easily. He stands normally on all four legs; he may rest a hind foot, but doesn't rest a front foot. He likes to eat, and drinks normally. He passes manure about eight times a day in normal manure balls (soft manure is usual for ponies on pasture), and his urine is clear or light yellow. His normal temperature (taken with a veterinary rectal thermometer) is between 100 and 101 degrees Fahrenheit.

A healthy pony

Signs of Sickness

Here are some important signs of sickness that should make you get help for your pony:

- *Colic* (belly pain): The pony may stop eating, break out in a sweat, look at or nip his belly, paw the ground, and stretch out as if to urinate. He may lie down and get up again, or roll from side to side, or even sit on his hindquarters, like a dog. All of these are signs of colic, which can be quite serious and even fatal. Call your veterinarian immediately, and while you are waiting for him, walk your pony slowly and don't let him roll.
- *Coughing* (especially a "wet" cough with mucus in his throat), *runny eyes and nose* (especially if mucus is white, yellow or green).
- *Diarrhea* (loose, runny manure), or *dry, hard manure balls.*
- *Pony is depressed:* He does not want to move, eat, or take an interest in what is going on. He may stand stiffly or hunched up. If lying down, he does not want to get up. He may act cranky and irritable, especially if you ride him.
- *Fever:* A fever of more than one degree above normal (102 degrees or higher). Fever in the feet (the feet will feel hot to your touch) can be serious, especially if the pony stands

◆◆

USPC D-1 TEST

Discuss what a veterinarian is.

◆◆

USPC D-2 TEST

Give one reason why the veterinarian might treat your pony.

◆◆

USPC D-3 TEST

Give two reasons to have your pony routinely checked by a veterinarian.

◆◆

with his front legs out ahead of him, moves stiffly or lies down and does not want to get up. (This could mean laminitis, or founder, which is an emergency. Call your veterinarian immediately.)

* *Not wanting to eat or not eating normally:* Pony refuses to eat, drools or drops food out of his mouth.
* *Losing weight, dull coat, change in usual eating habits or behavior.*
* *Injuries:* Cuts, swelling, heat or tenderness in a leg or elsewhere; a closed or swollen eye; lameness.

If you need to call your veterinarian, first write down all your pony's symptoms. If possible, get an experienced horse-person to take your pony's vital signs (his temperature, pulse rate and respiration rate). It is easier for the veterinarian to decide how serious your pony's problem might be if you give him all the information in a clear and organized way.

Recognizing Lameness

To tell if a pony is lame, lead him at a jog. Keep the lead line loose so he can move his head up or down freely. Jog him in a straight line on hard level ground, like a driveway. Sometimes you can hear that his hoofbeats are uneven; one may sound louder and one much quieter, like "CLIP, clop."

When a pony is lame, he favors his sore leg. He may stand with his weight on the good leg and rest the sore one. When he moves, he tries not to step hard on his sore leg. If it is a front leg, he throws his head up when he steps on the sore leg and down when he steps on the good leg. The sore leg usually takes a shorter step. If it is a hind leg, he carries his hip higher on the sore side and throws his head down as the sore hind foot touches the ground.

◆◆

USPC D-3 TEST

Give some symptoms of a sick or injured pony that would cause you to seek help.

◆◆

Signs of sickness

Colic signs: stretching out, pawing, biting or kicking at belly, sweating

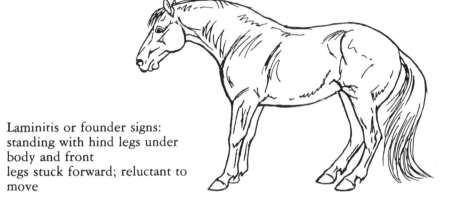

Laminitis or founder signs: standing with hind legs under body and front legs stuck forward; reluctant to move

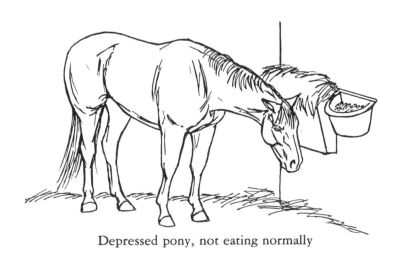

Depressed pony, not eating normally

How to tell when pony is lame

Lame in front leg:

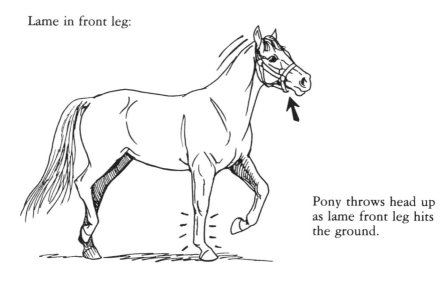

Pony throws head up as lame front leg hits the ground.

Lame in hind leg:

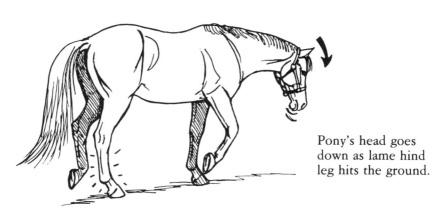

Pony's head goes down as lame hind leg hits the ground.

If your pony goes lame, clean out his feet and check for stones, a twisted or loose shoe, or something like a nail stuck in his foot. Feel his legs to see if you find a place that is tender (he flinches, or shows he's uncomfortable, when you touch or squeeze it), or that feels hot or puffy. (It helps to compare the lame leg with the other leg.)

Call your veterinarian or ask your instructor for advice, and don't ride him until you find out what the problem is and treat it. Some lamenesses can be made worse if you work the pony. (If you are out on a ride and your pony goes lame, it is okay to walk him back home slowly.) Don't put liniment or anything else on a lame leg until you get advice from your veterinarian.

HEALTH CARE AND RECORD BOOK

Good health care on a regular schedule will keep your pony healthy and prevent small problems from growing into big ones. Basic health care includes vaccinations ("shots"), regular de-worming, dental care and regular shoeing or hoof trimming.

To keep your pony's health care up to date, you will need a calendar and a record book. Mark on the calendar the dates when inoculations, de-worming, horseshoeing or other health care is due. Write down a note to call and make an appointment at least a week ahead of time. Visits from the veterinarian and other health care should be written down in your record book. Put down the date, what was done for your pony, and any notes or instructions. Shoeing and foot trimming should also be recorded in your book.

Worms and De-worming

Ponies are exposed to several kinds of internal parasites ("worms") all the time. They can damage a pony's intestines, heart and lungs, make him thin and unhealthy, and can even kill him. Every pony owner should have his pony treated for worms regularly.

De-wormer (usually a special medicated paste) is given to ponies every two to three months to kill the worms. There are many different kinds of de-wormers. Your veterinarian will advise you on how often your pony should be de-wormed and what kind of de-wormer is best to use.

Vaccinations

Every pony needs vaccinations, or "shots," to protect him against certain diseases. These should be given at least once a year. In most parts of the country, certain shots are necessary every six months or even every three months. Your veterinarian can tell you which shots are most important for your pony and in your part of the country. It is much better (and costs less) to prevent your pony from getting a serious disease than to have to treat one.

The most common diseases your pony should be vaccinated against are:

- *Tetanus:* It should be given once a year. A tetanus booster shot may be necessary if a pony gets a deep cut or a puncture wound.
- *Encephalomyletis* (sleeping sickness): In the North, one shot is given in the spring. In the South, shots may be needed every six months or every three months.
- *Influenza (flu):* If your pony goes to shows and events where he meets other ponies, this shot is especially needed. Protection from one shot lasts for three months.
- *Rabies:* If there is rabies among the wildlife in your area (especially foxes, skunks and raccoons), your pony must have a rabies shot every year.
- *Potomac Horse Fever:* This serious disease is thought to be carried by ticks or biting insects. Ask your veterinarian if it is a problem in your area.

There are several other diseases you may need to vaccinate your pony against, depending on where you live, or shots may be required by your club. Ask your veterinarian and your Pony Club D.C. for information.

BANDAGING LEGS
Kinds of Bandages

There are several kinds of bandages you might need to use on a pony.

- *Shipping bandage:* For protection against bumps and scrapes when traveling.
- *Stable bandage:* For protection and warmth in the stall and to prevent the legs from swelling after hard work.
- *Exercise bandage:* Protects legs against knocks and scrapes during work.
- *Treatment bandages:* For protection and treatment of injuries.

CAUTION: All bandages must be put on correctly or they can damage your pony's legs. Do not try to put on a leg bandage without hands-on help from someone who is experienced in bandaging legs correctly.

◆◆◆

USPC D-2 TEST

Give two reasons why you would bandage a pony's leg(s).

◆◆◆

USPC D-3 TEST

Describe what critical areas are protected by shipping bandages or boots, and give reasons for their use.

◆◆◆

Bandages are made up of leg wraps (usually knitted, flannel or special elastic material about 9 feet long), leg pads (made of sheet cotton, polyester, cotton quilts or special leg pads), and fasteners (Velcro, pins or masking tape). At Pony Club testings, sheet cotton must be used for leg pads.

Shipping Boots and Bandages

Ponies sometimes can slip or scramble in a trailer, or they may step on their own feet or another pony's feet if they should lose their balance. It's a good idea to use shipping boots or bandages on your pony whenever he travels.

Shipping boots or bandages should protect the legs from the hoof to the knees and hocks. They should cover the heels and the coronet, the pastern and fetlock joint, and the tendons up to the bottom of the knee or hock. A shipping bandage should be firm, snug, and well padded, to protect against bumps and scrapes.

Shipping bandage   Shipping boot

Because shipping boots are quick and easy to put on, they are sometimes used instead of bandages. They are a good choice for pony owners who do not know how to put on good shipping bandages. However, shipping boots must cover the coronet and heels as well as the tendons. Some shipping boots protect the knees and hocks as well as the lower legs.

LEARNING MORE ABOUT HEALTH CARE

- Be sure to read the books and pamphlets on your USPC reading list.
- You can get excellent information on such things as health care, de-worming and diseases from the Cooperative Extension (part of the U.S. Department of Agriculture), your county agent, the 4-H Horse Club Program, some horse health care companies, and horse books and magazines. Much of the information is free or inexpensive. You may want to start a file of magazine articles, pamphlets and other horse health care information for your Pony Club.
- Ask a veterinarian to come and speak to your Pony Club about such topics as first aid for ponies; which diseases to vaccinate against; de-worming and parasite control; and pony health problems.

NOTE TO PARENTS ON HEALTH CARE

Good health care is essential for the well-being of a pony. This requires visits from the veterinarian and some expense. Try to find a veterinarian who specializes in horses, and develop a good working relationship. If you use the same veterinarian, he will get to know your pony and can give you the best advice on health and pony management problems. Be sure to treat him or her in a professional manner: schedule appointments well in advance; give him all pertinent information in a clear and organized way; have the pony in the barn and be on hand to help when he is due to visit; and above all, pay his bill on time!

CHAPTER 10

Travel Safety and Trailering

Safety is important when you go places with your pony, whether you are riding with friends, going on a trail ride, or taking your pony somewhere in a trailer.

OUT AND ABOUT WITH YOUR PONY
Group Riding in an Enclosed Area

When you ride by yourself, you only have to think about yourself and your pony (and sometimes your instructor). When people ride together, everyone must follow certain rules in order to be safe and fair to the others. Here are some simple rules for riding together in a ring or an enclosed area:

- If others are riding in a ring when you arrive, ask permission before you open the gate and come in. If you open the gate suddenly, you could upset someone else's pony.
- Pay attention to your pony and keep him under control. Don't let him wander, crowd up close to other ponies or bother other ponies. Don't let him touch noses with another pony. This often makes ponies stamp and squeal.
- Keep a safe distance of at least one pony length from any other pony. Especially, don't crowd up close behind any other pony. This could make him kick.
- If you need to stop to fix something, go to the center of

219

the ring. Don't stop on the track, where you would be in the way of other riders.

- If you must pass a slower pony, turn and ride across the ring or circle back to an open space. Never pass close to another pony, or squeeze between another pony and the rail.
- When you are taking a riding lesson, be on time. If you pay attention to the instructor, obey commands promptly, keep good spacing and are ready when it is your turn to perform an exercise, you will make it a better lesson for yourself and others.
- If several people are riding in a small ring, it is easier if everyone agrees to ride in the same direction, with everyone changing direction from time to time. In a large and busy ring, people may ride both ways. When you meet another rider, pass like cars on the highway—left shoulder to left shoulder.
- Always be polite to others. If another rider is having trouble, slow down or stop and give him room. Don't interrupt a lesson or someone who is busy training or jumping. Thank anyone who gives you room or helps you, and remember to thank your instructor at the end of a lesson.

◆◆

USPC D-1 TEST

Know the basic rules of safe riding in a group in an enclosed area.

◆◆

Riding on Public Roads

- When you are riding outside, it is best to avoid riding on streets, highways or near auto traffic if you can help it. Some ponies are frightened by traffic, and even a well-trained pony may spook if something unusual happens. Even if you are careful, not all drivers are safe drivers.
- If you must ride along a public road, try to stay well off the pavement, on the shoulder. (However, this does not mean that you may ride on lawns or sidewalks.) Watch out for trash on the edge of the road, and drainage ditches.

Keep to a walk. Going faster is very hard on your pony's legs, and he might slip. In a group, ride in single file, not side by side. The whole group must stay on one side of the road.

- If you see a car coming from the front or the rear, pass a warning down the line to all the riders in front of you or behind you. Pass a warning along if you see a hazard like broken glass, wire, a hole or a hidden ditch.
- If you must cross a road with a group of riders, everyone should line up at a spot where you can see a long way in both directions. The riders at each end of the line look both ways for traffic. When it is clear, they act as crossing guards while all the riders cross at once between them.

CAUTION: It is *not safe* for one or several riders to cross a road, leaving some riders on the other side. Everyone should stay on the same side of the road and cross at one time when it is safe to do so.

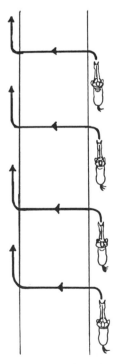

Procedure for crossing a road with a mounted group

◆◆

USPC D-2 TEST

Know basic rules for riding on public roads in your state.

◆◆

USPC D-3 TEST

Know the procedure for a mounted group crossing a highway.

◆◆

When you ride on public roads, you must obey the traffic laws and any special laws that apply to riders on the roads in your state. These laws are different in each state and in some towns, so you must learn what the traffic laws for riders are in your area.

To find out the traffic laws that horseback riders must know, contact your local Department of Motor Vehicles office. Also, the Town Clerk, Police Department or Sheriff's Department can tell you if there are any local laws you must obey.

Remember—*before you ride on a public road, you must know the traffic laws for your area and obey them.*

Be safe, not sorry—beware of cars and trucks *all the time*! Even if you have the right of way, a driver may not know—or care.

TRAILERING YOUR PONY

In Pony Club, you may often want to haul your pony in a trailer to a lesson, a rally or some other Pony Club activity. If your pony is well trained for trailering and you are careful and sensible, it is quite simple. However, if a pony has a bad experience with a trailer, he can become very hard to load or trailer, and it may even become dangerous for him and for you. It is very important to get help and advice from an expert when you are learning to load and haul your pony, especially if he is not used to loading and traveling in a trailer.

Preparing for Travel in a Trailer

Shipping a pony safely in a horse trailer requires some knowledge and planning. Before traveling, you will need to be prepared in the following ways:

- The trailer and tow vehicle must be safe, serviced and properly hitched, and the driver must be experienced in hauling horses. You will also need someone who is experienced in loading ponies safely and quietly to help you.
- The pony must be trained to load and unload easily and ride quietly. This takes experience and practice.
- The pony must have the right traveling gear for protection.
- You should take along the equipment you will need to keep the pony safe and comfortable while traveling and for after he arrives.

Equipment for Travel

To travel safely, your pony should wear the right equipment. He must never be saddled and bridled when traveling, because the tack could catch on the trailer when he is unloaded. This could hurt the pony and damage your tack. He should have:

- A strong, properly fitted halter and a strong tie rope.
- Shipping boots or bandages on all four legs, to protect against bumps or scrapes during loading or traveling.
- Tail bandage or tail guard, to protect his tail in the trailer.
- Sheet, blanket or fly sheet if the weather requires it. (A sheet can also be used to keep dust off the pony when traveling on dirt roads.)
- Head protector (used on ponies that throw their heads up and could bump themselves).

Some of this equipment (like bandages) should be put on by someone who has experience in bandaging. The person who helps you trailer your pony should be able to help you bandage his legs and tail, or you can use shipping boots, which are easier to put on.

What to Take Along

When your pony travels, you should take along the equipment you need to take care of him. This includes:

- Hay net filled with hay (to keep the pony contented in the trailer).

223

Pony prepared for shipping

- Water bucket. (You can get five-gallon pails with snap-on lids from a bakery. These let you take your own water with you.)
- Equine first aid kit, to let you take care of a cut or minor injury. (The basic items you should carry are described in detail in *The USPC Horse Management Handbook*. Ask your veterinarian or an experienced horse-person for advice, too.)
- Extra tie rope and chain-end lead shank. (For control if you need it.)
- Muck basket, rake and broom for cleaning up.
- Don't forget your tack!

LOADING AND UNLOADING
Loading an Experienced Pony

Before loading your pony, have everything else loaded and checked. The trailer should be on level ground, with the back step as low as possible, or the ramp steady. The front exit door should be open so that the trailer is lighter inside and the pony can see through, and you can get out that way. The trailer floor can be covered with shavings to give your pony better footing.

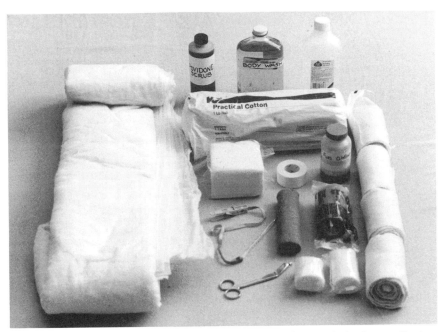

A simple equine first aid kit, which should always be carried when trailering a pony. (For details, consult *The USPC Horse Management Handbook.*) *Photo: Ruth Harvie.*

(If you have rubber floor mats, this may make the footing more slippery. Mixing the shavings with sand will help.)

If your pony is traveling alone in a double trailer, he should ride on the left (driver's side), so that his weight does not make the trailer drift toward the shoulder of the road. You can move the partition over to give him more room. Have a tidbit ready for him.

Lead the pony straight forward into the trailer. If your trailer has breast bars, you may walk in ahead of him and slip under the breast bar as he follows you in. If your trailer is the kind with a solid front, your pony should be trained to step into the trailer as you stand beside the door. It is not safe to walk into a closed trailer stall with a pony.

When your pony goes in, give him his tidbit and *wait until someone has fastened the tail bar or back door behind him before you tie him up.* CAUTION: *Never* tie a pony's head when the tail bar or back door is open behind him. This can cause him to pull back and panic. He could even flip over backwards.

Your pony should be tied with a quick-release knot or a special

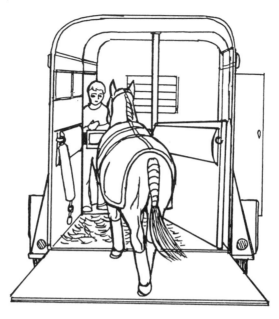

Loading in a ramp type trailer with breast bars: You can lead the pony into the trailer and go out the door in front.

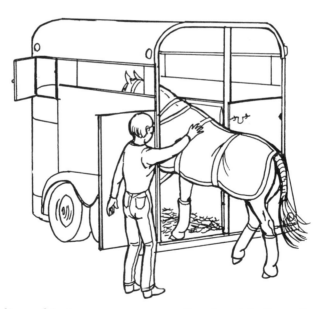

Loading safely in a step-up type trailer closed in front: Pony should be trained to go freely into the trailer on command. You should not go into the stall in front of him.

Safe trailer loading

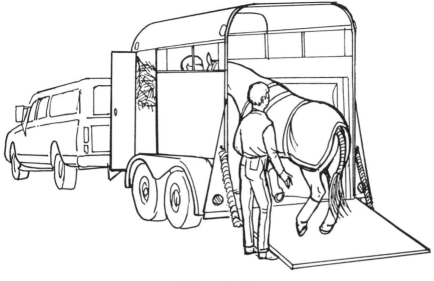

Safe unloading

trailer tie with a quick-release snap. The tie rope should be long enough so he can reach his hay net, but not so long that he can turn his head around or nip at his neighbor.

Unloading a Pony

Before unloading, the trailer should be parked on level ground. Avoid unloading on a highway, on slippery ground or too close to anything a pony could bump into.

CAUTION: Always untie your pony's head before you lower the ramp, open the back door or unfasten the tail bar.

A pony must *never* be tied up in a trailer when the tail bar is undone. If you forget to untie his head and he begins to back off while he is still tied, he can get frightened, pull back and flip over backwards.

When you are ready to unload, your helper should unfasten the tail bar. Back your pony out slowly, in a straight line. A helper should stand beside the ramp to keep him straight, so he doesn't step off the side of the ramp by mistake.

◆◆

USPC D-2 TEST

Know two ways to help your pony be safe in a trailer.

◆◆

USPC D-3 TEST

Know the safe procedures for loading and unloading an experienced pony.

◆◆

NOTES TO PARENTS ON TRAILERING

Trailering is one area in which children must have expert adult help. Unless you are experienced in loading and hauling horses, you should seek help from an expert before you try to trailer a pony yourself, even for a short distance. Asking a horse or pony to enter a closed box on wheels and stand quietly while traveling down a highway goes against the animal's natural instincts. If a pony is nervous or inexperienced, or if you make a mistake in loading in hauling, he may get upset and cause problems that are very difficult to handle, if not dangerous. It is also necessary to practice loading a pony before you must take him on a trip. A calm, confident and quiet attitude is everything in handling the pony during loading and unloading.

Hauling a horse trailer with live weight is not as simple as hauling other kinds of trailers. Driving too fast or making abrupt turns or changes of speed can upset the pony's balance and cause him to become frightened, to slip or scramble, or even to fall down. When hauling a trailer, you must drive especially smoothly, slowing down to 5 mph or less for sharp turns. Remember that the extra weight and length of a horse trailer requires more time and more room when stopping, accelerating, or pulling out into traffic.

If you ride along with a horse person who is experienced and sensible about loading, hauling and unloading and learn how to do it correctly, you will be safer and more confident when you are ready to take over the job of trailering your child's pony yourself.

PART 4

PONY KNOWLEDGE, TACK
AND
TURNOUT

CHAPTER 11

Pony Talk: Pony Parts, Colors and Conformation

When you talk about ponies, you will want to know the right names for everything.

PARTS OF A PONY

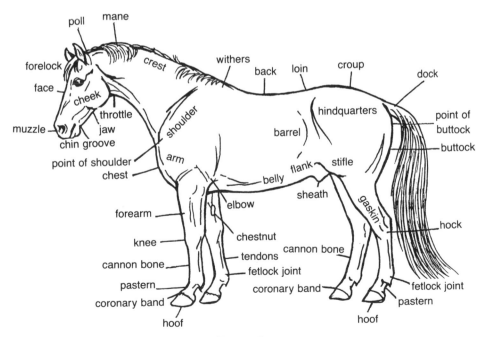

Parts of a pony

PONY COLORS

A pony's color means the color of his body and head, and his tail and mane. What color is your pony?

- *Black:* All black without brown highlights.
- *Brown:* Dark brown or nearly black with brown highlights.
- *Bay:* Brown or reddish-brown body with black "points" (mane, tail and legs).
- *Chestnut* (also called "sorrel"): Reddish-brown with the same color or lighter tail, mane and legs. May be dark chestnut, red chestnut or light chestnut. Mane and tail may be blond.
- *Grey:* Grey or white with dark skin, eyes and muzzle. Greys are born dark colored and grow lighter as they age, until they are nearly white. May be dark grey (iron grey), dappled grey, "flea-bitten" (speckled) grey, or white grey. True white ponies are born white with pink skin.
- *Roan:* Black, bay, brown or chestnut with white hairs mixed through the coat. May be "blue roan" (black or brown

USPC D-1 TEST

Name any ten parts of a pony.

USPC D-2 TEST

Name additional parts of a pony (fifteen).

USPC D-3 TEST

Know all parts of a pony.

USPC D-2 TEST

Know any six pony colors.

roan), "red roan" (bay or chestnut roan) or "strawberry roan" (light chestnut roan).

- *Dun:* Tan or mouse colored, with dark legs, mane and tail and a dark stripe down the back. A golden dun with dark legs, mane, tail and stripe is called a "buckskin."
- *Palomino:* Golden coat with white mane and tail.
- *Pinto:* Large, colored patches of any color and white. A "piebald" is black and white. A "skewbald" is any other color and white.
- *Appaloosa:* Has small round spots or speckles. May be dark with light spots, white with dark spots, roan with patches of spots, or dark with a white "blanket" and spots over the hindquarters.

PONY MARKINGS
Face Markings

Face markings are white areas on a pony's face and head.

Face markings. Left to right: star, snip, blaze, strip, and bald face

Leg Markings

Leg markings are usually described by saying how far up the leg the white reaches (for instance, "white coronet," "white half-pastern," "white half-cannon," etc.).

◆◆◆

USPC D-2 TEST

Know five face and leg markings.

◆◆◆

Other Marks

- *Brand:* A design burned into the skin to identify an animal.
- *Freeze brand:* A brand made by freezing instead of heat. The hair grows in white. Usually letters or numbers are used.
- *Scar:* A permanent mark left by an injury that has healed.

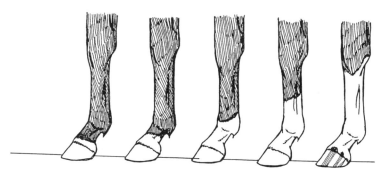

Leg markings. Left to right: Coronet, half-pastern, sock (white to top
of fetlock joint), half-cannon, stocking and ermine spots in stocking

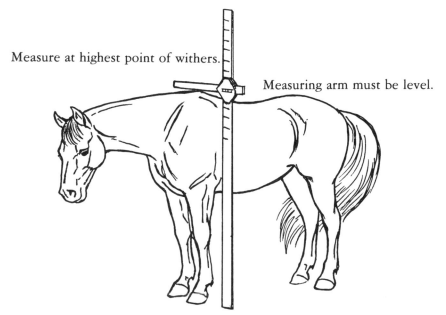

Measure at highest point of withers.

Measuring arm must be level.

How to measure a pony's height

SIZE AND MEASURING HEIGHT

The size of a pony is measured in "hands," from the ground to the withers. One hand equals 4 inches. A horse measuring stick is used for measuring.

In this country, a *horse* measures over 14 hands and 2 inches (written as "14.2 hands"). A *pony* measures less than 14 hands and 2 inches when it is mature (fully grown). There are small ponies (up to 12.2 hands), medium ponies (from 12.2 to 13.2 hands) and large ponies (13.2 to 14.2 hands). A pony is not a baby horse.

◆◆

USPC D-3 TEST

Describe how to measure the height of a pony.

◆◆

PONY TERMS

- *Mare:* A mature (fully grown) female horse or pony, four years old or more.
- *Filly:* A young female horse or pony, under four years old.
- *Colt:* A young male horse or pony, under four years old.
- *Foal:* A baby horse or pony of either sex, under one year old.
- *Yearling:* A horse or pony that is one year old.
- *Dam:* A horse or pony's mother.
- *Sire:* A horse or pony's father.
- *Stallion:* A mature (fully grown) male horse or pony, four years or older. He can be used for breeding.
- *Gelding:* A male horse or pony of any age that has been neutered. He cannot be used for breeding.
- *Near side:* The left side of a pony (the side of the pony we mount).
- *Off side:* The right side of a pony.
- *Green:* A pony that is untrained or inexperienced.

THE GAITS

Gaits are the ways in which a pony can move. There are four basic gaits:

Walk

The walk is a four-beat gait. It is the slowest and easiest to ride. A walk is about four miles per hour.

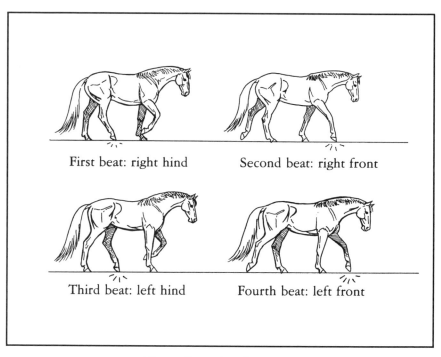

First beat: right hind   Second beat: right front

Third beat: left hind   Fourth beat: left front

The walk, a four-beat gait

Trot

The trot is a two-beat gait. It has suspension (bounce) because the pony goes up in the air between beats. It is about six miles per hour.

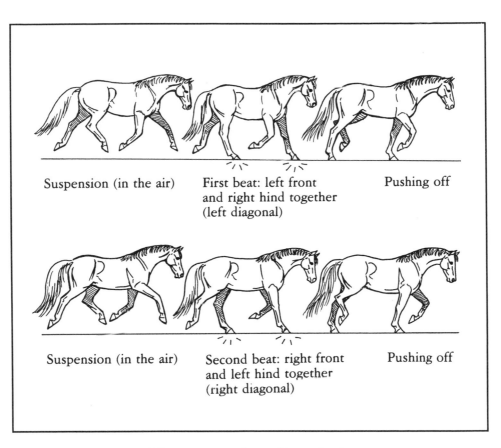

| Suspension (in the air) | First beat: left front and right hind together (left diagonal) | Pushing off |

| Suspension (in the air) | Second beat: right front and left hind together (right diagonal) | Pushing off |

The trot, a two-beat, diagonal gait

Canter

The canter is a three-beat gait. It has suspension because the pony goes up in the air between strides. It is about eight miles per hour.

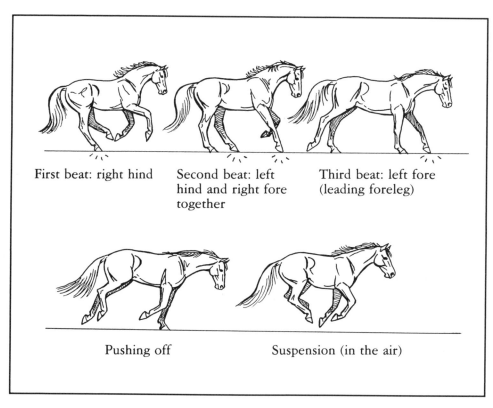

First beat: right hind   Second beat: left hind and right fore together   Third beat: left fore (leading foreleg)

Pushing off   Suspension (in the air)

The canter, a three-beat gait (left lead)

Gallop

The gallop is the pony's fastest gait. It is a four-beat gait with suspension because the pony goes up in the air between strides. It is about fifteen miles per hour or faster.

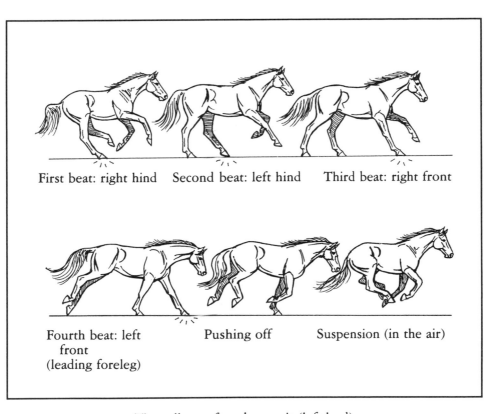

First beat: right hind   Second beat: left hind   Third beat: right front

Fourth beat: left front (leading foreleg)   Pushing off   Suspension (in the air)

The gallop, a four-beat gait (left lead)

HORSE AND PONY BREEDS AND TYPES

Any horse or pony may be a particular "type." A type of animal refers to its build and characteristics, which make it useful for certain kinds of work. Some examples are hunter type, pleasure type, western or stock type, gaited saddle horse type, and draft type. An animal does not have to be of any particular breed to be of a certain type.

A "breed" is a kind of horse or pony that has been bred for special purposes over a number of years. Most horses of a particular breed are "purebreds" (which means their sire and dam are both of the same breed), and have registration papers from their breed club. A *grade* horse or pony is one of unknown or mixed breeding.

Here are some horse and pony breeds that are popular in North America:

- *Arabian:* The oldest pure breed of horse, used today for endurance riding, showing, dressage and all kinds of pleasure riding. Arabians are usually small, high spirited and intelligent, with a "dished" (slightly curved) face, fine skin and coat, short back and a high tail carriage.
- *Thoroughbred:* First bred hundreds of years ago in England just for racing, but now also used as hunters and jumpers and for eventing and dressage. Many have been on Olympic teams. They are tall, lean and rangy, with long legs, necks and bodies. Thoroughbreds are fast, sensitive and powerful, with good endurance, and move with long, low strides.
- *Quarter Horse:* Originated in colonial America and bred for short-distance racing and cow ponies. Most Quarter Horses have some Thoroughbred blood. Today they are used for every kind of riding from ranch work to showing, jumping, pleasure riding, and racing. They have strong, muscular hindquarters and sturdy conformation, and are usually calm and intelligent.
- *Morgan:* Originated in the United States and descended from one small stallion, Justin Morgan. Morgans are compact, powerful and intelligent. They are used for driving as well as for all kinds of riding. Morgans are known for their endurance.

240

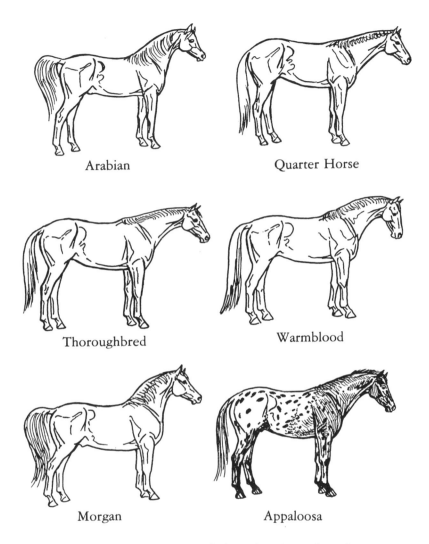

Arabian   Quarter Horse

Thoroughbred   Warmblood

Morgan   Appaloosa

Some common North American horse breeds

- *Appaloosa:* Originally came from the northwestern part of the United States. Appaloosas are a spotted breed with some Thoroughbred and Quarter Horse blood. Once bred as Indian ponies, they are now used for all kinds of riding, including western, English, jumping, trail and pleasure riding.
- *Warmbloods:* Not a single breed, but rather a group of breeds that cross "hot-blooded" Thoroughbreds and Arabians with "cold-blooded" draft horses. Many are imported

Some common North American pony breeds

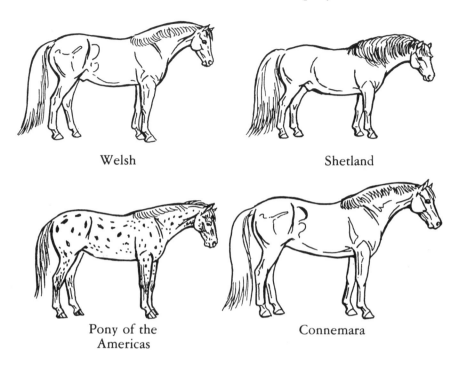

Welsh

Shetland

Pony of the
Americas

Connemara

from Europe. Warmbloods are usually tall, strong and athletic. They are bred for jumping and dressage, and some are used for driving. Many Olympic team horses are Warmbloods.

- *Welsh Pony:* Originally came from the mountains of Wales in Great Britain. Welsh Ponies have some Arabian blood. They are medium-sized, with beautiful heads, compact bodies and a "floating" trot. They are used for pleasure riding, jumping and driving.

- *Shetland Pony:* Originally came from the Shetland Islands off the coast of Scotland. Very small (under 12.2 hands) but sturdy, strong and smart, they are used as children's ponies for riding and also for driving.

- *Connemara Pony:* Originally came from Ireland. Some are medium to large ponies and some are small horses. They are tough, strong and hardy, with pretty heads, strong bones and good sense. Most are used for pleasure riding, hunting, jumping, eventing and driving.

- *Pony of the Americas:* A new beed of pony that is the size

◆◆

USPC D-2 TEST

Name four horse or pony breeds.

◆◆

of a Welsh Pony and has the color of an Appaloosa. POA's are used for children's ponies and are ridden English and western. They also jump and drive.

CONFORMATION

"Conformation" means the way a pony is built. Good conformation makes a pony a pleasure to look at, but it is more important than things like a pretty color or a long tail. It also means he can move and perform better, may have smoother gaits and is likely to be stronger and less likely to break down than a pony with poor conformation.

Here are some basic conformation points to look for in a pony:

Overall

The pony should look well balanced and all his parts should fit together well. (No part should look too big or too small for the rest of him, like too big a head, legs that are too short, or a back that is too long.)

Head

He should have a well-shaped, attractive head that is not too large, and is well set on his neck. It should be wide at the jaws, with large nostrils, large, kind eyes, and a pleasant expression. A well-balanced head with wide jaws makes it easier for a pony to respond to the bit and to balance himself. Large nostrils can take in more air, and large eyes with a kind expression usually mean a good disposition.

Faults A coarse, heavy head, a head that is poorly set on the neck, narrow jaws, small "pig eyes," small nostrils, and an unpleasant expression—all are undesirable.

243

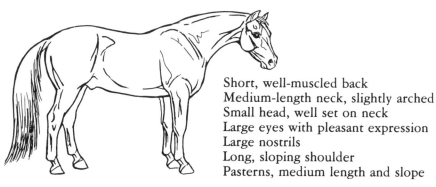

Short, well-muscled back
Medium-length neck, slightly arched
Small head, well set on neck
Large eyes with pleasant expression
Large nostrils
Long, sloping shoulder
Pasterns, medium length and slope

Good conformation

Poor conformation

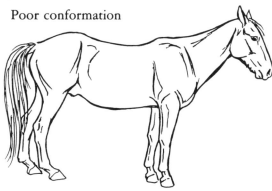

Long, hollow back
Short neck
Ewe neck (dips on top,
  bulges underneath)
Large coarse head, set
  on neck at awkward angle
Pig eyes, unpleasant
  expression
Small nostrils
Short, upright shoulders
Short, upright pasterns
Long, flat hind pasterns, too
  much slope

Conformation

Neck

A good neck is medium long and slightly arched, blending smoothly into withers of medium height. It is "clean" (not thick and puffy) at the throat, and neither too thick nor too thin. A good neck makes it easier for the pony to use his head and neck for balance, and to flex (or bend) his neck correctly when he responds to the bit.

Faults A short, thick neck ("bull neck") goes with short, choppy gaits and makes it harder to balance. A neck that dips on the top and bulges on the bottom is called a "ewe neck." It makes it hard for the pony to flex his neck properly, and he may carry his head too high.

244

Back

A good back is short and well-muscled, blending smoothly into a wide, well-muscled loin and medium-height withers. This makes his back stronger and able to carry weight better, and good withers help keep the saddle in place.

Faults A long back is weaker and hard to fit with a saddle, especially if it is also hollow. High withers are harder to fit with a saddle. Low withers (especially when covered with fat) do not hold the saddle in place well.

Shoulder

A good shoulder is long (from the end of the mane to the point of the shoulder) and sloping. This gives a longer stride and smoother gaits, and helps a pony jump well.

Faults A short, upright shoulder (nearly straight up and down) causes rough gaits and a shorter stride. It also makes it harder for a pony to fold his front legs well when he jumps.

Pasterns

The pasterns are "shock absorbers," so they must be strong and springy, with medium length and slope.

Faults Short, upright (almost straight up and down) pasterns cause rough gaits, which pound a pony's feet and legs and make him less comfortable to ride. Pasterns that are too long or that slope too much (almost flat) give smoother gaits, but they are weak and are easily injured.

DESCRIBING A PONY

There are many reasons you might have to describe a pony clearly—to tell someone just what he looks like. A complete description should give the pony's size, age and sex, color, markings, his breed or type, and any obvious conformation characteristics. (For instance, Dancer is a seven-year-old Welsh gelding, 13.2 hands, dark bay with a star and with his right hind leg white to mid-pastern. He has a long back and a Roman nose, and a scar on his left shoulder.)

245

◆◆

USPC D-3 TEST

Describe characteristics of a strange pony clearly enough for him to be identified.

◆◆

Write down a description of your pony below.

DESCRIPTION OF MY PONY

Name: Sex:

Height: Age: Breed or type:

Color:

Face markings (describe):

Leg markings (describe):

Scars or other markings:

Any other special characteristics:

Draw your pony's markings on the diagram below.

CHAPTER 12

Tack

Your pony's saddle, bridle and equipment are called *tack*. When you saddle or bridle a pony, you *tack him up. Untacking* is taking his tack off. A store that sells tack is called a *tack shop*. When you are talking about tack, you need to know the proper names for the different parts.

There are many kinds of tack, including English, Western, and special tack for certain kinds of riding, like racing. In Pony club, *English tack* is used because it is best for a balanced seat for riding and jumping. It's important to choose the right kind of tack for the kind of riding you do, and tack that fits both you and your pony. It's a good idea to get advice from your instructor when buying tack, to be sure that you get the right kind.

Knowing about tack and equipment is important for your safety and control. You should know what kind of bit you use on your pony, and how it works on his mouth. You must learn how to adjust your tack so it fits your pony properly, and to check it each time you ride. It's also important to learn how to clean and care for your tack, and how to keep it in safe condition and good repair. Good tack can be expensive, but if you take good care of it, it will last for many years. At Pony Club mounted events, every rider's tack must be checked for safety and proper fit before he is allowed to ride.

NAMES AND PARTS OF TACK
Parts of a Saddle

An all-purpose balanced seat saddle is the best type of saddle for Pony Club riders.

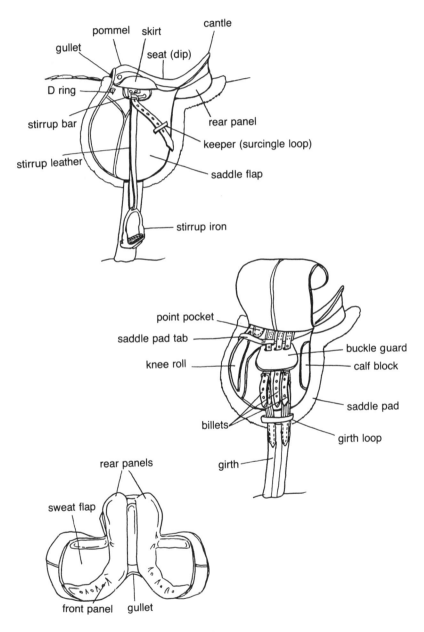

Parts of the saddle

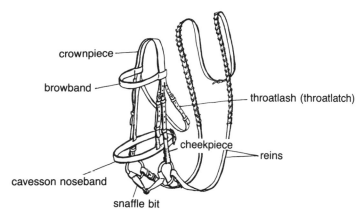

Parts of a snaffle bridle

Parts of a Bridle

A snaffle bridle is the simplest kind for Pony Club riders. There are other kinds of bits and bridles.

Halter, Lead Rope and Lead Shank

- A halter is used to handle, lead and tie a pony. It has no bit, so it can be safely used for tying a pony.
- A lead rope is used to lead and to tie up a pony. It may be made of cotton, hemp or a soft, braided synthetic material. Don't use lead ropes made of slippery plastic, which can come untied easily, or flat nylon, which can jam tight when tied.
- A chain-end lead shank is used for extra control when leading a pony. It may be of flat nylon or leather. It must *never* be used to tie a pony.

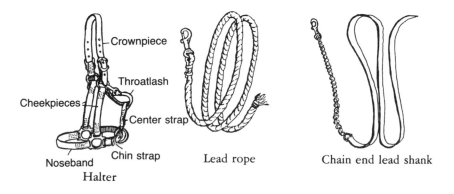

Halter

Lead rope

Chain end lead shank

◆◆◆

USPC D-1 TEST

Name any ten parts of a saddle and bridle.

◆◆◆

CAUTION: *Never* tie a pony by a bridle or snap a cross-tie into the bit ring. He may pull back and hurt his mouth badly, and may break the reins or the bridle.

The Bit and How It Works

The metal, rubber or nylon *bit* in your pony's mouth is important, because it lets you tell him what to do when you ride him. You should know how your pony's bit works, so you can control him without hurting his mouth.

Bits should work by pressure, not pain. Ponies are trained to listen to bit pressure and changes in pressure (stronger, lighter, left and right), and to obey by stopping, turning, slowing down or changing their balance, etc. If the bit hurts his mouth, a pony will be unhappy and confused, and he may get scared or angry. He then will not do what you want him to do, or will not be able to do it well.

THREE KINDS OF BITS

A Pony Club rider should use the mildest and simplest bit that will control his pony safely. This is usually some kind of snaffle bit. Some ponies may need a kimberwicke or a pelham bit, or some other kind.

Snaffle Bit

A snaffle bit has two rings and a mouthpiece, which is usually jointed and made of smooth metal, nylon or rubber. (Rough, sharp or twisted wire mouthpieces are discouraged for Pony Club riding.) Snaffle bits work by *direct pressure*. This means one ounce of pressure on the reins makes one ounce of pressure on the pony's mouth. Snaffle bits are fairly mild bits. They are used for training ponies and for advanced riding, as well as for pleasure riding and beginning riders.

A snaffle bit works by direct pressure on tongue, lips and bars of the mouth.

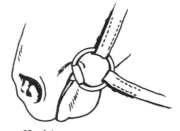

Jointed snaffle bit

Kimberwicke bit with rein slots

A kimberwicke bit acts like a mild curb bit, squeezing the mouth between the bit and the curb chain.

Curb chain

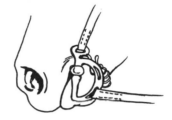

Rein in upper slot, mild curb effect

Rein in lower slot, stronger curb effect

Rein around ring, mildest effect (almost like snaffle bit)

Kimberwicke Bit

A kimberwicke bit is a mild curb bit, with a metal, nylon or hard rubber mouthpiece. Because it has a "curb chain" and "shanks," it works by *leverage* and multiplies the pressure. One ounce of rein pressure might cause two or more ounces of pressure on the pony's mouth. It is stronger than most snaffle bits, so riders should be careful when using it. A kimberwicke is quite mild compared to other curb bits. It is useful for ponies who don't pay attention to a snaffle bit, but whose riders cannot handle double reins.

A pelham is a double-action bit. The top rein acts as a snaffle and the bottom rein acts as a curb bit.

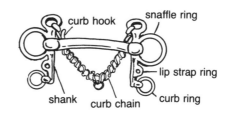

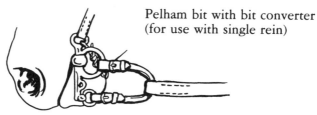

Pelham bit with double reins

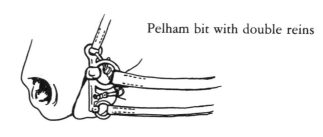

Pelham bit with bit converter
(for use with single rein)

One kind of kimberwicke bit has slots in which the reins can be fastened. The upper slot is the mildest and the lower slot makes the bit stronger. Putting the rein around the ring so it can slide freely makes the bit more like a snaffle, with very little leverage.

Pelham Bit

A pelham bit is a double-rein bit. The top rein goes to the "snaffle ring." When you use that rein, it acts like a bar snaffle bit with direct pressure. The bottom rein goes to the "curb ring." When you use that rein, it acts like a curb bit, with leverage. A pelham bit is always used with a "curb chain," which lies under the pony's chin in the curb groove. It has "shanks," which make it a leverage bit. Long shanks (more than 5 inches) make a pelham bit more severe, and are discouraged for most Pony Club riding. Pelham bits may have metal, nylon or rubber mouthpieces.

A pelham bit is stronger than most snaffle bits. Some ponies need the extra control of a pelham bit, but the rider must be able to handle double reins.

A "bit converter" is sometimes used to change a pelham into a single-rein bit. This is a pair of round leather straps that buckle to the snaffle and curb rings on each side of the bit. The single rein is attached to the loop of the bit converter. This makes a pelham bit act like a kimberwicke bit with only one rein. It is all right for beginning riders, but it would not be good for advanced riding.

CARRYING AND HANDLING TACK
Running Up Stirrups

For safety's sake, *English stirrups must always be run up whenever the rider is out of the saddle.* This keeps them from catching on things, banging into the pony, or hitting you. If a pony should bite at a fly on his side, he could catch his teeth on the loose hanging stirrup and get hurt. (For how to run up stirrups, see page 151.) Always run your stirrups up as soon as you dismount, and any time you see them hanging down on a saddle that is not being ridden.

TAKING CARE OF YOUR TACK

Good tack is expensive, but it can last for many years if you take good care of it. However, even the best tack can be ruined quickly if it is not cared for properly. There are four words to remember in taking care of your tack: *clean, condition, place,* and *repair.*

Four Steps in Tack Care

Clean   Each time you use your tack, it gets sweaty, dirty and dusty. This makes the leather harsh and dry and rough on the pony's skin and on your hands. It also makes the leather dry out and crack faster if it is not cleaned. It is unkind to ask a pony to take a rough, rusty or dirty bit in his mouth. Saddles, bridles and other tack should be cleaned each time they are used, and "stripped down" for a thorough cleaning each week. Washable saddle pads and girths or girth covers should be laundered each week.

253

Every time you clean your tack, check it for loose stitching or other problems. *Photo: Neena Ewing.*

Condition Leather is animal skin that has been treated, or "tanned," which seals the smooth side and leaves the underside able to absorb water, fat or oil. The natural fat and oil leather contains help keep it strong and supple. However, leather loses its natural fat when it gets wet and dries out, is exposed to heat, sweat, salt, and dirt, and when it is not cleaned or conditioned regularly. Conditioning means replacing the lost fat in the leather by working in fat or oil, usually neatsfoot oil or vegetable oil. This should be done after the leather is clean. After the leather has been cleaned and conditioned, apply glycerine saddle soap to seal the pores of the leather and protect it.

Tack hung up neatly in a well-organized tack room

Place Your tack must be kept where it is clean and dry and where it won't be dropped, scratched, knocked over, or chewed by animals. It should not be kept in a damp place like a cellar, or it will mildew. It must be kept away from heat (like a radiator), or it will dry out and crack. The saddle should be covered and put on a saddle rack. Things like bridles, halters and martingales should hang on bridle racks. Saddle pads should be hung on a clothesline or rack to dry, not left underneath the saddle. A sawhorse makes a good saddle rack, especially if you tack a strip of carpet over it to protect the bottom of your saddle. Pet food cans or small coffee cans can be nailed up to make inexpensive bridle racks.

Repair All tack must be checked for damage and wear every time you use it or clean it. You should make a careful check before any special event like a Pony Club rally. Small problems like loose stitching can be fixed easily if you notice them early. If you let repairs go, your tack can be ruined, and can become dangerous for you and your pony.

How to Clean Tack

You will need:

- Small sponges (two or three) and clean rags.
- Small bucket with warm (not hot) water.
- Leather cleaner (like castile soap or Murphy's Oil Soap—there are others).
- Leather conditioner (like pure neatsfoot oil or Lexol Conditioner).
- Leather protector (glycerine saddle soap).
- Saddle rack or sawhorse and a tack-cleaning hook to hold tack.

Cleaning tack is broken down into four steps: preparing, cleaning, conditioning, and protecting the leather. Here's how:

Preparing For a thorough cleaning, strip the saddle by removing the girth, stirrup leathers and irons, and the saddle pad. Rubber stirrup pads should be taken out of the irons. The bridle should be taken apart. The bit and stirrup irons should be placed in a bucket of warm water to soak while you clean the leather.

When you must do a quick wipeover instead of a thorough cleaning, take off the girth and saddle pad but leave the stirrup leathers and irons on. Unbuckle the leathers and run the irons down to the buckle ends. On the bridle, unfasten the reins and cheekpieces from the bit and undo all keepers and runners, but leave the bridle buckles in place. You can quickly clean the saddle, stirrup leathers, girth, bridle and reins while the bit soaks clean. This quick cleaning can be done daily if you are short of time, but you should do a thorough cleaning every week to keep your tack in good condition.

Cleaning Fill a small pail with warm (not hot) water. Dip a clean rag (or sponge) in the water and wring it out nearly dry. Rub it over the leather to remove dust, dirt and sweat. (If any water stays on the surface of the saddle, the sponge is too wet.) Don't forget to clean both the outside and the underside of the leather. Remove all the "jockeys"—dark, greasy dots or patches of dirt that stick to the leather. These are often found on the underside of the leather where it touches your pony. You may have to use

256

◆◆

USPC D-1 TEST

Know two reasons for cleaning tack.

◆◆

a plastic mesh dish scrubber to remove them, but be careful not to scratch the leather. Use lots of "elbow grease" but not too much water to get the leather clean. Use a rag to wipe away any excess water.

If the tack is really dirty, you may need a stronger cleaner. Use a damp sponge and a leather cleaner like castile soap or Murphy's Oil Soap. Don't use enough water to make the soap lather. If you do, the leather will get soaked and can be damaged. Rinse the cleaner off (along with the dirt) with a damp (not wet) sponge. Cleaners are too harsh to be left on the leather. If the leather isn't clean yet, repeat this step.

When you are finished, the leather should be clean and slightly damp. The stitching should stand out clean, and there will be no jockeys or dirty places.

Conditioning Now you must decide if the leather needs to be conditioned or oiled. Leather should be soft and supple, with no cracks, and it should not squeak when you ride. How often your leather needs oiling or conditioning depends on the climate you live in and the use and care the leather has had. You will not need to oil your tack every time you clean it. In fact, over-oiling can make leather too greasy and flabby, and it can damage the stitching. Only oil it if the leather seems dry or stiff.

If oil is needed, you can apply it by painting it on the *underside* of the leather in a thin coat, using a 1- or 2-inch paintbrush. It is better to oil the underside of the leather since it soaks up oil more easily than the outside or smooth side of the leather. Also, oiling the outside of your saddle will make oil stains on your pants. Next, bend the leather back and forth, and roll it and work it between your hands. This helps the leather soak up the oil or conditioner, and you can tell when it becomes supple. Use enough oil to make the leather easy to bend, but don't overdo it. Wipe off any excess oil with a rag.

Be careful not to get oil on suede knee rolls or on cloth (like the saddle pad)—it will stain.

Protecting the Leather This should always be done *after* cleaning and any oiling or conditioning. Glycerine saddle soap seals the pores of the leather, nourishes and protects it. If you use oil or conditioner afterward, it cannot get deep into the pores and the leather will be dull.

Use a damp sponge to apply the saddle soap. If you use bar saddle soap, dip the bar in water, not the sponge. The sponge should be sticky and soapy, not wet or lathery. Rub the soap in on both sides of the leather. There should not be any lather, but if the holes in the bridle or stirrup leathers get filled with soap, you can blow through them or use a toothpick to clean them out. If you have used just enough soap, you should be able to see a fingerprint on the leather after you have rubbed the soap in, and the leather will feel smooth and supple. Any excess soap should be wiped off with a rag.

Other cleaning hints:

- Bits, stirrup irons and spurs should be cleaned by soaking them in warm water and scrubbing them with a pot scrubber or steel wool. For a special shine, polish them with metal polish (except for the mouthpiece of the bit), and buff them with a dry rag.
- Washable saddle pads, girths and girth covers should be laundered once a week. Don't use bleach, and be sure to rinse them thoroughly. Bleach or soap left in a pad can mix with the pony's sweat and irritate his skin.

For more information about tack care and cleaning, see *The USPC Horse Management Handbook.*

TACK SAFETY CHECK: CONDITION AND REPAIR

Tack must be in good, safe condition or it may break while you are riding and cause an accident. Worn, cracked or dirty tack can also cause sores on the pony or the rider. Check the condition of tack before you buy or borrow it, when you clean it and every time you use it. If you find a problem (like cracked leather or stitches coming loose), don't use that tack. Show it to your parents or your instructor and arrange to get it fixed.

Parts to check include:

Saddle Tree

The saddle tree is the framework inside your saddle. If it is cracked or broken, the saddle can hurt your pony's back or fall apart. Saddle trees can be broken by using a narrow saddle on a wide-backed pony (especially with a heavy rider), by a pony rolling on his saddle or by a rider pulling on the cantle and twisting the tree while mounting. To check the tree, push against the pommel and cantle and look for tell-tale wrinkles across one or both sides of the seat. Pull sideways on the head or front of the saddle—any movement means the tree is broken. Some broken trees can be repaired by a saddler, but it is quite an expensive job.

Leather

All leather must be strong and supple (easy to bend), free from cracks and not dried out. Bend the leather back and forth and check for cracks. Cracks with brown powder in them are called dry rot. Stiff leather can sometimes be restored with cleaning and oiling, but dry-rotted or cracked leather cannot be used safely. Any leather that bends around a piece of metal (like bit and rein fastenings or stirrup leathers) is likely to wear out and crack faster.

Saddle seat should not move or wrinkle when pressed end to end.

There should be no movement in the gullet when you try to squeeze and pull side to side.

Checking for a broken tree

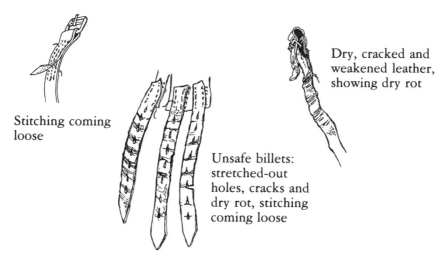

Stitching coming loose

Dry, cracked and weakened leather, showing dry rot

Unsafe billets: stretched-out holes, cracks and dry rot, stitching coming loose

Dangerous conditions

Stitching

Check the stitching on all your tack—saddle, bridle, girth and all other items. Any stitching that is broken, missing or coming loose should be fixed before you use that item again.

Billets

The billets must be sound and must be stitched firmly to the webbing. Billets that are thin, stretched, worn out or cracked could break—the saddle would fall off. The holes in the billets should not be cracked or stretched out. The stitching that holds the billets on must not be broken, worn or missing any stitches. Billets can be replaced easily.

Stirrup Leathers

The stirrup leathers must be sound or you could lose a stirrup suddenly. The leather must be strong, without cracks or too many extra holes too close together, which weakens the leather. The area where the stirrup iron rests must also be checked for cracks. The stitching that holds the buckle must be strong, If a stitch or two is missing, or if the thread is wearing through, the leather is not safe to use and must be re-stitched. This is a simple but important repair.

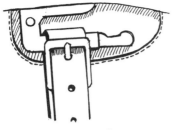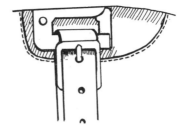

SAFE Stirrup bar open   DANGER! Stirrup bar closed

Safety stirrup bars

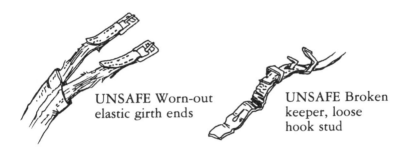

UNSAFE Worn-out elastic girth ends   UNSAFE Broken keeper, loose hook stud

Stirrup Bars

The stirrup bars should always be in the open position to be safe for riding. They are supposed to let your stirrup leather slide away in case your foot gets caught in the stirrup during a fall. They should not be loose, bent or slanted downward. If they are rusty, they may need oiling.

Girth

The girth must be smooth, clean and strong. Check the stitching that holds the buckles on. If you have elastic ends on your girth, the elastic will eventually wear out and need replacing. On a string girth, be sure there are no broken or worn-out strings.

Keepers and Runners

Keepers and runners are little pieces of leather near the buckle that hold the end of a strap in place. They keep straps from flapping loose and getting caught on things and keep buckles from un-

261

USPC D-2 TEST
Give three examples of unsafe equipment.

◆◆

buckling by accident. If a keeper or runner gets so loose that it won't hold its strap, it should be fixed. The most important keepers are the ones at the bit fastenings on reins and cheekpieces. If one of these keepers breaks, your rein or bridle could come undone. The little hook that goes through the hole in the fastening is called a hook stud. It must not be loose or bent, because it keeps the bit fastening from coming off. Some bridles and reins fasten with buckles instead. These must not have loose stitching, and the buckle must not be bent.

Synthetic (Non-Leather) Tack
Synthetic tack (made from nylon or other materials instead of leather) is fine for Pony Club use. It must be in good repair, just like leather tack. Some synthetic saddles must have synthetic stirrup leathers and girths, because the oil in leather fittings can damage them.

If you use a nylon or synthetic halter, you *must* use a *leather "breakaway" crownpiece* for safety's sake. This should be one piece

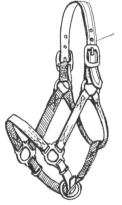

Breakaway leather
crownpiece

Nylon halter with leather safety crownpiece

of leather, not doubled and stitched. A breakaway crownpiece is necessary because nylon or synthetic halters are so strong that they might not break in an emergency if your pony should get his halter caught on something. This could hurt your pony badly. Synthetic bridles should also have a leather breakaway crownpiece for safety.

ADJUSTING AND FITTING TACK

It is very important that your tack fits your pony and that all parts are correctly adjusted. Improperly adjusted tack can:

- Hurt your pony by pinching, slipping or rubbing him.
- Make your pony act up or make you lose control of him.
- Make your saddle unsafe for you.
- Make you uncomfortable when you ride.

Every pony should have his own tack that is properly fitted to him. If you buy or borrow other tack, it must be carefully adjusted before you can ride with it. *You should check the adjustment of the tack every time you ride.*

To adjust tack, you will need:

- A leather punch.
- A sharp knife to cut off long ends.
- A nail or pencil to mark where extra holes should be punched.

Saddle Fitting

How to Check the Fit of Saddle to Pony A saddle must fit your pony's back without pinching, rocking, or pressing on his spine at any point. When the saddle sits on his back without a saddle pad, you should be able to see an open space all the way down the center of the gullet over the pony's spine. When you are sitting in the saddle, you must be able to fit at least two fingers between the head of the saddle and your pony's withers. The front of the saddle must be wide enough to fit his "saddle muscles" comfortably, without pinching or pressing on the top of his shoul-

Checking saddle fit

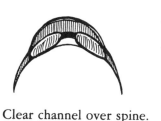

Clear channel over spine.

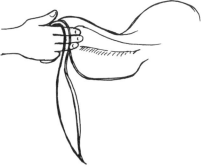

Three fingers fit between front of saddle and pony's withers.

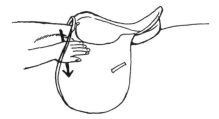

Slide hand under front of saddle, behind pony's shoulder blade— no pinching.

Sweat mark showing pressure point (dry spot).

der blades. To check this, slide your hand down each side under the front of the saddle to check for pinching while a rider is mounted. The panels must fit the pony's back muscles evenly, without rocking, rubbing, or making pressure points. When you remove the saddle after a ride, check the sweaty "saddle mark." If you see smaller dry patches in the sweat mark, these show where the saddle makes pressure points and is hurting the skin and the tissues underneath.

Saddle Too Wide If a saddle sits down too low on a pony's withers and spine, it is too wide for his back. (This can happen if a pony is thin or has a bony back.) If it is not too bad, it can be fixed by having the panels re-stuffed. A temporary solution is a "back protector pad," which fills in the hollows on each side of the pony's spine, raising the saddle and protecting his back. This pad is always

Saddle fitting

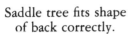

Saddle tree fits shape of back correctly.	Tree too wide, presses down on withers.	Tree too narrow, digs into back muscles, pinches shoulder blades.

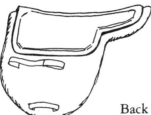

Back protector pad (always use over a regular saddle pad).

used on top of a regular saddle pad. Just stuffing padding under the front of the saddle will not do—this will lead to sore withers.

Saddle Too Narrow A saddle that is too narrow will press down into the pony's back muscles and pinch the tops of his shoulders. This makes him sore and can make a pony move stiffly, buck or even rear. This cannot be fixed by padding; the only solution is to use a wider saddle.

Balance of Saddle The seat of a saddle should be balanced so that the "dip" or lowest point is in the center, not at the back. If the saddle is too high in front or if the back panels are too flat, it will throw the rider backward out of balance. This can give your pony a sore back. The best way to fix an unbalanced saddle is to have a saddler re-stuff the panels to fit your pony's back. A "lift-back pad" can be used temporarily to balance the saddle, but you must be sure that this doesn't make the tree points dig into the pony's saddle muscles in front. Many saddles ride too high in front because they are really too narrow for the pony.

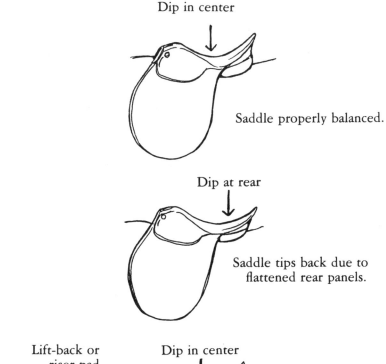

Dip in center

Saddle properly balanced.

Dip at rear

Saddle tips back due to
flattened rear panels.

Lift-back or
riser pad

Dip in center

Saddle balanced (tempo-
rarily) with lift-back
pad. (Saddle's panels
should be re-stuffed.)

Saddle balance

Girth Fitting

It is very important for the girth to fit right, because it holds your
saddle on. A girth that is too long cannot be tightened enough to
be safe. It can make the saddle slip. A girth that is too short is
hard to do up and may be tightened too much, making the pony
uncomfortable.

A girth should have two spare holes above the buckles on each
side when it is tightened, and at least one spare hole below the
buckles.

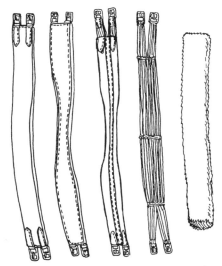

Left to right: folded leather girth, shaped girth, elastic end shaped girth, string girth and fleece girth cover.

Types of girths

Some ponies get sores behind their elbows from the girth. This is usually caused by a rough or dirty girth, but the kind of girth and the way it fits can make a difference.

Types of Girths A "shaped girth" is made narrow at the elbows so it won't rub the elbow skin. A "string girth" grips tightly but lets air get to the skin, which may help prevent sores. "Elastic-end girths" make it easier to tighten the girth and allow the pony more room to breathe. A "girth cover" is a soft, washable fleece cover that fits over the girth to protect the pony's skin.

Stirrup Leathers

Stirrup leathers should be long enough and have several spare holes so you can adjust them to a normal riding position. You may need to punch extra holes to make them adjustable to your best riding length. It's important to get the holes evenly spaced, so you won't ride crooked. Don't punch lots of extra "half-holes" in your leathers—this weakens the leather. Changing your leathers from one side of the saddle to the other will help keep them even as they stretch out.

How to measure spacing when punching extra holes

Use another nail to scratch a mark in the bottom leather, through each hole.

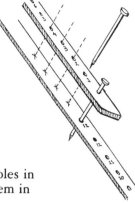

Use a leather punch to cut new holes at the marks.

Put a nail through the holes in both leathers to keep them in place.

Here's how to measure stirrup leather hole spacing:

1. Put a nail through one hole in both leathers.
2. Use a pencil to scratch a mark in the bottom leather, through the holes in the top leather.
3. Punch the holes with a leather punch.

FITTING BITS AND BRIDLES

Bits and bridles must be carefully fitted because your control depends on them. If the bit fits badly, it can hurt your pony's mouth and make him toss his head, fuss with his mouth, pull or even rear. The only way he can tell you it hurts is to act up.

All bits should be about ¼ inch wider than your pony's mouth. They must be smooth and comfortable, with no rough or rusty spots. They should not pinch or rub the pony's lips.

Snaffles

A snaffle bit must rest high in the pony's mouth so he cannot get his tongue over it. A properly fitted snaffle should make one or two gentle wrinkles at the corners of his lips, like a smile. If you use a "full-cheek snaffle," you should use keepers on the upper cheeks so that the pony cannot catch the upper cheek of the bit on something and cause an accident.

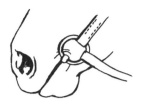

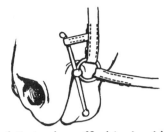

A snaffle bit should be adjusted so it makes two small wrinkles in the lips. It must not hang too low in the pony's mouth.

A full-cheek snaffle bit should have bit keepers on the upper cheeks.

Fit of snaffle bit

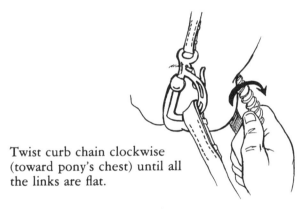

Twist curb chain clockwise (toward pony's chest) until all the links are flat.

Making the curb chain lie flat

Pelhams, Kimberwickes, and Curb Chains

Pelhams and kimberwickes should rest against the corners of the pony's mouth without making more than one small wrinkle. The curb chain must be flat against the pony's chin. It must not be too loose, or the bit will turn too far and you will have no control. It can also pinch the pony's lip. If it is too tight, it will make the bit "grab" and hurt the pony's mouth. The curb chain should be adjusted so that the bit turns 45 degrees to tighten the curb chain against the chin groove. It is usually right if you can fit two fingers (held sideways) between the curb chain and the chin groove.

A lip strap may run through the center link on the curb chain and buckle to the tiny rings on the bit shank. This keeps a pony from grabbing the side of the bit with his lip.

Adjusting the curb chain

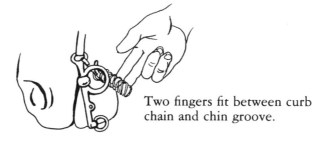

Two fingers fit between curb chain and chin groove.

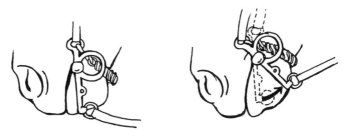

When curb chain is properly adjusted, bit will rotate 45 degrees to tighten curb chain.

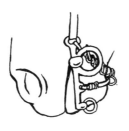

Lip strap in place (through center ring of curb chain).

Fitting Other Parts of the Bridle

Other parts of the bridle should be snug, not loose and sloppy. You should be able to slip a finger under every part of the bridle. All straps should have their keepers and runners fastened.

Browband Must be long enough so that the bridle doesn't rub and pinch the base of the ears.

Throatlash Should be loose enough to allow the pony to flex his neck without binding at the throat. You should be able to fit a fist between the throatlash and the pony's cheek.

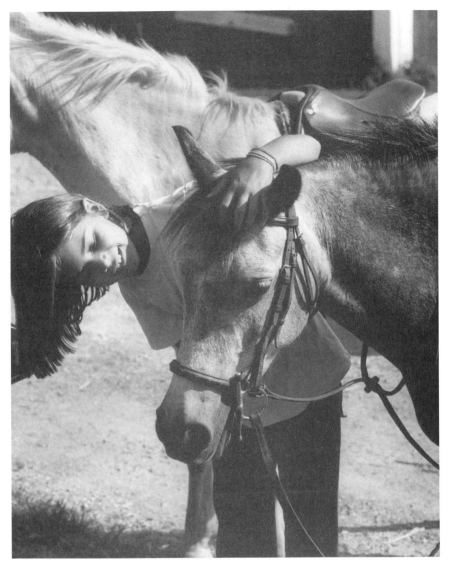

A Pony Clubber checks her pony's bridle for proper fit before riding. (Notice the keepers on the full cheek snaffle bit.) *Photo: Neena Ewing.*

Crownpiece Should have two extra holes above the cheekpiece buckles when the bit is correctly adjusted.

Cavesson (headstall) Adjusts the height of the noseband. It goes inside the crownpiece and cheekpieces.

Cavesson (noseband) Should rest 1 finger below the pony's cheekbones. It goes inside the cheekpieces, next to the pony's face. It should be snug but never uncomfortably tight.

Proper fit of bridle parts

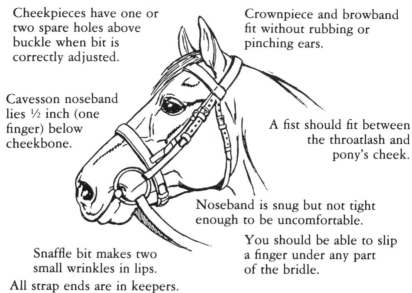

Cheekpieces have one or two spare holes above buckle when bit is correctly adjusted.

Crownpiece and browband fit without rubbing or pinching ears.

Cavesson noseband lies ½ inch (one finger) below cheekbone.

A fist should fit between the throatlash and pony's cheek.

Noseband is snug but not tight enough to be uncomfortable.

You should be able to slip a finger under any part of the bridle.

Snaffle bit makes two small wrinkles in lips.

All strap ends are in keepers.

HOW OTHER ITEMS SHOULD FIT
Saddle Pads

A saddle pad (the British term is "numnah") should fit the saddle with a 2-inch border all around—unless it's a square pad. It fastens to the billets with billet tabs or a Velcro strip, above the buckle guard. Some use a "pocket" that fits over the lower panels and sweat flaps of the saddle. A girth loop helps keep the pad from slipping back or wrinkling. A "baby pad" is a washable cotton pad that is used alone or underneath a show pad, next to the pony's skin. It is easy to wash and it keeps the show pad clean.

Breastplate (Hunt Style)

A breastplate keeps the saddle from slipping back. The yoke fits around the shoulders, and the center strap goes between the front legs and fastens around the girth. The two top straps attach to the D-rings at the front of the saddle. There should be room to fit one hand at the top of the yoke, and the center strap should be slightly loose so it will not cause a sore between the pony's front legs. The best breastplates have adjustable buckles on each side of the yoke.

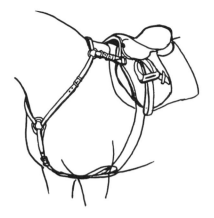 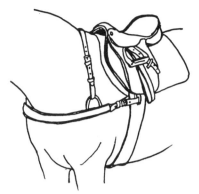

Hunt-style breastplate   Event or polo style breast collar

Breast Collar (Event or Polo Type)

A breast collar keeps the saddle from sliding back. It should fit across the chest without binding at the base of the neck. It is buckled around the girth on both sides. The upper strap should be snug enough to keep the breast collar from slipping down.

Standing Martingale

The martingale strap attaches to the cavesson noseband (never to a dropped noseband!) and runs between the front legs to the girth. The neckstrap buckles on the left. It should be secured by a rubber ring at the chest, so that the martingale cannot hang down in a big loop, which is unsafe. The martingale should be adjusted so that it can be pushed up to almost touch the pony's throat when his head is in a normal position. (NOTE: In Pony Club competitions, standing martingales are only allowed for D Level riders.)

Running Martingale

The martingale strap fastens around the girth and splits at the chest, with each strap ending in a rein ring. The reins run through these rings. For safety, the reins must have "rein stops," which prevent the martingale rings from getting caught on the bit fastenings. The martingale should be adjusted so that it has about an inch of slack when the pony's head is in a normal position and

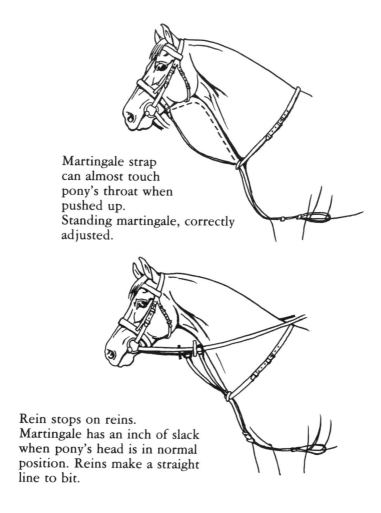

Martingale strap
can almost touch
pony's throat when
pushed up.
Standing martingale, correctly
adjusted.

Rein stops on reins.
Martingale has an inch of slack
when pony's head is in normal
position. Reins make a straight
line to bit.

Running martingale, correctly adjusted.

the reins make a straight line from the bit to the rider's elbows. The neck strap buckles on the left, and should be secured with a rubber ring at the chest. (NOTE: Running martingales are training aids that should be used only by riders who know how to use them correctly. They are not for beginners!)

Dropped Noseband

A dropped noseband is used to keep a pony from opening his mouth to evade the bit. The noseband rests on the end of the nose bone, just above the soft part of the nose. The chin strap is buckled below the bit, in the curb groove. The noseband should be snug but not too tight. You should be able to slip a finger under it, and the pony should be able to chew easily.

Flash Noseband

Also used to keep a pony's mouth closed, but it lets you use a standing martingale attached to the upper cavesson noseband. The cavesson noseband is adjusted fairly high and snugly. The chin strap buckles below the bit, in the curb groove. Both should be snug but not tight—you should be able to slip a finger underneath.

Nosebands

Dropped noseband: rests on end of nose bone with chin strap below bit in chin groove.

Flash noseband: cavesson noseband adjusted high (just below cheek-bone) and snugly; chin strap below bit in chin groove.

Figure 8 noseband: upper jaw strap adjusted snugly above bit, just in front of cheekbone. Chin strap below bit in chin groove.

Figure-8 Noseband

Also used to keep a pony's mouth closed, but it rests higher on his face and lets his nostrils expand better for fast work. The upper strap goes under the jaw behind the cheekbones, inside the bridle. The lower strap buckles below the bit, in the curb groove. A small pad rests high on the nose bone, where the straps cross. Both straps should be snug but not tight—you should be able to slip a finger underneath.

SELECTING THE RIGHT TACK

There are many different kinds of tack. It is important to choose the right kind of tack for you, for your pony, and for the kind of riding you do in Pony Club. The wrong kind of tack can be an expensive mistake, and it can make it much harder to ride well.

Tack may be bought new or used. Often good used tack that has been well taken care of is a better buy than very cheap new tack. If you buy used tack, it should be checked carefully for soundness and condition. Many Pony Clubs have used tack sales from time to time, where you may be able to find good used tack and outgrown riding clothes at reasonable prices.

Here are some things to remember when buying tack:

Saddle

An all-purpose balanced seat saddle is best for Pony Club riding. This type of saddle makes it easier to learn a good balanced seat for riding and jumping. Either leather or synthetic saddles are acceptable.

Some types of saddles are not suitable for Pony Club riding. These are special-purpose saddles, which are designed to make the rider sit in a certain way for special events. This can make it difficult to ride with a good all-purpose balanced seat. Some examples are:

- Western saddles
- Australian stock saddles
- Saddle seat show saddles (also called "Lane Fox" saddles)
- Racing saddles

- Polo saddles and old-fashioned "park" saddles
- Forward seat or "flat" jumping saddles (okay for jumping only, but not suitable for general-purpose Pony Club riding)
- Dressage saddles (okay for dressage and flat work, but not for general purpose Pony Club work and *never* for jumping)

Types of saddles

A. 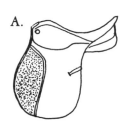 B. 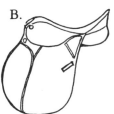 C.

Recommended for Pony Club use: A, B, and C.
All-purpose, balanced seat saddles (leather or synthetic).

D. Flat jumping saddle

E. Forward seat jumping saddle

F. Dressage saddle

  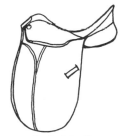

D and E are less suitable for balanced seat riding and are best for jumping only.

Suitable for dressage only. Do not use for jumping.

G. Old-fashioned park saddle

H. Saddle seat show saddle

G and H are unsuitable for balanced seat riding and jumping.

Fitting Saddle to Rider A saddle must be the right size for the rider. A saddle that is too small makes a rider feel stuck in a too-upright position, and his knees may be jammed against the knee rolls. A too-large saddle puts a small rider too far back to ride safely in a good balanced position, and the stirrup bars are too far forward to let him keep his legs in position underneath his body.

To check for rider fit, sit in the middle and deepest part of the saddle (preferably on a pony). Adjust the stirrup leathers so that the stirrups hang evenly to touch the bottom of your ankle bones.

Saddle fits rider. Rider can sit in balanced position with one hand's width of cantle behind him, knees behind knee rolls.

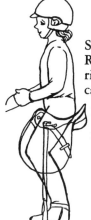

Saddle too small. Rider is stuck in up-right position between cantle and knee roll. No extra space behind seat or in front of knee.

Saddle too large. Dip in seat is too far back and stirrup bars are too far forward, causing rider to sit in "chair seat" with legs ahead of seat.

Fitting saddle to rider

When you sit in the center of the saddle in a good position, with your feet in the stirrups, there should be room for one hand behind you at the cantle, and your legs should fall easily into the hollow of the saddle flap, behind the knee rolls. It should be easy to sit in a good position, to post, and to balance in a half-seat. The stirrup leathers should hang vertical (straight up and down) when you are in a good balanced position. It's a good idea to ask your instructor to check your position in a new saddle, to see if it helps you ride well.

The saddle must fit the pony, too. (See pages 263–264, on fitting and adjusting tack to make sure it fits.)

Bridles and Other Tack

Bridles, breastplates, martingales and other equipment may be leather or synthetic. (Synthetic bridles and halters must have a leather breakaway crownpiece for safety.)

Tack comes in several sizes:

- *Pony:* Fits most small to medium ponies (up to about 13 hands).
- *Cob:* Fits large ponies, smaller ponies with large heads and small horses or those with fine heads, like Arabians.
- *Horse:* Fits most full-sized horses.

◆◆◆

USPC D-1 TEST

Inspection: Tack safe and neat; properly adjusted, with assistance if necessary.

◆◆◆

USPC D-2 TEST

Inspection: Tack safe and clean, with attention to stitching, girth and stirrups; properly adjusted by Examiner if necessary.

◆◆◆

USPC D-3 TEST

Tack to be properly adjusted, safe and clean.

◆◆◆

Peacock stirrup iron

CAUTION: Bridles for ponies should not have horse-sized reins, long enough to make a very long bight (the loop of extra rein behind the rider's hands). A child's foot can get caught in this loop, which can be dangerous. It is not safe to shorten the loop by tying the end of the reins in a knot. If the reins are too long, they can be shortened by a saddler, or you can buy shorter, pony-size reins.

Bits A bit should be ¼ inch wider than the pony's mouth. It must not be rusty, rough or worn thin. Avoid nickel bits—they bend and develop thin spots and sharp edges as they get old.

Fittings Since your safety depends on your girth, stirrup leathers and other tack, it makes sense to get strong, sound items of the right size. Stirrup irons should be 1 inch wider than the rider's foot. If they are too big, the foot can slip right through. If they are too small, the foot can get stuck. Safety stirrups can be used, especially for small children. These may free the foot from the stirrup in case of a fall. If the Peacock type of iron is used, the rubber band should be on the outside of the iron.

LEARNING MORE ABOUT TACK

Here are some things you might like to do to learn more about tack:

- Go through a tack catalog and look up different kinds of tack and equipment. Compare the difference between various brands and models. How much do they cost? Which ones would you like best?

NOTES TO ADULTS ON TACK FITTING AND CHECKING TACK

There is nothing more important than making sure your child rides with safe equipment, correctly adjusted and in good working order. Children should be taught to check their own tack every time they mount, but this is too important not to be double-checked by a responsible adult, especially where small children and inexperienced riders are concerned. This is also important for the comfort and welfare of the pony.

Be sure to examine your child's tack and equipment regularly for condition and wear. Helping with a thorough tack cleaning once a week is a good way to see that small problems don't develop into big hazards, and it emphasizes to the child the importance of taking good care of expensive equipment.

If you or your child spot a problem or a needed repair, get it mended right away. This is not something that children can do for themselves, and if you put it off, it can add up to a real riding hazard.

Make a "wish list" of the tack you would like to have. You might like to cut out pictures of the things you would buy if you were outfitting a stable, and paste them in a scrapbook.

- Visit a tack shop with your Pony Club. (Your instructor can call ahead to see if it's okay to bring a group and when would be a good time.) Ask what kind of tack they recommend for Pony Club. Do they have bargains in used tack? Ask for tips on checking to see if a saddle fits the pony and the rider, and on breaking in new tack. How can you tell if tack has good leather, just okay leather or poor leather? What should it cost?

- Visit a saddler (a person who makes and repairs tack), or perhaps invite him to come and talk to your Pony Club. Maybe he can show you a saddle tree and how a saddle is put together. Ask if he can teach you some simple tack repairs you can do yourself. How can you tell if a saddle needs repairs? Ask for tips on taking care of tack.

- Have a tack cleaning party with your friends. Everyone brings his own tack and tack cleaning equipment. You all clean and check the tack for safety. (Maybe your parents or Pony Club District Commissioner can help do minor repairs, too.) Music, friends and maybe pizza can help make it fun.

- Play Tack Parts Tag. To learn parts of tack, write the name of each item on tape or Post-it notes. Each person draws a tag and tries to stick it on the correct part of the saddle or bridle.

- Bridle Assembly Race. Each team (two or three people) gets a snaffle bridle (taken apart), with all the pieces on a blanket. The first team to put their bridle together *correctly* wins. (If you're really experienced, try it blindfolded!)

- Whatizzit Game. Three or four people each bring an odd piece of tack. It can be something old or unusual that *they* know all about but that others would not know. Each person holds up his piece of tack and tells what it is and what it is used for. *Only one* tells the truth—the others make up a story. The rest of the club tries to guess who is telling the truth about their tack and what each object really is. (Set a time limit or a number of guesses.) If the audience can guess who is telling the truth, or what the tack really is, they win. If not, the person with the tack wins. After the guessing is over, each person tells what his tack really is and what it is used for.

- Tack Trunk Game (can be played anywhere—in the car, on a trail ride). The first person says, "I'm going to a Pony Club rally, and in my tack trunk I've got an *ankle boot* (a piece of tack beginning with A). The next person says, "I'm going to a Pony Club rally, and in my tack trunk I've got an *ankle boot* and a *bit* (piece of tack beginning with B). The next one has to say the whole thing, including *ankle boot, bit,* and a piece of tack beginning with C. How far can you go before somebody goofs?

CHAPTER 13

Dress and Turnout

"Turnout" means the way you and your pony are dressed and prepared to ride. Good turnout means being safe, neat, clean and "workmanlike," not fancy. Workmanlike means ready to work— to do the job. This means having the right clothes, tack and equipment, having everything in good condition and fitting properly, and having your pony clean, properly prepared and in good condition. You do not have to have expensive clothes or equipment to do this, but you do need to know what the proper turnout means.

Turnout can be everyday, informal or formal. "Everyday turnout" means the way you dress, groom and prepare yourself and your pony for ordinary riding at home. "Informal turnout" is for riding lessons, clinics and some Pony Club rallies. "Formal turnout" is for special occasions like competitions, and for formal Pony Club inspections, which may be required at some rallies.

WHAT TO WEAR FOR RIDING AND WORKING AROUND PONIES
Everyday Attire

Your everyday riding clothes should be safe and easy to work in. They should fit comfortably and should be washable.

Boots or Shoes The first thing you need is safe boots or shoes in which to ride and work around ponies. Riding shoes or boots with a heel, like leather, synthetic or rubber hunt boots, jodhpur

Dressed in turnout for an informal Mounted Games practice, these riders have correctly fitted helmets and safe footwear. *Photo: Neena Ewing.*

boots or paddock shoes are best. Riding boots must have enough heel to keep them from slipping through a stirrup (no sneakers or loafers!) Deep-tread hiking boots or "waffle" soles are unsafe for riding, as they can catch on a stirrup.

For working around ponies on the ground, any substantial shoe that is securely fastened, covers the ankle, is entirely closed (no sandals or open toes!) and has a thick sole is okay. *Never* work around ponies in cloth or canvas shoes, sandals or open-toed shoes or in bare feet!

Helmet You must wear an ASTM/SEI safety riding helmet whenever you are mounted, at home or anywhere else. It must be of the approved type that meets the ASTM (American Society for Testing and Materials) standards. The helmet must have a seal from

Unsafe footwear

DANGER! Sneakers or shoes without heels can slip right through a stirrup.

DANGER! Stirrup can get caught in the gap between the heel and the deep tread of this kind of boot.

the SEI (Safety Equipment Institute), which proves that it has been tested. *No other type of helmet will do,* as this is the safest type of helmet currently available. Your helmet must be worn with the harness and chin strap in place and properly fastened whenever you are riding, and at Pony Club pre-riding inspections. It's a good idea to wear your helmet when you are working around your pony, even if you are not riding, as it can save you a bang on the head if he should bump into you.

Your helmet must fit properly so it will protect you if you fall, and will be comfortable when riding. It should sit down on your head so the brim shades your eyes (not on the back of your head). It should fit as snugly as you can comfortably wear it, but it should not give you a headache. With the harness and chin strap on, your helmet should stay securely on your head without rocking, even when you bend over and shake your head; if you wiggle it gently, you should feel your scalp and the skin of your forehead move with it.

If your helmet is slightly loose, use the "spacers" (pieces of foam with Velcro or sticky backs) that come with the hat to adjust the fit, according to the manufacturer's directions.

Never get on a pony, even for a minute, without your helmet on, and never let anyone ride your pony unless they are wearing a helmet. Wearing a helmet isn't just a silly rule—*it can save your life!*

Safe footwear and an ASTM/SEI certified helmet must always be worn when riding or working around ponies. Here are several types of suitable helmets, boots and shoes. *Photo: Ruth Harvie.*

Pants For comfortable riding, you need long pants that fit snugly in the lower legs and that don't ride up and wrinkle under your knees. Breeches or jodhpurs are best for riding because they are made to be comfortable when you are in a riding position. Jeans (especially stretch jeans) or slacks are okay if they fit right and don't give you sore knees from wrinkles. You can use pants clips with elastic straps that fit under your boots and hold the pants down.

Gloves Gloves can save you from getting blisters on your fingers. Stretch cotton gloves are good for summer. Some have rub-

Riding clothes

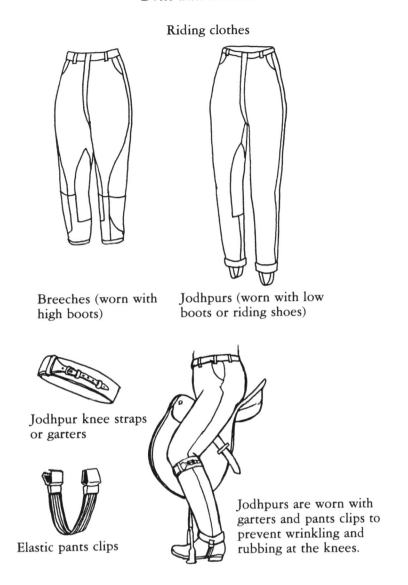

Breeches (worn with
high boots)

Jodhpurs (worn with low
boots or riding shoes)

Jodhpur knee straps
or garters

Elastic pants clips

Jodhpurs are worn with
garters and pants clips to
prevent wrinkling and
rubbing at the knees.

ber or plastic "grippers" that hold the reins when they are wet.
For winter, be sure your gloves are not too bulky to hold the
reins easily.

Accessories Don't wear dangle earrings, rings or other jewelry
that could catch on the reins or the pony's mane. Don't wear
combs, barrettes or pins in your hair that could hurt your head
if you took a spill. Don't wear loose scarves or belts that could
catch on things. Never chew gum or eat candy while you are

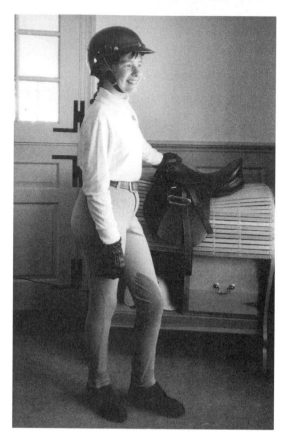

Everyday attire. This attire is proper for lessons, riding clinics and working rallies. It should be neat and workmanlike. *Photo: Ruth Harvie.*

riding. If something should happen to make you gasp, you could choke!

When you are riding outside in the sun, use sunscreen to prevent sunburn. In cold weather, wear layers of clothes to keep warm, but be sure your clothes let you move freely.

Informal Attire

This is what you should wear for a riding lesson, a clinic, informal hunting or a rally. You should be neat and tidy, with clothes clean, shirt tucked in and boots clean and polished. Informal turnout is expected at most Pony Club rallies and tests.

Helmet Must be properly fitted, ASTM/SEI certified hunt cap type or event type.

Footwear Riding boots, jodhpur boots or equivalent, as described above. Black or brown. Clean and polished.

Pants Breeches (worn with high boots) or jodhpurs (worn with jodhpur boots or paddock shoes), preferably beige, grey, rust or other conservative color. Garters (leather knee straps) and/or elastic foot straps should be worn with jodhpurs. Belt must be worn if pants have belt loops.

Shirt Ratcatcher, turtleneck or plain collar, white or plain light color. Shirt should have sleeves, as a white shirt with sleeves (not a T-shirt) may be worn when coat requirement is waived due to

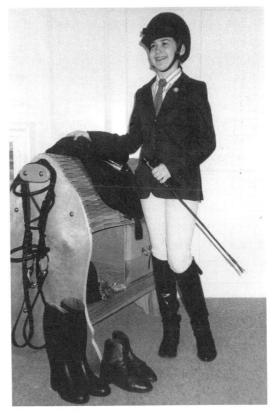

Informal attire. This attire is correct for Pony Club shows or rallies where informal attire is specified. (Jodhpurs and jodhpur boots or paddock shoes are also correct.) *Photo: Ruth Harvie.*

◆◆

USPC D-3 TEST
Describe informal and formal attire.

◆◆

hot weather. A plain polo shirt, worn tucked in, is acceptable for riding lessons in hot weather.

Tie Not required with turtleneck. Stock tie (colored) with plain gold safety pin (fastened horizontally through knot), or choker (pin optional) with neckband shirt. Plain or regimental stripe necktie optional with plain collar-style shirt.

Coat Hunt coat of any color other than solid black or solid dark navy. In cold weather, a plain form-fitting sweater over a turtleneck is acceptable for riding lessons and clinics, instead of a riding coat.

Gloves (optional) Brown or black (not white), cotton, synthetic or leather.

Jewelry Pony Club pin should be worn on front of helmet or jacket lapel. No other jewelry except plain stock pin or tie tack.

Hair Neat and tidy. Long hair should be braided, done up in a bun or put up under the helmet. Medium hair should be put into a hair net. Hair should never be in the rider's eyes or cover his or her number.

Formal Attire
For formal competitions, hunts and formal Pony Club inspections at rallies.

Helmet Same as informal. Black ASTM/SEI hunt cap or event helmet with black cover.

Boots Black field or dress boots (jodhpur boots for young children). Clean and polished.

Pants White, buff, canary or tan breeches (jodhpurs for young

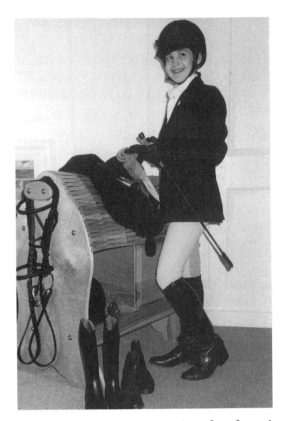

Formal attire. Correct attire for formal competitions, hunts and rallies where formal attire is specified. (Jodhpurs and jodhpur boots or paddock shoes are also correct, especially for younger children.) *Photo: Ruth Harvie.*

children, with leather garter straps and elastic foot straps). Belt is required if pants have belt loops.

Shirt White riding shirt with neckband collar. Should have long sleeves, as white shirt with sleeves may be worn when coat requirement is waived due to hot weather.

Tie White stock tie with plain gold safety pin, fastened horizontally through the knot. "Ready-tied" stock ties are not allowed.

Coat Solid black, solid navy blue, or dark grey (charcoal) hunt coat (no pinstripes).

Gloves (optional) Black or brown, white for dressage only. Cotton, synthetic or leather.

Jewelry Pony Club pin worn on front of helmet or jacket lapel. Plain gold stock pin. No other jewelry.

Hair Same as informal. (Even if hair is put up in a twist, braid or bun, a hair net must be used.)

Formal and informal dress should not be mixed. (For instance, don't wear a turtleneck sweater (informal) with a formal black coat. Clothes should fit well, be in good repair (no rips or missing buttons) and be clean and pressed. Boots should be clean and polished. Remember to wear your Pony Club pin on your helmet or jacket lapel.

TURNOUT FOR PONY CLUB INSPECTIONS

Pony Club inspections are held before Pony Club mounted events to be sure that all Pony Club riders are safely dressed for riding, ponies are clean and comforable, and tack is safe, clean and correctly adjusted. Most Pony Club inspections are informal. You will be told before the event whether informal or formal turnout is required.

Tack

Your tack should always be safe, clean and fit well when you ride, but it should be especially clean, neat and well adjusted for a Pony Club inspection. Tack is checked for safety, neatness, cleanliness, adjustment and condition. Old or worn equipment is not penalized as long as it is in safe condition and shows proper care. The Examiner or judge will check and inspect your tack and turnout according to the requirements for your rating level.

It is better to take good care of your tack from day to day than to try to do a super cleaning of dirty, neglected tack right before a rally or competition. Good regular cleaning and conditioning will show up in the condition of the leather. Your leather should be clean and supple, with the stitches showing clearly, no "jockeys" (sticky dots of dirt) and the metal parts clean and bright. The saddle pad (and girth cover, if you use one) should be freshly laundered, and rubber stirrup pads should be scrubbed clean.

The condition of your tack is most important, as you will not be allowed to ride in a Pony Club event with tack that is broken or in need of repair. All tack must be in safe condition—all stitching must be sound and leather parts must be free of cracks and dry rot. The billets must not be worn out, and the stirrup leathers must be sound and cannot have cracks or loose stitching. The bit fastenings of the reins and bridle must be strong, supple and tight, and there should not be any loose keepers, cracked leather or missing stitching on the bridle or reins.

Adjustment of tack will be checked by the Examiner or judge to be sure your tack is safe and comfortable for you and your pony. The girth must have two buckles at each end and must be fitted so that after it is tightened there are at least two spare holes at the top and one at the bottom of the billets. You must have buckle guards in place. Your stirrup bars must be down (in the open position) for riding. If you wear rubber-soled boots, rubber stirrup pads are discouraged (but not penalized) because they make it harder to take your foot out of the stirrup. (Some stirrups—"Fillis" style or "knife edge" irons—are made to be used only with stirrup pads.) Your stirrup irons must be 1 inch wider than your boots for safety. The bit and bridle and any other equipment must be correctly adjusted (see page 263 for how to adjust tack).

When you come to the place for your inspection, all your tack should be adjusted ready to ride. Your girth should be tightened and your stirrups should be run up.

Your Pony

Your pony should always be clean and comfortable when you ride, whether at home or in the most formal competition. For ordinary riding, he should at least be brushed clean (especially under the saddle and girth), and have his feet picked out. For Informal Turnout and Formal Turnout inspections, he will be checked for grooming and cleanliness, care and condition of his feet, and condition and fitness to do his job. If you have taken good care of your pony by grooming him thoroughly every day and taking regular care of his feet, he will show good care and will be in much better condition than if you just tried to do a big cleanup the day before the rally. Good care shows! (See pages 204–205 for how to groom and pick out feet.)

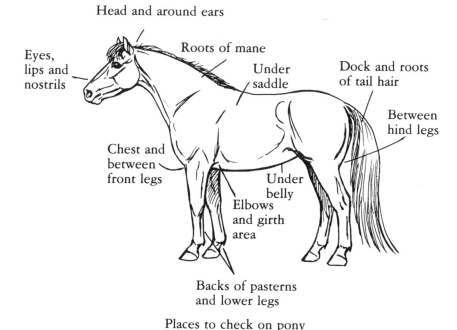

Head and around ears

Eyes, lips and nostrils

Roots of mane

Under saddle

Dock and roots of tail hair

Between hind legs

Chest and between front legs

Under belly

Elbows and girth area

Backs of pasterns and lower legs

Places to check on pony

Grooming and Turnout Your pony should be curried and brushed clean, so that his coat is free from dirt, dust and scurf. Some places to check are:

* Under the saddle and girth.
* Under the belly and between the hind legs.
* The backs of the pasterns and the lower legs.
* The head and around the ears.
* The roots of the mane and tail hair.
* The elbows and between the front legs.

You should clean the skin around your pony's eyes and eyelids, his nostrils and lips, and under his tail. (Use damp cotton balls.)

Any botfly eggs should be removed. (They can be scraped off with a styrofoam block after being lubricated with a dab of shampoo.)

Mane and Tail The mane and tail should be brushed out and free of bedding and dirt. The roots of the hair should be clean. Light-colored tails should be washed to remove stains. Braiding the mane or tail is not permitted for Pony Club events, except for Dressage competitions at the upper levels. (See *The USPC Rules for Competitions.*)

Feet and Shoeing Feet should be picked out. They must show evidence of regular trimming or shoeing. If you clean the feet and apply hoof dressing to the hoof, sole and frog the night before turnout inspection, the feet can be toweled off in the morning, and they will be shiny and easier to pick out clean.

◆◆

U.S. PONY CLUB TEST REQUIREMENTS FOR TURNOUT
D-1 Test:

1. Rider neatly and appropriately dressed. Wearing Pony Club pin (no other jewelry).
2. Pony neatly brushed. No bedding, burrs, etc., in mane or tail. Feet picked out (with assistance).
3. Pony's feet trimmed and/or shod, showing farrier care.
4. Tack safe and neat (properly adjusted with assistance if necessary).

D-2 Test:

1. Rider neatly and appropriately dressed. Wearing Pony Club pin (no other jewelry).
2. Pony clean (no obvious dirt) and neatly groomed (no obvious sweat). Eyes, nose, lips and dock wiped off.
3. Feet picked out. Well trimmed or shod, showing farrier care.
4. Tack safe (especially stirrups, girth and stitching), properly adjusted by Examiner if necessary. Tack clean (no obvious dirt, "jockeys" or heavy dust).

D-3 Test:

1. Rider in safe, clean, neat and appropriate attire. Wearing Pony Club pin (no other jewelry).
2. Pony well brushed and neatly groomed (no sweat or dirt). Eyes, nose, lips and dock wiped off.
3. Feet picked out. Well trimmed or shod, showing farrier care.
4. Tack safe, clean and properly adjusted. All stress points clean, stirrup pads clean (if used), bit clean, no "jockeys" or dust on tack.

◆◆

Turn-back Inspections

A turn-back inspection is held at a working rally or competition after riding. The pony's grooming and care after riding, care of tack, equipment and personal gear, and the neatness of the stable area are all inspected. Ponies are not tacked up, and Pony Clubbers do not dress in formal attire for turn-back inspections. Requirements for turn-back inspections are found in *The USPC Horse Management Handbook* and *USPC Rules for Competitions.*

NOTES TO ADULTS ON TURNOUT AND PONY CLUB INSPECTIONS

Turnout inspection is intended to be sure that all Pony Club riders are safely dressed for riding, ponies are clean and comfortable, and tack is safe, clean and correctly adjusted. It also teaches children the value of neatness, regular and conscientious care of the pony and tack and pride in a job well done. Turnout should be approached with commonsense and intelligent attention to details, not nitpicking. Planning ahead with your child for assembling necessary clothes and equipment, regular care and cleaning, and preparation of the pony can help your child learn to be prepared, organized and well turned out. Children should receive the help they need, appropriate for their age and level, but Pony Clubbers are expected to take as much responsibility as possible for preparing themselves and their ponies.

Index

Note: Page numbers in *italics* refer to illustrations.